Vito Marcantonio, Radical in Congress

A *Men and Movements* book

Men and Movements

ALAN SCHAFFER

Vito Marcantonio, Radical in Congress

SYRACUSE UNIVERSITY PRESS

Manufactured in the United States of America

Preface

Vito Marcantonio, as a man as well as a public figure, always fascinated me. When I began the work that resulted in this book, I had hoped to write a full-length biography of him. From the very beginning I was frustrated in this attempt.

The Marcantonio Papers, the keystone for this study, contain little of a personal nature. There are places where the collection quite obviously has been culled; just enough intimate material is left to give the impression that there once was more. There are certain blocks of time, when the correspondence between Marcantonio and others must have been heavy, that are not covered at all in the papers made available to me. I assume the existence of more documentary material and can only hope some future historian will have access to it.

Documents are the historian's "hard" evidence, but there are other approaches to the life of a human being. The historian working on a nearly contemporaneous individual can, for example, interview those people who knew the subject and were involved with him. The utility of this kind of evidence can be seen in the spate of books completed on the basis of material in the Oral History Collection at Columbia University. Yet, for me, personal interviewing was an unsuccessful tool, and I think the reader deserves to know why.

Personal recollection, oral or in print, is useful only to the extent that it can be corroborated. Confirmation was the first problem; given the limitations of the Marcantonio Papers, I frequently had no way of checking oral information. What is one to do when three people, all of whom knew the congressman, give three widely differing accounts of the same event? My own answer has been not to use such information.

The second problem, one that came up as soon as I started trying to interview, relates to the controversial nature of Vito Marcantonio. Individuals who had known him quite well at one point in history chose not to be connected with him in any way in the 1960's. A writer who was a personal friend of Marcantonio's in the 1930's denied ever knowing him. Others would not reply to letters or calls requesting interviews.

Some people would talk and therein lies the third problem. If they were not of the same political persuasion as Marcantonio, what they told me, in light of what I already knew, was frequently outlandish. If they had agreed with him politically, they could not be made to relate fact but felt called upon to defend the congressman to me; in thus defending his position in the past they were, of course, justifying important aspects of their own lives.

The fourth and last problem was that, of those individuals who would talk to me and who had worked with Marcantonio, almost no one knew much about him personally. More than one person was momentarily taken aback when I asked if he knew anything about Marcantonio's brother, a long-time invalid in a hospital, supported by the congressman. No one I spoke to had known of the brother's existence.

For all the reasons mentioned, this book is limited to a study of Vito Marcantonio's public life and particularly to his career as a congressman. To the reader who wants more I can only say that I do too, and I am terribly sorry I do not have it.

This book owes much to a great many people while I, of course, am responsible for its faults. I cannot here acknowledge all my debts, but several individuals and one group must be singled out. The late Mrs. Miriam Sanders Marcantonio deserves special mention for having had the foresight to preserve her husband's voluminous collection of documents and for depositing them at the New York Public Library. Dr. Edward Younger, now Dean of the Graduate

School of Arts and Letters at the University of Virginia, saw this volume begin as a paper in his graduate seminar on Recent American History and actively contributed to the development of both the book and its author. Librarians, too many to be singled out, in New York, Washington, D.C., and Virginia, contributed in important ways as they do to every work of scholarship. My wife Carole, for reasons obvious to her and too personal to mention here, without writing a line deserves listing as co-author.

ALAN SCHAFFER

East Lansing, Michigan
December 1965

The author wishes to thank the following for their kind permission to quote from works held in copyright:

J. B. Lippincott—Quotation reprinted with permission from *La Guardia: A Fighter Against His Times* by Arthur Mann. Copyright 1959 by Arthur Mann. (New York: J. B. Lippincott, 1959)

McGraw-Hill Book Company—Quotations reprinted with permission from *The Heart Is the Teacher* by Leonard Covello and Guido D'Agostino. Copyright 1958 by Leonard Covello. (New York: McGraw-Hill Book Company, 1958)

The Macmillan Company—Quotation reprinted with permission from *Life with Fiorello* by Ernest Cuneo. (New York: Macmillan, 1955)

University of Pennsylvania—Quotation reprinted with permission from Henry F. May, "The End of American Radicalism," *American Quarterly*, Volume II, No. 4 (Winter 1950), pp. 291-292.

Vito Marcantonio Memorial Association—Quotations reprinted with permission of the editor from *I Vote My Conscience*, edited by Annette T. Rubinstein. (New York: Vito Marcantonio Memorial Association, 1956)

Alfred A. Knopf, Inc.—Quotation reprinted with permission of the author from *Politics in the Empire State* by Warren Moscow. (New York: Alfred A. Knopf, Inc., 1948)

The author is grateful to the Franklin D. Roosevelt Library, Hyde Park, New York, for permission to quote from the Roosevelt Papers, and to Mrs. Fiorello La Guardia and the Municipal Archives and Records Center, New York City, for permission to use and quote from the La Guardia Papers.

Contents

Contents

Vito Marcantonio,
Radical in Congress

Introduction

Vito Marcantonio served as congressman from Manhattan's upper east side for fourteen of the most critical years in American history, an era spanning the period of the Depression, the Second World War, and the origins of the present conflict with the Communist world. Until his defeat in 1950 by a coalition candidate representing the diverse interests of the Republican, Democratic, and Liberal parties, Marcantonio was frequently the sole spokesman in Congress for America's radical left. Because of the unique role he played, his importance was nationwide rather than merely local.

Historians of the most recent period in American history have either ignored Marcantonio completely or have given him brief and generally derogatory mention in their books. Reinhard Luthin included a sketch of Marcantonio in his *American Demagogues: Twentieth Century,* where the "splinter-party leftist" was compared with men like Joseph McCarthy, Huey Long, or Theodore Bilbo. To Luthin, Marcantonio was an out-and-out demagogue with no redeeming features; it was my own dissatisfaction with Luthin's account that led ultimately to the present study.

Richard Sasuly, a long-time friend of the congressman, wrote what amounted to a eulogy, "People's Politician," published in a book edited by Harvey Goldberg, *American Radicals: Some Problems and Personalities.* Equally eulogistic is the brief biographical account of Marcantonio's career contained in a memorial volume of his speeches, *I Vote My Conscience,* edited by Annette T. Rubinstein. While both of these

1

sketches are diametrically opposed to Luthin's profile of the congressman, they are no more satisfactory.

Demagogue, people's politician, or something in between —whatever the label—Marcantonio deserves more than this inadequate treatment. Admittedly, he was never a congressman of first-rank importance and his accomplishments during fourteen years in the House of Representatives were notably slight. But Marcantonio presents the student of recent American history with the opportunity of studying the radical in a position of relative responsibility rather than on the ubiquitous soapbox. With a voice and a vote in Congress, Marcantonio represented the most radical section of the American left on a host of issues. What did he support? What did he fight against? How did his position change under the stress of events? What were the reasons he gave for the positions he adopted?

Equally intriguing is what we might call the Marcantonio phenomenon. Considering the almost constant and frequently violent opposition to his biennial candidacy, in the press and among politicians belonging to the two major parties, how did he manage to win election after election? On two occasions the New York State Assembly attempted to legislate Marcantonio out of office, once by gerrymandering his district, again by passing a special election law. Undaunted, the congressman went before the voters and with remarkable obstinacy his constituents sent him back again and again to represent them in Washington. In two primary elections he managed to garner the nomination of all three major parties in New York, thus obviating the necessity for any general election campaign.

Called on to explain this phenomenon most commentators have either recorded their bewilderment or have hinted darkly at violence, collusion, or a subterranean political machine of immense power. The question still remains unanswered: How and why did Vito Marcantonio, an outspoken radical, win seven terms in the House of Representatives, six of them in succession?

Several times in the foregoing paragraphs and throughout the remainder of this book I have used some terms—"radical," "left-wing radical," and "the radical left"—that demand explication if not precise definition.

The key word, "radical," has itself undergone enormous changes in usage during the past century. In its earliest political sense in the nineteenth century, the word encompassed those individuals who advocated advanced views of political reform along democratic lines. Thus, the radicals in England after 1800 were those who demanded the broadest extension of the suffrage, while in America during the era of Reconstruction the radicals in Congress were those who urged the extension of the suffrage to the Negro. But for most of the twentieth century the word has connoted much more than a particular political view on the question of voting rights.

While "radical" is a sharply positional word, heavily dependent on the views of the individual using it, I think we can agree to at least the broad manner in which the word was used in this country between 1930 and 1950, the period covered in this book. Necessarily we have to investigate the word from at least three different positions: political, social, and economic.

Politically, "radical" still maintained its earlier meaning of one who advocated reform along democratic lines, but not only in terms of the suffrage, for it was broadened to include the totality of laws and methods of government. To this we might add the element of immediacy, for the radical wanted such reform *now* or with the least possible delay.

Socially, I believe the best conclusion we can come to is that the radical was anti-middle class, anti-bourgeoisie, by which he meant a society in which all things were measured by pecuniary values. In social matters the radical consistently gave primacy to human rights over property rights and in fact allowed few, if any, rights to property. It makes no difference that many if not most of those who considered themselves radicals in America during much of this period were card-carrying members of the middle class; within the American framework they were critics of their society who stood outside the consensus.

Economically, "radical" referred to one who was anti-capitalist and certainly against whatever was meant by the term "free enterprise." There was not always unanimity among radicals about capitalism's ultimate replacement; but regardless of the form, all of the "new societies" called for the elimination of the private profit motive as understood by advocates of capitalism.

If this three-pronged attack is sufficient to define the word "radical" as used in America between, roughly, 1930 and 1950, why the further subdivision into "left-wing radical" or "the radical left"? Primarily because there was one issue, outside the broad framework of the political, social, and economic, that served to split the radical movement in America: the question of foreign policy. Here we can become infinitely more specific than we could in defining the more general term, "radical." I think we can simply classify the left-wing radicals or the radical left as those individuals or groups that, *for whatever reasons,* tended substantially to follow the lead of the American Communist party on questions relating to foreign policy.

I do not imagine that this attempt at definition will satisfy all readers; few words are more positional and emotive than "radical," and even fewer words are so constantly used with little or no attempt at precision. We have witnessed, for example, over the past decade the widespread dissemination of the phrase, "the radical right," when what is meant is either a reactionary or an irresponsible political position. I neither hope nor intend to turn back the tide of linguistic "progress," but I do hope I have made clear my own understanding of this important political word and its variations.

I

East Harlem and a
Politician's Youth

Vito Anthony Marcantonio was born in the heart of New York City's East Harlem at 112th Street and First Avenue on December 10, 1902. Few men in public life have been so intimately linked with a particular urban neighborhood. Born and reared in East Harlem, Marcantonio's permanent home was never more than four city blocks from his place of birth, and for fourteen years he represented the district and its people in Congress. In many ways the man was the product and personification of the neighborhood.[1]

Occupying the northeastern tip of Manhattan Island, East Harlem was an urban slum through all the years of Vito Marcantonio's life. Bounded roughly by the Harlem and East rivers to the north and east and by 96th Street and Fifth Avenue to the south and west, the neighborhood consisted primarily of tenements which varied substantially only in height and condition. Four, five, and sometimes six stories high, their original colors shaded by the city's dirt and grime, the buildings provided little more than shelter from the elements. Through the first four decades of this century, private baths and hot water remained a luxury while central heating, for many of the buildings, was nonexistent.

While primarily residential, East Harlem had its local shops, light manufacturing plants, and on its periphery, some heavy industry: the Knickerbocker Ice Company, Jacob Rupert's massive brewery, the Consolidated Gas Company, and along the East River waterfront the coal yards from which

5

the wind scattered a perpetual rain of fine black dust over the tenements.[2] But much more important than any of these as far as the people of East Harlem were concerned were the small, single-owner retail shops spotted along the 160 square blocks that constituted the district.

According to a survey taken in the mid-1930's, some 685 grocers carried on a cut-throat competition and managed to eke out a precarious living in East Harlem. More than 500 candy stores sold newspapers, magazines, school supplies, and sodas; they sometimes served as headquarters for bookies and numbers racketeers, provided a social center for East Harlem's youth, and occasionally sold penny candy. There were 378 restaurants that together served an international and inexpensive cuisine and 156 bars, one for almost every square block, that made it possible for the adults to drink without going too far from home. More than 230 tailor shops serviced the area, and 26 different junkyards provided a variety of cheap items and added to the aura of urban blight. Nearly 300 doctors sent out bills, 14 loan offices provided an "easy" method of payment, 8 labor organizations strove to increase the weekly paycheck of the predominantly working-class populace. Spiritual needs were met by 42 churches, synagogues, and missions, none of which seems to have suffered from a shortage of communicants. And finally, 11 funeral parlors buried the dead.[3]

Above and beyond geography, East Harlem was its people, a population in excess of 200,000 who gave the neighborhood its color and life. A classic slum since before the turn of the century, East Harlem was both home and steppingstone to successive waves of immigrant groups, "a community always in transition, always on the move, its people ever looking forward to the day when they can break away, shake off the stigma of being identified with it."[4]

A more heterogeneous ethnic grouping would be hard to find in a similar-sized district in any of the world's major cities. Between twenty-seven and thirty-four different nationalities roamed East Harlem's streets and occupied its dilapidated buildings. Every language and dialect of the Western world was spoken along with a few from Asia; every faith, non-faith, and anti-faith was professed. A sprinkling of southern and northern Negroes rubbed shoulders with the majority whites; Italians, Spaniards, Czechs, Jews, Germans, and Irish lived down the street from each other in various stages of ethnic disintegration in the great American "melting-pot." Here and there, sprinkled at random through the district, "refugees" in their own land, a handful of old-stock Americans heroically held their ground against the overwhelming tide of immigrants.[5]

Until the First World War, more than 150,000 Jews lived in both East and Central Harlem. But the influx of Negroes into Central Harlem and of Italians into East Harlem, along with improved economic conditions after 1917, contributed to the escape of many Jews from the slum to the then-suburban areas of the Bronx and Brooklyn. By 1930 less than ten thousand Jews lived in a tight cluster in the western section of East Harlem, their number decreasing each year.[6]

Replacing the Jews and maintaining ethnic dominance in the neighborhood from at least 1920 until after the Second World War were the Italians. They came in such overwhelming numbers that East Harlem became one of the two important "little Italy" areas within the city's limits.[7] Concentrated around Thomas Jefferson Park near the East River and radiating west, north, and south, more than 150,000 first and second generation Italian descendants made East Harlem a faithful reproduction of "bella Napoli" to more than one observer in the 1920's.[8] It was here that Samuel Marcantonio, American-born but of Italian descent, met and married Angelina de Dobitis, a newly arrived immigrant; and it was here they raised their family.[9]

Their oldest son, Vito, grew up in a slum that was as Italian as it was American. Coffee shops labeled *Torroni e Biscotti* dotted the sidestreets and avenues. The grocery stores featured "rabbits and kids, eels and octopuses, watercress and garlic, lemons and chestnuts"—all staples of the Southern

Italian diet. The streets rang with an Italo-American jargon filled with such linguistic perversions as "bisinisso," "giobba," "aisacrima," or the insulting "sonomogona."[10]

Raised as a Catholic, Vito participated in the festivities surrounding the great religious holidays, especially the feast day of San Gennaro, the Neapolitan patron saint. On that day "Little Italy's" drab streets became fragrant arcades of flags and flowers, banners and bonbons, lights, laughter, and much liquid. Bright-robed priests led winding processions of the barefooted faithful who carried statues of the honored saint through the district, bringing a touch of medieval drama to the New World metropolis. Prayer gave way in the evening to a carnival spirit during which bands played tarantellas and fireworks exploded. Practiced hawkers enticed the participants into games of chance, with a percentage of the "take" going to the church instead of to the "house."[11]

But feast days came infrequently, and for the remainder of the year young Marcantonio's East Harlem was preeminently an underdeveloped section of a bustling city. At one period in the mid-1920's, the district had the dubious distinction "of having the most populated block in the city. . . . Five thousand human beings in one city street; as many as fifteen to a four-room flat; two, three, and even four hundred to a tenement intended for fifty!"[12] The Depression of the 1930's had less apparent effect in East Harlem than it did in many other sections of the nation simply because the area was so poor prior to the fateful crash of October 1929. The working-class residents tightened their belts, and more men, young and old, were seen walking the streets during working hours. Those who did continue working frequently had both their hours and wages cut. It was primarily among the small businesses of the neighborhood, run by those marginal operators who had survived the "prosperous" 1920's, that the Depression was most noticeable to the visitor to East Harlem. "The black store windows of small ventures which had gone under," wrote one newcomer, "stared out onto the shabby streets like empty eyeball sockets."[13]

Within this economic context, the family of Samuel Marcantonio seems to have been somewhat better off than the
average in East Harlem. Samuel was a skilled carpenter, his
immediate family was small, and he apparently made a living
wage during Vito's youth if ability to provide for education
is taken as a criterion. After completing primary schooling at
Public School 85 in East Harlem, Vito was, by his own account, one of but two boys who went on to matriculate in
high school. It was not the normal course for an East Harlem
teen-ager; and stung by the derisive laughter of neighborhood
friends, the other boy "dropped out before the end of the
first year."[14]

Each school day for four years, young Marcantonio made
his way across the city to DeWitt Clinton High School at 59th
Street and Tenth Avenue.[15] The location is significant because
it reinforces the impression of familial well-being; the Marcantonios were sufficiently affluent to forego any income their
son might have brought into the household and also to bear
the expense of daily carfare and lunches. War-borne prosperity was undoubtedly a factor in enabling the young man to
pursue his education, for he entered high school in September
1917, six months after the nation declared war on Germany.

His late teens were exciting growing years for Vito, both in
high school and in East Harlem. Early in his school career,
during which his last name was informally shortened to
"Marc," the boy evinced an interest in politics.[16] His class-
mates at DeWitt Clinton tabbed his as a Socialist, perhaps
because the boy constantly discussed "world affairs, politics,
and labor conditions"[17] or possibly because he was active in
some of the Socialist student groups formed during this
period. Leonard Covello, one of Marcantonio's teachers, re-
members him berating a group of fellow students in heated
fashion: "You birds don't even know you're alive. I'll bet you
that this very minute there's somebody, some guy outside
there figuring how he's gonna make money off of your hides
when you go look for a job. You don't even know that!"
Covello does not indicate whether it was the idea of exploita-

tion or the ignorance of his fellow man that upset the young Italo-American.[18]

It was relatively easy for an East Harlem youth to grow up with an interest in politics, for the area was a hotbed of political conflict with every shade of the political spectrum in evidence. The Twentieth Congressional District, the political subdivision covering most of East Harlem, was nominally a Tammany stronghold for the first two decades of the century. The Democrats, however, frequently had difficulty with the Socialist party which was strong in the area; so much so, in fact, that in 1920 Morris Hillquit, a leader of the Socialists, narrowly missed election to Congress. Followers of "the cause," with more hope than accuracy, afterwards referred to East Harlem as "Hillquit's District."[19]

Marcantonio's own entrance on the political scene came in 1920, when he was seventeen years old and still in high school. It was only indirectly connected with the election campaigns. At the end of the war, landlords throughout the city attempted to raise apartment rentals and the courts were flooded with hundreds of eviction cases and countersuits by enraged tenants. Along with fighting in the courts, tenants throughout the city organized in order to effect a political solution to the problem. Marches, meetings, and other forms of peaceful protest were undertaken; but the most popular form of protest became the "rent strike," the purposeful withholding of rent in order to force the landlords to institute suits against hundreds of tenants rather than against a few individuals. Young Marcantonio played a major part in organizing and leading the East Harlem Tenants' League which conducted just such a "strike against post-war rent gouging."[20]

While studying the workings of politics in practice as well as in his textbooks, the boy also attempted to pass on some of his knowledge by conducting citizenship classes at *La Casa del Popolo*, an adult education center established in East Harlem by the Methodist Reverend Amadea Riggio. Here, in each of his classes, "intent, but not without humor," the seventeen-year-old "expounded the elements of American history to some twenty Italian workingmen" who were studying to become citizens. Having learned something about America, he left nothing to chance and periodically shepherded his charges downtown to the naturalization center to guide them personally through the bureaucratic maze.[21]

His activity in East Harlem was matched by his activity in high school, where young Marcantonio showed an early talent for political manipulation. Denied the presidency of a student cultural organization at DeWitt Clinton, *Il Circolo Italiano,* possibly because of his leftist political leanings, perhaps because of his brash personality, Marcantonio fought back. He "managed to have the organizational setup revised and had himself elected chairman of the executive committee, with powers over the president himself."[22]

With all this extracurricular activity, Marcantonio still managed to do well academically during his high school years. He graduated with an 84 average, his only consistently low grades coming in mathematics and the sciences; he barely scraped through elementary algebra and suffered with chemistry for one year. Low grades in these two fields were compensated for by his achievements in social studies, where his marks were uniformly high. His average in this general field was 90.7 per cent, while in American and European history and in the study of economics he was a straight-A student. There seems to have been little doubt in his mind that he was headed for higher education. Except for a one-semester course in business law, he followed an academic curriculum and avoided the many industrial art and commercial courses offered at DeWitt Clinton.[23]

All these experiences—high school, the Italian cultural movement, *La Casa del Popolo,* and the Tenants' League— were important in laying the foundation for a future career. But the single most important event in Marcantonio's teen-age life was a speech he delivered in his senior year of high school.

Behind him on the platform, as the short, slight Italo-American moved to the front of the stage, sat the chubby President of the city's Board of Aldermen, Fiorello La Guardia, the guest speaker of the day.

"This morning," Marcantonio announced, "I am going to talk about old-age pensions and social security." What La Guardia thought as he watched the slender, swarthy student launch into an impassioned defense of a proposal that was extremely radical in 1921 remains shrouded in the past. But given his own social attitudes, he must have been impressed as Marcantonio eloquently concluded, ". . . for, if it is true that government is of the people and for the people, then it is the duty of government to provide for those, who, through no fault of their own, have been unable to provide for themselves. It is the social responsibility of every citizen to see that these laws for our older people are enacted."[24]

La Guardia moved to the front of the platform, "shook Marc's hand, slapped him on the shoulder in a congratulatory gesture," and used the boy's speech as the basis for his own which began with the phrase, "Our neglected citizens. . . ." Within three years they were to meet again as mentor and protégé in a relationship that was severed only by the older man's death.[25]

In September 1921, after receiving his diploma from DeWitt Clinton's principal, Dr. Francis Paul, Marcantonio entered New York University's Law School as a full-time student. Interestingly enough, he registered not as Vito but as Victor Marcantonio.[26] Not yet nineteen, moving for the first time beyond the sharply restricted immigrant world of East Harlem and his Italian circle at DeWitt Clinton, the simple name change undoubtedly indicates a weak attempt at Americanization. Whatever the motive, the aberration was momentary and "Vito" was soon again in use.

Marcantonio's law school grades are worth looking at in some depth for two reasons: first, as a clue to his activities at this period; second, as an indication of how high one can rise on what was, at best, a miserable law school record.

He enrolled in a total of twenty-four courses—ten for one

semester, fourteen covering the full year—and received a total of thirty-eight grades: one A, two B's, twelve C's, twelve D's, and eleven F's. He squeaked through three courses with the lowest possible grade, sixty. He had to take re-exams to pass two other courses. One course, taken in his senior year and a prerequisite to graduation, he flunked in both semesters with grades of 40 and 56. Even a re-exam would not have helped him at this point, and he was passed by special action of the faculty. Thirty-six credits were necessary for graduation; Marcantonio had to take forty-five to accumulate the requirement. That he managed to accomplish it in four years is surprising, but the LL.B. was conferred upon him in 1925 by what one imagines must have been a very relieved dean.[27]

There were several explanations of, if not excuses for, this unpromising record. Marcantonio worked evenings in the adult education department of a new neighborhood social agency, Haarlem House, where his work was an outgrowth of earlier labors at *La Casa del Popolo*. While attending law school, he was not firmly committed to law as a profession. Social work, politics, and teaching American history remained as possible careers in his still youthful mind.[28]

Haarlem House played another and more significant role in his life at this time, for it was there the young law student met and fell in love with Miriam Sanders, a member of the professional staff. Five inches taller and eleven years older than Vito, Miriam Sanders seemed, on the surface, to be worlds apart from the Italo-American.

Her family traced its lineage back to seventeenth century New England, and she had been born in Boston in 1891 and raised in Ossipee, New Hampshire. Devoid of luxurious tastes, thrifty in both person and speech, a devout believer in the social responsibility of her Protestant faith, Miss Sanders had been educated at New Hampshire State University and had studied social work at the Chicago School of Civics and Philanthropy. She did social work in Boston for a short period; then her work brought her to New York City, Haarlem House, and Vito Marcantonio.

Intellectually and culturally the two young people found much in common, and the age and height difference seemed to make no difference in their love affair. On May 20, 1925, even before Vito's graduation from law school, Miss Sanders became Mrs. Marcantonio in a civil ceremony at New York's Municipal Building. New England succumbed permanently to East Harlem.[29]

Another factor explaining Marcantonio's law school grades was his entrance into East Harlem politics in the fall of 1924, the start of his senior year. The not yet "twenty-two-year-old youth then in his political swaddling clothes"[30] suddenly became Fiorello La Guardia's campaign manager in the congressional election of that year. The chance meeting between the two men three years before on the auditorium platform at DeWitt Clinton High School had apparently deepened into a more permanent relationship. If any single fact can explain the emergence of a politician, in Marcantonio's case it was definitely his tie to La Guardia dating from the elections of 1924.

La Guardia's entrance into East Harlem politics, so decisive in Marcantonio's career, needs some explanation. In 1921, the same year Marcantonio entered law school, La Guardia bucked the Republican party machine in New York and tried to wrest the nomination for mayor from the party's choice, Henry Curran.

With neither funds nor an organization, the rotund insurgent was soundly trounced; and after the Democratic victory in the municipal election, he stepped down as president of the Board of Aldermen. In 1922, having mended his political fences, La Guardia accepted the Republican nomination for Congress in the Twentieth Congressional District. In a bitter, three-way campaign filled with much personal invective between the Republican and his Democratic and Socialist rivals, La Guardia squeaked to victory by a margin of 168 votes.[31]

In 1924, incapable of accepting the position of the old-guard Republicans, La Guardia again broke with his party and endorsed the presidential aspirations of the Wisconsin progressive, Robert La Follette. Since La Follette's Progressive party was not formally on the ballot in New York, La Guardia himself accepted the endorsement of the Socialist party in the congressional race in his district. The move involved smart politics rather than ideological commitment. La Guardia was sure of the vote in the Italian section of East Harlem; but the voters in the western section of the Twentieth Congressional District, the still heavily Jewish area, had almost defeated him in 1922. The alliance with the Socialist party undoubtedly strengthened his total position in the campaign.[32]

Marcantonio, possibly a member of the Socialist party at the time, joined the campaign as Fiorello's manager and zealously organized the "hundreds of volunteers, many of them youngsters like himself, who streamed into La Guardia headquarters ready to do what they could to send their Congressman back to Washington."[33] Popular in the district by virtue of his work at Haarlem House, Marcantonio was well-equipped for political campaigning in multinational East Harlem. He already had command of Yiddish and Italian, the two languages most important for political success in the area. Public speaking came easily to him even at that early age, and he was a "natural born leader to whom the common people were attracted because they knew he was one of them . . . only smarter."[34] At any rate, he attacked his political responsibilities with more energy than his books on equity, quasi contract, bills, and notes.

La Guardia's strategy and Marcantonio's labors paid off in the congressman's most sweeping victory; he outdistanced his Democratic opponent, Henry Frank, by 3,615 votes, an enormous differential in the Twentieth Congressional District.[35]

Either as a reward for his efforts or out of the affection La Guardia formed for Marcantonio, the latter was installed early in 1925, before he graduated from law school, as a clerk in the law firm Foster, La Guardia & Cutler. "I am going to take this boy on eventually," the childless, affectionate La Guardia explained to his partners, "as I want to make him my professional heir." The young law clerk's salary was ten dollars a week.[36]

While the congressman fought against the rising tide of Republican "normalcy" in Washington, Marcantonio labored in East Harlem helping constituents who needed legal aid, keeping his "chief informed about the release of immigrants from Ellis Island, the political knifings going on in the district, family feuds, evictions, the loss of jobs," and other matters of local importance. The young law clerk served "as the New York window" for La Guardia in Washington.[37]

Equally important, he kept intact for La Guardia the political organization constructed during the campaign of 1924, ready to become operative at each biennial election. The organization served as La Guardia's personal machine, insuring him against dependence on the Republican party even after he formally returned to the GOP in 1926. Composed of a cross-section of East Harlem's residents, "all of whom rang door bells, distributed leaflets, and cheered" La Guardia's street corner speeches, the organization took legal form in 1929 when it became the F. H. La Guardia Political Club with headquarters on East 116th Street, East Harlem's major traffic artery. Under Marcantonio's astute leadership the club grew to a membership of more than one thousand persons.[38]

Through the congressional campaigns of the 1920's, the personal and political relationship between the two second-generation Americans grew stronger. "Marcantonio," one of La Guardia's biographers insists, "was like a son to the childless and widowered Fiorello."[39] And like a father, La Guardia was brutally frank in criticizing his law clerk and political right arm.

When Marcantonio sent the fiery Fiorello a memorandum covering two cases and enclosed the valuable original papers, La Guardia wrote back, "It was not necessary to send me the papers. In fact it was very stupid to do so."[40]

Refusing to be intimidated, acting much like an unfairly criticized son, the brash beginner fired back a letter reminding La Guardia that his telegram had specifically asked for "papers." Sardonically he added, "I think that the language indicates clearly that you wanted the papers in the case. . . . I may have been 'stupid' to have sent them, according to your interpretations of your own words." In reply to another La Guardia criticism, this time relating to generally shoddy work, Marcantonio wrote, "I have been very hard pressed for time. I have been busy interviewing people that have come in to see you, taken care of your matters, and have ten negligence cases to prepare for trial. . . . I am not as bad as you make me in your letter."[41]

Whatever face La Guardia showed his protégé, he brooked no interference from his partners when it came to Marcantonio's position in the firm. From the beginning La Guardia hinted that the law clerk's salary would have to be raised in the near future, and he became angry upon learning the Marcantonio had not been asked to sit in when the firm's case load was reviewed—a major honor for a young man then on the verge of flunking out of law school.[42]

A significant picture of Marcantonio at this period in his life can be derived from a letter La Guardia wrote the twenty-two-year-old youth in 1925. Always free with advice to the young, La Guardia poured out his heart to Marcantonio, whom he addressed as "Dear Sonny":

You are young, you have a lot to learn and a long way to go before you will be a lawyer in the real sense of the word. I am fond of you and want to help you. Were I not interested in you, I would not have planned as I did looking far into the future. . . . You have an opportunity presented to you such as very few boys have, other than those who can step into their own father's office and know that one day it will be theirs. That is what I am offering you. You must make up your mind to be fair with me. You are going to be a politician, a social worker, or a lawyer. If you are satisfied, as I told you, to make a living from the Magistrate and Municipal Courts, with General Sessions as the possible limit, you can keep up your social and political activities. If you love your profession, want to be proficient in it and intend to follow it, then you have got to change your attitude and your whole mode of living. You have to cut out your evening appointments, your dances, your midnight philosophers, for the next five years and devote yourself to serious hard study of the law. . . . Be careful in your personal appearance. Get a Gillette razor and keep yourself well groomed at all times. Be always respectful and courteous to all, the humble as well as the high and for goodness sake keep your ears and eyes open and keep your mouth closed for at least the next twenty years. Now my dear boy take this letter in the fatherly spirit that I am writing it.[48]

It was reasonable advice in part, and in part Marcantonio accepted it. He was at this time "often unkempt, in need of a shave, and badly dressed; he quickly learned . . . the value of conservative suits, regular haircuts, and a clean shaven face."[44] But the brash youth became a brash adult; and when La Guardia suggested the tough young denizen of the East Harlem slum learn to keep his mouth closed "for at least the next twenty years," he was asking the impossible given Marcantonio's character. La Guardia's moderating influence operated only at Marcantonio's choice, and at times the older man was forced to sigh, "My son, my son, my erring son."

Through the era of Republican ascendancy, Marcantonio labored in East Harlem for his political mentor and helped him retain his seat in Congress in the elections of 1926, 1928, and 1930. In that last year La Guardia's protégé received an appointment as assistant United States attorney general for the district of New York, a position he held without particular distinction until 1932.[45] During this same period the young lawyer established his own firm, Pinto & Marcantonio, specializing in labor law.[46] When La Guardia made his final race for Congress in 1932 and lost to the magnetic attraction Franklin Delano Roosevelt had for the voters that year, Marcantonio again managed the campaign with frenetic zeal.

Ernest Cuneo, another La Guardia law clerk of the period, described Marcantonio at work during the election of 1932 as "one of the smartest cookies I ever encountered, one who

could trade political punches blow for blow with any comer.
He was a really tough guy," despite his size. Short, slight, with
long black hair that frequently spilled over his forehead,
Marcantonio had a pinched face accentuated by prominent
cheekbones. His dark eyes were large and liquid, his lips full,
and to Cuneo he had "the Bourbon look of combined sensu-
ousness and asceticism."[47]

Unaccustomed to politics in East Harlem, Cuneo was
shocked by the violence, fraud, and mayhem that punctuated
the 1932 campaign between La Guardia and his Tammany
opponent, James J. Lanzetta. During that campaign "La
Guardia gangs matched Lanzetta gangs in smashing plate-
glass windows which contained the picture of the enemy."[48]
He also could not understand Marcantonio's physical as well
as political commitment to La Guardia's cause. Writing about
the rough-and-tumble tactics of street-corner campaigning,
Cuneo reported seeing a fight that broke out near the tailgate
of a truck from which Marcantonio spoke one evening. "Suddenly Marc launched right out into the air and landed on
top of a milling group . . . flailing away at a great rate."[49]

While Cuneo failed to appreciate the publicity value of
such physical involvement, he fully recognized Marcantonio's
power as a speaker and has left us a superb portrait of the
young politician at work:

> Marc then took over the microphone and there ensued what
> can only be described as a mass phenomenon. He started
> slowly and spoke for some time. Then abruptly he struck his
> heel on the truck bed; it made a loud hollow noise and the
> crowd stirred. The cadence of his talk increased, and soon the
> heel struck again. Again the pace quickened. . . . His voice
> rose, and now the heel struck more often with the beginnings
> of a real tempo. It began to sound like a train leaving a sta-
> tion. The crowd mirrored his growing excitement. At the cli-
> max, Marc was shouting at the top of his lungs and he was
> stamping his foot as hard and as rapidly as a flamenco dancer.
> The crowd pulsed to the rhythm and at last found release in a
> tumultuous, prolonged roar of applause. Because it was good
> theater, it was also great politics.[50]

Defeated in the Democratic landslide of 1932, La Guardia rode a wave of reform into office as New York City's mayor in 1933, thus removing himself from the narrower confines of politics in East Harlem.

With La Guardia out of the way the road was now clear for Marcantonio's own emergence into the political spotlight. The growing-up years were behind him. He had learned what he could from La Guardia, he had definitely determined on politics as a career, and he now prepared himself to apply the lessons learned in political combat in East Harlem since 1924.

The path to political success in New York City is marked by two obvious road signs. One counsels membership in either the Republican or Democratic parties. The other advises an appenticeship at the local or clubhouse level with slow movement up the machine-made ladder. Both signs generally have to be followed before an individual can hope to present his name to the public in candidacy for an important elective position. It is possible to ignore the advice, but only with much risk. There are men who have bolted into the political limelight without serving the apprenticeship, but they are rare. Ignoring the two major parties is an even rarer occurrence. The election laws drawn up by representatives of those same parties work effectively against the independent and favor the organization man.

Vito Marcantonio had carefully met both major criteria by the time he decided to run for Congress in the 1934 campaign in the Twentieth Congressional District. He had served a ten-year apprenticeship in East Harlem under La Guardia, one of the most masterful modern politicians. Working with his mentor, Marcantonio had helped build La Guardia's personal machine into a superb political instrument and had wielded that instrument with skill in five election campaigns between 1924 and 1932.

Whatever his own political predilections, the young man was a Republican through his association with La Guardia.

As one of the best-known younger politicos in East Harlem, Marcantonio should have had little trouble getting the Republican nomination for the congressional race. In addition, he had the apparent advantage of La Guardia's unqualified support. By 1934 "The Little Flower" was not simply an ex-congressman; he was the recently elected mayor of the city and thus the most important Republican in New York. Paradoxically, Marcantonio's association with La Guardia proved to be a handicap.

La Guardia had a long record as a progressive, maverick Republican who had twice bolted the established GOP machine. At best, he wore his Republican label lightly; some members of his own party would have preferred the word "invisibly." On some of the major issues of those Depression days, "The Little Flower" stood far from the orthodox Republican position.

While his own party and a series of Republican presidents backed the "noble" experiment in Prohibition, La Guardia set up a still in his congressional office and defiantly brewed beer for the doubly delighted Washington press corps.[51] It was the Republican La Guardia who successfully led the battle in Congress against one of President Herbert Hoover's major legislative recommendations, the national sales tax.[52] In addition, La Guardia was the kind of man who had organized a personal machine, independent of the GOP in his district, to provide himself with insurance against being dropped by the party with which he was ostensibly allied.[53]

The local Republican party organization balked at giving the nomination to the mayor's young protégé, from whom they expected the same type of behavior. Marcantonio's only recourse was to fight for control of the GOP machine in his district; success would enable him to dictate his own nomination.

Luckily for the young politician, the entire New York County Republican leadership was under fire in 1933 from an insurgent group directed by Chase Mellen, Jr. Marcantonio, looking for support in his own battle, allied himself with this "progressive" opposition against the "old guard" Republicans led by Samuel Koenig. Koenig was a "man of character and integrity," who had been chairman of the New York County Republican organization for some twenty years prior to 1933. His machine's position had frequently run counter to public opinion, and to some observers Koenig himself possessed an almost uncanny ability at losing elections.[54] The primary election fight between these two Republican factions was bitter, especially in East Harlem with its long heritage of political conflict. The physical proximity of the contending factions, both of whom had headquarters on East Harlem's 116th Street, added fuel to the raging political fire.[55]

On September 26, 1933, in an election enlivened by physical contact between the two groups—Marcantonio supporters charged that they had been barred from their own clubhouse by "gangsters and thugs" working for the opposition—Marcantonio won control of the Republican organization by the barest of margins, one vote.[56] Two days later, the "old guard" capitulated and Chase Mellen, Jr., was elected chairman of the Republican County Committee by unanimous vote. Winning in his own district, Marcantonio found himself on the victorious side in the county and thus cleared the road for his own nomination in the congressional campaign the following year.[57]

Beating an anachronistic Republican organization in 1933 was one thing; defeating an incumbent Democratic congressman in 1934 was something altogether different. Marcantonio was fortunate on this point too, for James J. Lanzetta, the Tammany man who had upset La Guardia in the election of 1932, had not compiled a sparkling legislative record for himself.

It would have been difficult for any ordinary politician to follow La Guardia as East Harlem's representative in Washington. "The Little Flower" had a national reputation, an instinctive rapport with his constituents, and a highly developed sense of the dramatic that made him one of the most formidable campaigners of his time. It was difficult to read a New York City newspaper during his tenure in Congress without finding his name in one context or another.

Lanzetta had comparatively little press coverage during his two-year term; he had none of La Guardia's flair for either politics or public relations. One of the Democrat's longest speeches in Congress was, in fact, an indiscretion as far as East Harlem was concerned. During the debate over H.R. 5240, a bill "to provide emergency relief with respect to home mortgage indebtedness," Lanzetta urged his fellow legislators to consider the plight of the poor landlord of the slum. "Many tenants have been unable to pay rent," he explained, "but they, nevertheless, have been permitted to remain because of the friendly feeling existing between the owner and the tenant, from a long and intimate association."[58] This idyllic picture of landlord-tenant relations in East Harlem hardly depicted reality. The only regular contact between building owner and apartment dweller occurred on rent collection day, a relationship hardly conducive to warm friendship. The majority of slum real-estate was owned or controlled by either banks or real-estate syndicates and not by middle-class individuals living at a level barely above that of their tenants as indicated by Lanzetta.

In one area Lanzetta showed himself to be an astute politician. He recognized the importance of the growing Puerto Rican minority in East Harlem, which slowly but steadily infiltrated into the area of former Jewish preponderance between "Little Italy" and Fifth Avenue.

Lanzetta took every opportunity on the floor of Congress to remind the legislature of its responsibility to America's closest island possession. In particular, he offered an amendment to the Agricultural Adjustment Act designed to remove discriminatory restrictions on raw and refined sugar produced in Puerto Rico. On the final day of the Seventy-third Congress he pleaded for passage of his measure, pointing out that otherwise the Congress would tacitly condemn the islanders to poverty and ultimately to disorder.[59] Such labors paid off politically. In October 1934, in the midst of the election campaign, Senator Antonio Barcelo of Puerto Rico came to East Harlem to assist the congressman in his campaign for re-election in return for Lanzetta's work "in Congress on behalf of Puerto Rico." On the night of October 15, 1934, more than two thousand Puerto Ricans boisterously paraded through East Harlem carrying signs and banners in support of Lanzetta's candidacy.[60]

Marcantonio had neither the advantages nor the disadvantages inherent to the incumbent. His only connection with politics was through La Guardia, at the time the most influential politician in New York City. It was through La Guardia that Marcantonio succeeded in winning the nomination of the City-Fusion party as well as that of his own Republican organization. The endorsement he received from the Knickerbocker Democrats and the Liberal party—both reform, anti-Tammany, Democratic organizations—undoubtedly also came through the mayor.[61]

Because of his work as a labor lawyer, Marcantonio counted on the support of many labor leaders and their unions; in fact, a labor committee for Marcantonio opened a separate office on Lexington Avenue at the start of the campaign. The most important backing from labor came through his good friend, Luigi Antonini, general secretary of the solidly Italian Local 89 of the International Ladies Garment Workers Union (ILGWU), one of the strongest labor organizations in East Harlem.[62]

Marcantonio's platform was more negative than positive as far as can be determined. He favored more liberal immigration laws, a safe position in heavily immigrant East Harlem; and he called for a more conscientious home relief program, another appealing measure in a slum neighborhood riddled with unemployment. But as the outsider fighting his way in, Marcantonio spent much more time insulting Tammany Hall, detailing Lanzetta's failure as a congressman, and berating the Democrats for their failure to alleviate the effects of the Depression.[63]

Taking a cue from Tammany's methods, Marcantonio inaugurated a technique during the 1934 campaign that he later refined into pure political gold. Residents of East Harlem developed the habit of dropping into Marcantonio's headquarters, the old La Guardia Clubhouse on East 116th Street, to ask advice on matters pertaining to relief. The young candidate and his supporters, some of whom had a social work background, gave freely of their time and knowledge; this modified form of social service undoubtedly won votes. The technique was little different, if perhaps of more lasting value, that the older Tammany device of distributing Christmas food packages.[64]

But the young challenger's most telling weapon in the campaign was La Guardia's enthusiastic endorsement which burst over East Harlem the week before the election. "I have confidence in you," the mayor wrote, "and that you will join with the progressive forces of the House for good government and progressive social welfare laws." He concluded with, "I know that you will support the President," surely one of the strangest endorsements for one Republican to give another concerning a Democratic president.[65] La Guardia's pronouncement went a long way toward confirming whatever doubts regular Republicans might have had about Marcantonio's reliability.

The election campaign almost ended in disaster for both sides when Marcantonio and Lanzetta planned election eve rallies for the same location, Lexington Avenue and 116th Street, the heart of East Harlem. La Guardia traditionally had completed his campaigns at this same spot, his famous "Lucky Corner"; Marcantonio, campaigning on the mayor's record, chose the spot naturally as La Guardia's political heir. Lanzetta apparently hoped to profit from whatever audience appeared.

The possibility of excitement drew people from all over the district, and the crowd meeting under arcades of lights and election banners was estimated by reporters at fifteen thousand people. From loudspeakers set up at opposite corners, some sixty orators berated the multitude in English and

Italian (Spanish had not yet come into prominence in East Harlem and Yiddish was no longer important). Two police emergency squads and seventy-five blue-coated patrolmen kept the peace between the contending factions. While there is no record of the bilingual oratory convincing any uncommitted voters, neither is there evidence of any injury among the crowd—a tribute to New York's sharp-eyed police force.[66]

After the evening's activity, election day itself was anticlimactic. When the 27,145 ballots cast in the district had been counted, thirty-two-year-old Vito Marcantonio had defeated James J. Lanzetta by the slim margin of 257 votes.[67]

Lanzetta had laid the basis for contesting the election earlier in the campaign and almost immediately cried "foul," filing notice with the clerk of the House of Representatives that he would contest Marcantonio's seating. The Democrat charged that Marcantonio had bought votes by extending or promising relief funds to otherwise unsympathetic voters and was aided and abetted in this chicanery by Edward Corsi, director of the Home Relief Bureau, and by William Hodson, New York City's commissioner of public welfare. As proof Lanzetta cited a New York *Daily Mirror* gossip column, "City-Hall-Run-a-Round." The evidence turned out to be useless, the reporter having no more proof than Lanzetta himself.[68]

Marcantonio termed his opponent's charge "silly and ridiculous." Basically the charge referred to the Republican's developing program of social service for the residents of East Harlem. "It is true," the congressman-elect explained "that people came to us at our political club with relief problems, and we did help them when we could, showing them how they could get relief, but further than that Lanzetta's charges will not stand. I'm willing to have a hearing on them."[69] As with most such attempts, the complaint was eventually rejected by the House of Representatives.[70]

It is difficult today to separate the elements leading up to Vito Marcantonio's emergence in 1934 as a Republican member of the House of Representatives. Indeed, how can one account for the election of *any* Republican in the year that saw the Democrats increase their large majorities in both houses of Congress? Arthur Krock of *The New York Times* called the Democratic sweep of 1934 "the most overwhelming victory in the history of American politics"; when the returns were all in, there were only seven Republican governors left in the nation.[71]

The electorate in East Harlem, despite its endorsement of Republican Vito Marcantonio, did not really go counter to the national trend. If anything, it elected a man who seemed to be more New Deal-oriented than his Democratic opponent. La Guardia's endorsement, "I know that you will support the President," was the key to the limits of Marcantonio's Republicanism. His personality, the excitement he generated as a campaigner, his lifelong connection with East Harlem— these too were factors accounting for his victory. Beneath all of this there was the Depression itself, which enabled many political neophytes to win election to Congress.

Whatever the cause, the effect was clear; by virtue of 257 votes Vito Marcantonio was a newly elected member of the House of Representatives.

II

The Off-Color Republican

The Seventy-fourth Congress, the first in which Vito Marcantonio served, convened in Washington on January 3, 1935, in the fifth year of the worst depression the nation had ever suffered. The overwhelming mood of despair, the sense of national crisis Franklin Delano Roosevelt faced immediately after his election in 1932, had been overcome. But the economic recovery he promised the nation remained in the future as far as the average man was concerned; the gross national product was twenty billion dollars less than in 1929 and more than ten million people were still unemployed.

Critics of the administration, quiescent through 1933 and 1934, now loomed up at every point on the political spectrum ready to pick up the pieces when and if the New Deal faltered. Despite the sweeping Democratic victory at the polls in 1934, there was hope for the opposition. Some of the problems met by Roosevelt and his supporters were not solved finally, for much of the important New Deal legislation was to be reviewed by the Supreme Court within two years and the Court could reverse New Deal progress.

In addition, the first two years of New Deal legislation was limited in scope, no matter how revolutionary it appeared to some Americans at the time. Depression on the farm was vigorously attacked primarily through the Agricultural Adjustment Act of 1933; the National Industrial Recovery Act of that same year, the act that gave birth to the famous Blue Eagle, was designed to help the businessman. But the administration depended on these and a mixed bag of fiscal tricks to institute recovery and, through general recovery, to put the large mass of unemployed back to work. By 1935 the strategy had not succeeded and the unemployed workingman received scant direct attention from the New Deal. Of the countless laws passed by Congress during the first hundred days of the New Deal, only the acts establishing the Civilian Conservation Corps and the Federal Emergency Relief Administration, and these only in a very limited way, had much bearing on the day-to-day suffering of the urban unemployed. Late in 1933 Roosevelt created the Civil Works Administration (CWA) and through it pumped federal funds into the trickle of relief available during the winter of 1933–1934. But the CWA was short-lived and died a quiet, officially unmourned death in April 1934, while the number of unemployed remained substantially the same.

The leaders of every political group, from the conservative Liberty Leaguers through the two major parties to the Communists, fully realized the tremendous significance of the Seventy-fourth Congress which would lead the nation into the presidential elections of 1936. There was no doubt about which political party would ultimately bear the responsibility for congressional action or inaction on the unsolved problems of the Depression. The elections of 1934 gave the Democrats absolute control of both houses of Congress; 69 Democratic senators ruled over 25 Republicans, while in the House of Representatives the newly elected Congressman from East Harlem, Vito Marcantonio, was one of only 103 Republicans in a body dominated by 319 Democrats.

Some spice was added to politics in the House by a sprinkling of Farmer-Laborites and other midwestern "progressives" who formed the nucleus of the group Arthur Schlesinger, Jr., later referred to as that "lively generation of radicals" brought into the House by the congressional elections of 1934.

From the moment the House convened, this group—numbering as many as thirty-five congressmen—made up an unorganized radical bloc under the informal leadership of Maury Maverick (Dem., Texas). At various times the bloc attempted to push the House further to the left than it wanted to go; while these radicals had almost no substantive success, they did succeed in dramatizing issues and viewpoints that otherwise would never have been made public. It was in this informal group—with men like Maverick, Ernest Lundeen (Farmer-Laborite, Minnesota), Tom Amlie (Prog., Wisconsin) and George Schneider (Rep.-Prog., Wisconsin)—that young Marcantonio soon found those with political leanings and thoughts similar to his own.[1]

It took time, however, for Marcantonio to join the group, for the "members" were almost all from the Midwest and were as unfamiliar to him as he was to them. Thus, in his first legislative action the congressman from East Harlem voted with the Republican minority for Bertrand Snell (Rep., New York) as speaker of the House rather than for the nominee of the radical bloc, George Schneider of Wisconsin.[2] Regularity in this essentially meaningless way was rewarded with assignment by the minority leadership to three committees: Civil Service, Labor, and Territories.[3]

Within a few months, certainly before Congress adjourned in August, the freshman congressman had exhibited a legislative position far to the left, not only of his own party, but also of the most fervent New Dealers. Some of his own most important and ardent supporters gasped at the extent of his radicalism. "What is on your mind?" asked Luigi Antonini of the ILGWU, baffled by Marcantonio's stand. "Surely you cannot expect to get the approval [of] and count on labor organizations."[4]

The gulf between Marcantonio and the majority of both political parties became apparent with his maiden speech late in February 1935. The immediate issue was the War Department Appropriations Bill of that year. In his attack Marcantonio concentrated on two aspects of the measure, and these same two factors appeared repeatedly in his speeches during the Depression years, almost like some personal leitmotiv.

First was the simple contradiction Marcantonio saw in a bill that called for "one of the largest annual outlays in peacetime history for strictly military purposes" while at the same time upwards of ten million people walked the streets without jobs. The unemployed were, in his thinking, the central tragedy of the Depression, the people who paid for it with day-to-day suffering. Under such conditions, he insisted, no administration had the right to demand huge sums in preparation for some future war when the same funds might more properly be used for the relief of the jobless.

Second, and the issue that really raised Marcantonio's ire, was one small section of the measure providing funds for compulsory Reserve Officer Training Corps (ROTC) programs in colleges and universities. Innocuous to most congressmen, involving nothing more than an attempt at providing military officers in case of emergency, this section of the bill raised in Marcantonio's mind the question "whether or not the freedom of choice and the liberty of the young men of this Nation are to be completely annihilated and abolished?" Compulsory ROTC programs, he explained with more than a slight reference to Nazi Germany, involved an attempt at forcing American youth "to goose step through the classroom and mentally goose step on the campus"; it was a device intended "to stifle liberal thought in our educational institutions." Behind it all he saw "a strong tendency toward government by edict . . . an urge for regimentation."[5]

His speech, which was called "the most stirring of the day," whipped up an acrimonious two-hour debate in the House over the pragmatic value of military training. But Marcantonio's amendment to eliminate funds for compulsory ROTC programs from the Appropriations Bill received scant support among his fellow legislators, the few votes coming mostly from the group of similar thinking young radicals.[6]

If nothing else, Marcantonio's attack on the administration brought him to the attention of that informal group on the left led by Maury Maverick. Less than one month later the Democratic congressman from Texas invaded the Republican cloakroom and presented his colleague from East Harlem with "an elaborately decorated scroll in which" Marcantonio was described as "an OFF-COLOR Republican, . . . the said Marcantonio being hereinafter known and designated as: THE PINK PACHYDERM OF CONGRESS."[7]

Fulfilling the trust thus given him, Marcantonio admirably demonstrated just how far "off-color" he was during the legislative battle over the administration's Social Security Bill that occupied the Congress for many weeks during 1935.

The Republican party and conservative elements throughout the nation attacked the president's bill on predictable grounds. Marcantonio, ostensibly a Republican, attacked the measure because it did not go far enough in protecting the workingman and because the imposition of a payroll tax on employees was "a vicious anti-social system of having the poor carry the burden of caring for the poor."

Against the measure backed by Democrats he supported H.R. 2827, the Frazier-Lundeen Bill, a proposal for a much broader system of social security. When the bill came up for discussion, both Democrats and Republicans characterized it as Communist-inspired, which led Marcantonio to characterize the opposition as those "superdetectives" of the House who "went around snooping and . . . hurled the cry of 'communism' . . . the only manner in which this bill has been attacked thus far."[8]

Thirty years after its introduction, the bill would still be considered the height of radicalism. It provided for a system of unemployment insurance covering all the unemployed, regardless of occupation, for the full period of unemployment and paying benefits equal to the prevailing local wage and rising with any rise in the cost of living. This unemployment insurance feature was to be administered through commissions elected by members of labor and farm organizations; thus effective control would be kept in the hands of the working classes. Other forms of insurance covering sickness, old-age, maternity, and industrial accidents were to be studied and immediately instituted by the Secretary of Labor. Funds to pay for this vast program of social insurance were to come, not from the workers themselves, but by the imposition of higher taxes on all inheritances, gifts, and individual and corporate incomes exceeding $5,000 a year.[9]

There was no doubt in Marcantonio's mind that a social security measure of some kind was going to be passed by the House in 1935. The administration's bill, he admitted, was an attempt at solving a pressing national problem and was laudable in all ways but in the method used to pay for the program. The method of payment was the key question "before the nation at this time."

The administration's bill was designed "to afford security against the large bulk of unemployment in the future." While Marcantonio agreed with this aim, he could not overlook the immediate effects of the measure. The imposition of a payroll tax, he insisted, would further reduce the pitifully low purchasing power of the American working class. "Everybody recognizes," he explained, "that America's problem today is the lack of purchasing power on the part of the American workers; they have practically no purchasing power left. When we attempt to remove a further portion of this purchasing power," through a direct tax on their pay, "we only accentuate the problem, we do not alleviate it. . . ." The Frazier-Lundeen approach was more logical, he insisted, since under it the worker retained his purchasing power, his standard of living, and his self-respect.[10]

It did not matter to Marcantonio that the Communist party supported the Frazier-Lundeen Bill and probably played an important part in formulating its provisions.[11] What mattered was the worth of the measure itself. Since it fit into his radical view, since it would detract only from the purchasing power of what he thought of as the upper classes, he threw what little force he had behind the more radical proposal. It was the administration's bill that won congressional approval; the Frazier-Lundeen Bill never even received serious consideration.

It must be added that, despite the value the Social Security Act had in later years, at the time of its passage it provided few benefits for the nation's workers and did, as Marcantonio explained, sap their purchasing power to the extent that it taxed their wages. The act did nothing to solve the pressing problems of unemployment and the physical deprivation caused by the Depression. It was legislation for the future and a hesitant step forward at that.

To Marcantonio, the Social Security Act was little more than a key to the essentially conservative character of Roosevelt's New Deal. This particular attitude on his part was deeply buttressed when, early in 1936, the administration asked Congress to appropriate $1,500,000,000 for unemployment relief, compared with nearly $5,000,000,000 appropriated for the same purpose the preceding year. According to Marcantonio, who estimated the number of unemployed exceeded twelve million, the need for unemployment relief had not changed in one year; yet Roosevelt recommended slashing the relief budget by more than two-thirds. The reason was clear enough to Marcantonio: Roosevelt was playing the "numbers racket," attempting in an election year to establish a statistical case for recovery by pointing to lower expenditures for relief.[12] President Hoover had attempted to solve the problems of the Depression, Marcantonio reminded his fellow congressmen, "by waiting for Lady Prosperity. . . . The New Deal is trying it by proclaiming loudly and smilingly that she has kept her date and is now promenading with the President of the Chamber of Commerce along Main Street." The administration's request for reduced relief funds "constitutes a sweet victory for the Liberty League over the unemployed." The unemployed, he concluded ominously, "can expect nothing from those in power. They must depend on themselves."

Representative John McCormack (Dem., Massachusetts), an administration spokesman, took exception to Marcantonio's remarks and angrily asked, "Where would [the unemployed] be if the present administration had not engaged in the humane policy that it has?"

"You should ask me," Marcantonio replied, uncovering the

huge gulf between himself and the New Dealers, "where would the administration be?"

"We have given $3,000,000,000 a year," McCormack insisted, averaging the figures for the two years.

"That is not enough . . . you started in the right direction. Now you retreat. What kind of leadership is that?"

McCormack, probably thinking he was engaged in a debate with a normal Republican, shot back, "It is $3,000,000,000 a year more than Hoover gave."

"Is the gentleman proud," Marcantonio asked, "of being just a little better than Hoover? Is that all the gentleman has to offer?"

When Congressman Thomas Fletcher (Dem., Texas) rather sarcastically asked Marcantonio how he would solve the seemingly insoluble unemployment problem, Marcantonio responded by calling for an immediate appropriation of six billion dollars, equally divided among direct relief, grants to the states, and work relief programs. The unemployed, he insisted, were victims of an economic system that had failed and were without work through no fault of their own. Providing them with employment at a living wage was not, he pointed out, a question of charity, but of right.

"Where are we going to get the money?" he rhetorically asked. "Reduce to a minimum the more than a billion dollars appropriation made for war purposes. Apply the British tax rate on all individual and corporate incomes, inheritances, and gifts over $5,000 a year."[13]

His program had as little chance of passing as did the Frazier-Lundeen Bill. After all, Marcantonio himself termed the Seventy-fourth Congress "hopelessly reactionary" in a report to his constituents after only six months in Washington.[14]

If Congress were "hopelessly reactionary," what path could a radical like Marcantonio follow? The problem bothered at least three other members of Congress, for in April 1935 Marcantonio, joined by Ernest Lundeen, George Schneider and Thomas Amlie, issued a call to a private conference to be held in Washington in May to discuss the possibilities of organizing a new party. There was practical unanimity among themselves, they wrote, "that a new party on a national scale is becoming necessary, but [there was also] some difference of opinion as to the possibility of action by 1936." There was similar agreement "that the basis of united action by progressives must be recognition of the fallacy of any attempt to preserve the old economy of scarcity, and the necessity of moving towards the establishment of an economy of abundance through production for use, employing the immense productive capacity known to exist in this country."[15]

The fruit of this May gathering was a public meeting in Chicago two months later attended by 250 "native American radicals" and presided over by Professor Paul H. Douglas of the University of Chicago. The aim of the meeting was to discuss the preparations necessary for the "organization of a political federation to be held ready for action in 1936, if necessary."[16]

On the first day of the meeting, July 5, 1935, Tom Amlie, congressman from Wisconsin, introduced a discordant note by announcing, "Our aim is to unite all the groups who want a change to come through the ballot box, which excludes Communists."[17] Amlie's statement was in accord with the view of the majority attending the meeting, but it was distasteful to Marcantonio.

On various occasions in the past, Marcantonio had declared his insistence on working with any individual and any party that favored ends similar to his own. Yet, when he withdrew from the Chicago conference the following day, his statement to the press was equivocal and avoided any direct confrontation with the policy of excluding Communists. "The formation of a new party at this time," he announced, "is not only premature, but also wrong, and the conference is not at present so constituted as to fully express the opinions and demands" of the various groups that would ultimately compose the new political coalition.[18]

At the very least the statement was illogical since he had been one of those who called the conference together to investigate the need for a new party. Less than two weeks before his withdrawal, he had been absolutely certain about the same issue. "Please be ready," he advised a correspondent in June, "to write a requiem for the New Deal."[19] If anything, the statement mirrors the confusion in his own mind, the paradox that the New Deal presented to the radical mind during the Depression. In less than one year he was once again talking about the formation of a left-led farmer-labor party organized on a national scale, but for the elections of 1940 rather than 1936.[20]

Essentially the problem for Marcantonio and other leftists was that they felt the New Deal was bad, but not as bad as was the Republican party. While he talked about requiems and frequently spoke out against the limitations of the New Deal, he just as frequently voted for important administration measures and at times found himself fighting for legislation that later became hallmarks of the New Deal.

He favored, for example, the Wealth Tax Act and the Snyder-Guffy Act to stabilize the bituminous coal industry, though he had reservations concerning both measures. He suggested three important amendments to the tax bill. First, he called for an increase in the tax rate applied on corporate and personal income exceeding $5,000 annually. Second, he asked for the elimination of tax credits for depreciation and depletion, "one of the widest doors through which tax dodging is accomplished." Third, he offered an amendment to tax all gains arising from exchanges of property or from the acquisition of securities through reorganizations or the formation of holding companies. All three amendments were voted down, the first by a lopsided majority of 169 to 16.[21]

When the Wagner-Connery Labor Relations Bill was debated in the House during the warm month of June 1935, Marcantonio again had his own ideas about the legislation but was nevertheless "whole-heartedly for the bill."

As a member of the Labor Committee, the freshman congressman from New York found himself disagreeing with the majority of the committee members on the question of whether the proposed National Labor Relations Board (NLRB) should be placed under the jurisdiction of the Department of Labor or should be established as an independent regulatory agency. The majority opinion favored the first procedure, while Marcantonio signed a minority report upholding the latter view. The issue was crucial to Marcantonio; he foresaw the distinct possibility of the legislation being emasculated if left in the hands of the Labor Department. He had seen the intent of the famous section 7(a) of the National Recovery Act destroyed when committed to the hands of politicians, and he predicted that an NLRB under the thumb of the Secretary of Labor "would quickly be swallowed up in the general policies of the Department of Labor," which are "susceptible to political repercussions."[22]

This was one of the few times in his political career that Marcantonio found himself on the winning side. When the Wagner-Connery Bill became law, the NLRB was established as an independent agency and its status in the difficult and complex field of labor-management relations was very definitely enhanced.

An unusual note in his wholehearted espousal of the Wagner-Connery Bill came when Marcantonio, the representative from the city slums, introduced an amendment to include farm laborers under the provisions of the bill. "The same reasons," he told his congressional colleagues, "urged for the adoption of this bill in behalf of the industrial workers are equally applicable in the case of the agricultural workers, in fact more so as their plight calls for immediate and prompt action." The amendment won little support and was defeated easily. Legislators from farm areas were usually more interested in the farm owners than in farm labor; and the migrant workers, moving with the crop and the season, rarely met the residence requirement that would have given them the power of the vote.[23]

Marcantonio put up his strongest fight and used some of his most outspoken language in defense of Roosevelt's Public Utilities Holding Company Bill of 1935. The congressional battle over this segment of the New Deal program was particularly bitter and revolved around two issues, one in the bill itself and one a natural concomitance of the measure. These were, respectively, the "death sentence" clause, which called for the outlawing of public utility holding companies, and the intensive lobbying in which both the utility companies and the government engaged.

When critics of the public utility companies denounced the swarm of lobbyists who urged congressmen to repudiate the bill, defenders of the utilities pointed to government emissaries Benjamin Cohen and Thomas Corcoran, who lobbied intensively for the measure. Marcantonio, favoring the bill, came to the defense of the two young government lawyers. They have, he insisted, "no financial or selfish interest in the outcome of the issues involved here." Whether this bill failed, whether the "death sentence" clause remained or was omitted, "they are not going to be financially rewarded, nor are they going to the punished." He won a storm of applause from the galleries when he announced that he intended to introduce a resolution calling for an investigation of "the lobbyists and the political cockroaches that have infested the corridors of our National Capitol during this great fight."[24]

It was during the battle over the "death sentence" clause itself, a battle the administration won only in compromised form, that Marcantonio delivered one of the blazing speeches for which he later became famous in East Harlem and in the closed world of the American left.

> Mr. Chairman, charges have been made that this proposition of the so-called "death sentence" for public-utility holding companies [is] radical. We are always accused of radicalism when we advance an idea for the benefit of the American consumers. Let me say this in answer: If it be radicalism to believe that when God said, "Let there be light," that that light should be used for the sole benefit of all of the American people and not for the sole benefit of a few exploiters; if it be radicalism to believe that our national resources should be used for the benefit of all of the American people and not for

the purpose of enriching just a few; if it be radicalism to smash, to abolish, and to surgically eradicate these companies which have been throttling the life of American consumers, then, Ladies and Gentlemen of this House, I accept the charge; I plead guilty to the charge; I am a radical, and I am willing to fight it out on this issue until hell freezes over.[25]

The printed words fail to convey the rising, emotion-packed voice, the pugnacious look, the stamping foot, or the fist slammed into an open palm for punctuation—the rhetorical flourishes used to deliver this and similar speeches throughout Marcantonio's career. But even in print, few congressmen were so outspoken or so eloquent in defense of New Deal legislation.

When fellow legislators tried to pin Marcantonio down to something more than the bill under discussion, he tried at first to sidestep a definite commitment to government ownership of public utilities, insisting only that the government "should aid every municipality that wants to go into the public utility business . . . if you call that Government ownership, then it is Government ownership." One month later he apparently had decided that there was no sense in pussyfooting with the issue. "I believe," he told the House flatly, "in public ownership of power."[26]

The fight over public utilities was not the only political occurrence during Marcantonio's first congressional term that indicated his essentially radical approach to almost all problems of American life. For example, when the Supreme Court invalidated the Railway Pension Act, the National Industrial Recovery Act, and the Frazier-Lemke Farm Mortgage Act early in 1935, the New Dealers reacted by trying to rewrite the legislation so as to conform to the opinions of the Court. As far as Marcantonio was concerned such action was cowardly appeasement. With three other congressmen—Amlie, Schneider, and Lundeen—Marcantonio called for a second Constitutional Convention to rewrite the basic law of the land "in order to realize the new age of economic liberty and democracy which lies before us if we have the courage and intelligence to strive for it."[27]

In 1936, after the Supreme Court had voided the Agricultural Adjustment Act, Marcantonio took the occasion of Lincoln's birthday to give the House a lesson in history and urge it to even more rapid action than that afforded by either an amendment to the Constitution or a Constitutional Convention. The radical from East Harlem compared his own era to the situation of the United States in 1857 when the "power of Congress to legislate for the welfare of the American people was challenged by the Supreme Court in the Dred Scott decision." The position adopted by the Republican party in answer to the Court's ruling was essentially a revolutionary one, Marcantonio explained. More important, when Lincoln, the Republican president, was actually confronted with a Court that attempted to frustrate his wartime policy, "he changed the Court. From 5 members he increased it to 10 members on March 3, 1863, by act of Congress." This was the kind of political courage Marcantonio called for in 1936. "Lincoln did not wait for a constitutional amendment. He faced realities. . . . The Court had issued a challenge. He met that challenge."[28]

Ironically, the gauntlet Marcantonio thus threw down before the House was taken up by the Democratic president a year later when Roosevelt presented his "court-packing" scheme to a stunned Congress. There is no causal relationship in the two actions; the president and the congressman arrived at their respective proposals independently. Roosevelt did not need Marcantonio to teach him history. Nevertheless it is interesting to note that the essentially revolutionary approach Marcantonio advocated as a solution to a pressing national problem became, in the space of one year, the wedge used by a profoundly conservative president to force the Supreme Court to a more liberal viewpoint.

On legislative matters not directly connected with the New Deal, Marcantonio's viewpoint was always far to the left of

his congressional colleagues. As might be expected he served
as the legislative watchdog over the civil liberties of the radical left, frequently rising in the House to challenge the anti-
Communists in both parties. Emphatically refusing to join
Congressman Thomas Blanton (Dem., Texas) in a move to
deport Communists, he insisted, "I disagree with the Communists, but they have a perfect right to speak out and to advocate communism."[29] Holding to this basic belief, he fought
against all legislative attempts aimed at curtailing the Communist party's freedom of speech or freedom of the press; he
based his stand largely on the contention that the real danger
to American liberties came not from the left but "from the
right, from the extreme reactionaries." It was fascism not
communism that threatened America in 1935 and 1936, an
obvious fact to a man who thought that the tactics of the
Liberty Leaguers, of the Chambers of Commerce, and of the
financial and industrial interests of the nation "point irresist-
ibly to this conclusion: they are forming a united front to
overthrow the basic fundamental democratic principles of the
United States."[30]

Characteristically, this attitude on his part had nothing to
do with any political benefits that might accrue to him. There
was no reason to believe that supporting Communists in
Washington would win him votes in East Harlem; as a matter
of fact the Communist party in New York had opposed his
election in 1934.[31]

Far from being ideologically based, Marcantonio's approach
seems to have been that of a totally pragmatic politician fighting for a radical viewpoint against virtually impossible odds.
He would, he wrote his friend Luigi Antonini in the summer
of 1935, make common cause with "anyone who joins me . . .
irrespective of the politics of the person. Red-baiting and
Communist baiting is the assault of the forces of dictatorial
reaction."[32] In this same vein he fought against the tendency,
even among his supporters, to connect him with groups that
backed a specific part of the program he favored. "The fact
that a Communist or a Democrat speaks on the same platform

as me," Marcantonio wrote the Italo-American journalist Girolamo Valenti, "does not mean that I am a Communist or a
Democrat. The mere fact that a Communist or a Democrat
endorses any of my bills does not mean that I have become a
Communist or a Democrat."[33]

Outside Congress Marcantonio matched his radical language with radical action. When the House adjourned in
August 1935, the congressman raced home to East Harlem
and immediately became involved in legal and extralegal activity in support of his legislative views. In September, when
nine Communists were brought to trial in New York for having ripped the Nazi flag off the mast of the new German liner
Bremen, Marcantonio served as their counsel and won acquit-
tal on the basis that the Nazi emblem, the swastika, was
insulting to American ideals.[34]

Later that same year, as counsel for the Association of
Workers in Public Relief Agencies, Marcantonio blasted New
York City's Emergency Relief Bureau for its announced cut
in staff at a time when "the number of people needing relief
is on the increase." He told a wildly cheering audience of
union members that American labor must go to the left when
thus pushed. "The workers of our city," he shouted, "are going
to fight for their rights with or against the police. . . . if we go
on the picket line," the congressman-labor lawyer added, "I
will be with you."[35]

When the cuts went through as planned, Marcantonio
charged his good friend and political supporter, La Guardia,
with responsibility in the case, caustically commenting, "I
have always felt that Mayor La Guardia was a friend of labor.
Now is the time for him to prove it."[36] La Guardia had been
proving his attitude toward labor since before Marcantonio
was out of his teens and did not feel it necessary to reply to
the congressman's blast. The incident is an interesting comment on Marcantonio's independent frame of mind; he was,
after all, slashing out at the most influential politician in New
York City.

The incident, moreover, was not an isolated event. Marcantonio had a more violent run-in with the city administration in February 1936, when he led a mass demonstration of unemployed in a protest against further cuts in the WPA program for the city. A crowd, estimated by police at about 15,000 people, showed up at Madison Square Park in downtown Manhattan to hear the fiery congressman lambaste the Roosevelt policy of cutting relief aid in the face of continued high unemployment. In the body of his speech Marcantonio referred to La Guardia's "Mussolini-like administration"—a reference to the mayor's refusal to grant a permit for a parade in conjunction with the demonstration.

At the completion of his speech Marcantonio called for the singing of the "Star Spangled Banner" and at the last vibrating note, with the police standing rigidly at attention, he yelled, "Forward March," starting the forbidden parade. The police, only momentarily caught off guard, swarmed into the parading marchers and threw Marcantonio and twelve others into waiting patrol cars. They were held for several hours in what Police Commissioner Lewis Valentine called "protective custody."[37]

Released later the same day Marcantonio was asked by reporters if he had fought back against the police? "Against a whole cordon of police?" the congressman asked. With typical cockiness he added that he would be more than happy to take on Commissioner Valentine in a gymnasium on a man-to-man basis.[38]

Valentine met the congressman's challenge without any noticeable fear. "I'll let him come in with any weapon he wants and I'll meet him with a flit gun." Then, more seriously, "His is the immaturity and arrogance of youth. It is an example of a publicity seeking demagogue who would love to don a martyr's crown."[39] Valentine's analysis of Marcantonio in 1936 was as incorrect as those of later, supposedly more objective observers. If Marcantonio wanted to wear a martyr's crown, he had ample opportunity in 1936 and later; yet he never acquired that particular "honor," an indication that he was not as anxious for the crown as Valentine thought. That the congressman was "a publicity seeking demagogue" is a more difficult charge to analyze, for by the very nature of his job any politician is open to that particular accusation by anyone who disagrees with him politically. There was nothing particularly demagogic in Marcantonio's action; he believed in the right of the unemployed to demonstrate in their own behalf and acted on that belief in defiance of the law. The police commissioner's viewpoint might have had more validity if he had explained why a permit for a peaceful political demonstration had been summarily denied.

Aside from such frenetic activity on behalf of the unemployed and in favor of increased social welfare legislation, Marcantonio seems to have paid little attention to the Italian majority in his congressional district. He apparently relied on the personal services provided by his organization to keep the voters on his side in the coming election of November 1936. But the closeness of the vote in 1934 led Marcantonio to search for new sources of political support; thus he turned to the Puerto Rican minority in East Harlem, an ethnic group that had been behind Lanzetta in the previous contest. He took extraordinary steps to win the allegiance of the Puerto Ricans.

Marcantonio would have backed the islanders in their fight against "American imperialism" even if none of them had voted in his district. He had unsuccessfully tried to include agricultural workers under the provisions of the Wagner Act,[40] and through his work on the Committee on Labor he had successfully forced a change in Labor Department regulations concerning working conditions in coal mines; there were few agricultural workers and fewer coal miners among his constituents.[41] In these matters it was his basic radicalism that had dictated his stand, and it was the same radicalism that dictated his position on Puerto Rico.

Marcantonio's own statement on his interest in Puerto Ricans and their problems can be accepted at face value. It was, he insisted, "due not only to the fact that I represent the largest Puerto Rican constituency," a true statement in light of the peculiar second-class citizenship offered Puerto Ricans in Puerto Rico, "but also to my desire as a progressive to defend the most exploited victims of a most devastating imperialism."[42]

There was no doubt in Marcantonio's mind concerning this last statement. Others might see the relationship between the United States and the Caribbean island as something other than European style colonialism, but to Marcantonio it was imperialism of the most vile kind. While he introduced several bills designed to relieve the islanders from the distress they suffered during the Depression, bills calling for heightened relief expenditures and less-stringent sugar quota restrictions, he also put his radical view into legislative form by introducing a measure providing for immediate independence for the island colony. Independence was to be accompanied by a substantial monetary indemnity "to make up in part for the years of hardship that [the Puerto Rican people] have undergone, and to enable them to better find their feet and take boldly the path of freedom they ardently desire."[43]

Having lined up with the extreme left wing among Puerto Rican political parties by this legislative action, Marcantonio was now called upon for a personal confrontation with the forces of imperialism that he had blasted in Congress. In August 1936 he flew to Puerto Rico in an abortive attempt at defending Pedro Albizu Campos, leader of the Puerto Rican Nationalist party, who had been arrested earlier in the year and charged with conspiring to overthrow the government. In July, Marcantonio requested a postponement of the trial until such time as he could arrive in San Juan and familiarize himself with the legal issues at hand.[44] The request was denied, and moving with almost unseemly haste the government tried the Nationalist leader and sentenced him to ten years in prison on the day before Marcantonio arrived in Puerto Rico.[45] After conferring with Albizu Campos on August 1, Marcantonio accused the prosecution of chicanery, called for a new trial, and returned to New York. The brief visit had reinforced any ideas he had formed previously concerning the relationship between the nation and its island possession.[46]

When the congressman continued to lash out at the government in Puerto Rico for its handling of the case, efforts were made to divert him. Ernest Gruening, then administrator of the Puerto Rico Reconstruction Administration, wrote to him stating that after studying the case he had come to the conclusion that the trial was fair and the conviction just. "My study of the case," he wrote, "causes me to regret that you have gone into it. I think your good nature has been imposed upon. . . . I wish for your own sake and repute that you could withdraw from the case."[47] Marcantonio spurned Gruening's advice and three years later he made public a letter from one of the jurors in the trial which indicated that the jury had been stacked by the prosecution.[48]

The political benefit derived by the representative of "the largest Puerto Rican constituency" from this particular activity was debatable in the fall of 1936. On the one hand, few Puerto Ricans in Marcantonio's district or on the island were Nationalists or favored the immediate break with the United States that Marcantonio had proposed, with or without indemnity. On the other hand, the fiery leftist from East Harlem had given tangible evidence of his interest in Puerto Rico and its problems and this fact alone was enough to win support from this important minority among his constituents.

By the time Marcantonio returned from Puerto Rico early in August 1936, the political parties were preparing for the November elections. The congressman had earlier announced his intention to run for re-election and his position appeared strong to those who would attempt to defeat him.

III

Defeat and Victory

Without any doubt the elections of 1936 rank among the most important such contests in American history. On the national scene Franklin Delano Roosevelt put the New Deal and all it stood for squarely before the voters in the face of violent opposition from the Republican party and its front organizations. Like many incumbent presidents, Roosevelt had certain built-in advantages over Alfred Landon, the Republican nominee; in New York City's Twentieth Congressional District the incumbent congressman, Vito Marcantonio, seemed to have similar advantages over his opponent. Marcantonio looked strong in the fall of that election year, and anyone attempting to predict the outcome of the balloting in November would certainly have made him the favorite.

There were gaping holes in the congressman's political armor, however, and while they were not apparent to the outside world they were none the less real. Not the least of his problems were with his own Republican party.

On any imaginary scale of loyalty to the Grand Old Party, Marcantonio's standing would have been slightly lower than that of such people as Harry Hopkins or Harold Ickes. True, Marcantonio had frequently opposed Roosevelt and the New Deal during his first term in Congress; but his opposition differed qualitatively from that of most Republicans. Marcantonio did not fear the developing of the welfare state; he insisted it was not coming rapidly enough and that it was not providing sufficient welfare. On almost any given issue he was not only to the left of the Republicans in the House, he was also further to the left than most of the Democrats.

His relationship to the Republican party was not merely

peculiar; in a sense it was impossible. He had become a Republican because of his connection with La Guardia; he maintained the label while rejecting the party's program because there was no other political party in which he could fit and which gave him a chance at election. Marcantonio might have been more at home in a political sense in the Democratic party, but the party in Manhattan meant Tammany Hall; there was not the slightest chance, in 1936, that the Democratic machine would have accepted him had he offered his services.

Although Marcantonio retained sufficient control of the Republican organization in his own district to insure renomination, William Bleakley, Republican candidate for governor in 1936, favored ridding the party of the East Harlem radical and made sure that Marcantonio received neither financial nor organizational aid during the election campaign.

Just prior to the election Marcantonio returned a $100 campaign contribution to his friend, Congressman Hamilton Fish, Jr. (Rep., New York), writing: "Thanks a lot for the check which you sent me and which I am herewith enclosing. I certainly appreciate your sentiments but I feel that I cannot accept it, especially in view of my severance from the Republican Party." He detailed for Fish the difficulties he had had with Bleakley and the organized Republican opposition he had faced in winning renomination. This was, he indicated, only one of the reasons causing him to sever his relationship with the party on the state and national level. Another factor was the difference in viewpoint, for, as he explained to Fish, "the campaign of the Republicans is in the hands of the worst reactionaries in the country. I feel that this country needs a real political realignment," he added, a viewpoint voiced by American radicals in every decade. Marcantonio closed the letter with a sentence at once revealing of his character and sufficient to set him apart from the average American leftist: "I shall always respect you," he told Fish, "as an honest conservative even though we shall be on opposite sides of the fence."[1]

As important as the break with the Republican party was the rupture Marcantonio's radical position created in the ranks of his own supporters. Unlike La Guardia, Marcantonio vigorously assailed Fascist Italy and spoke out openly against Benito Mussolini.[2] In August 1935, for example, he participated in a *Grande Dimonstrazione Contro Il Fascismo* held at Madison Square Garden.[3] This stand undoubtedly lost the congressman some votes among the fiercely patriotic Italian elements in East Harlem; it also cost Marcantonio the political support of Luigi Antonini, one of the most influential labor leaders among the Italians in New York.

Antonini was not upset with Marcantonio's stand against Mussolini and fascism. What bothered the labor leader deeply was Marcantonio's insistence on aligning himself with Communists in the anti-Fascist movement. Antonini had fought the Communists for control of his own union, and the sight of Marcantonio now consorting with them was personally insulting. On several occasions he remonstrated with his old friend, the exchange of letters between them becoming more and more acrimonious.

Marcantonio stubbornly insisted he could continue to make common cause with anyone without losing his own identity, but paradoxically he refused to permit Antonini the same freedom of action. The congressman hurled the charge of guilt by association back at his friend, charging that because Antonini was in a union affiliated with the A. F. of L. he was becoming too conservative. In one of the last exchanges of personal letters between them, Marcantonio pleaded with Antonini not to "permit the soon dead cigar smoking orthodox labor leaders of the A. F. of L. to lead you from the path which you so successfully followed in the past." He urged his friend to continue as a liberal labor leader "in the class struggle which is ever present," despite the personal cost. "I fully realize," he explained, "that men must pay a great price in order to adhere to ideals. I fully realize that one needs guts to pursue such a course. I also thought that you had them. I trust that you have not recently undergone an operation."[4]

Antonini did not feel any obligation to keep Marcantonio informed on the current medical status of his "guts" or to render any aid to the congressman during the election campaign of 1936. Within a short time the two old friends were insulting each other in two languages with equal facility. Marcantonio became *Fritto Misto* or "mixed fry" to Antonini and his supporters, a reference to the congressman's confusing mixture of political supporters; and the labor leader soon blossomed into *testa di cappuccio*, or "cabbage head," in Marcantonio's literature.[5]

The loss of Antonini's support was particularly harmful to Marcantonio politically since his former friend was one of the key figures in the formation of a third party which came into prominence in the 1936 campaign, the American Labor party (ALP). Organized primarily to win support for Roosevelt in the crucial state of New York, the party had wide labor and left-wing support and could have been important to Marcantonio, who was closer to this left-oriented organization than to either of the major parties. But with the ILGWU among the strongest of the labor organizations backing the newly founded ALP, and with Antonini as the new party's first secretary, Marcantonio received no support from that particular quarter.[6]

Whatever the political losses, the gains Marcantonio had made since 1934 seemed adequate to balance them. In 1934 Marcantonio had been unknown beyond the restricted world of East Harlem; by 1936 his name had appeared on the front pages of the city's newspapers on more than one occasion and frequently in a manner that endeared him to his primarily working-class constituents. The social services rendered the voters from his clubhouse on East 116th Street continued during his term in office and became an effective weapon in his fight to retain his congressional seat. An important portion of the support his opponent had received in the 1934 campaign was now on his side in an active way, compensating in part for the losses he had suffered. Antonio Pacheco Padro, a Puerto Rican Nationalist leader who "previously attacked Con-

gressman Marcantonio in the bitterest tones of political violence," now switched allegiance in an open letter to the Puerto
Ricans of the Twentieth District.[7]

Support for the previously unknown freshman congressman
also came from a host of people comparatively well-known on
the national scene and representing a mixed political orienta-
tion. Such prominent individuals as Senator Gerald Nye (Rep.,
North Dakota), Clarence Darrow, General Smedley Butler,
Senator Elmer Benson (Farmer-Laborite, Minnesota), Max
Lerner, Babette Deutsch, Quincy Howe, Elmer Rice, George
S. Kaufman, and Professor John Dewey sent the congressman
from East Harlem their warmest support.[8] Heywood Broun,
Morris Ernst, Paul Kern, and Oswald Garrison Villard headed
a "Non-Partisan Committee" for Marcantonio's re-election.
The leadership of this last-named committee circulated a letter
that read in part, "His consistent record of struggle . . . for
maintenance of civil rights, rights of labor, adequate unemployment relief, protection of the foreign born, for Puerto
Rican independence, for peace, and against discrimination, . . .
entitles him to the support of progressive citizens everywhere."[9]

Predating the support from well-known personages of stage,
literature, and politics came the endorsement of the Communist party. As previously indicated, the Communists had opposed Marcantonio's election in 1934 when his political position was still unknown; but his stand in and out of Congress
on the most important issues of the day, along with his
willingness to work with Communists for mutually desired
goals, made him a natural ally of the party. At a Communist
party meeting held in May 1936 to discuss the approaching
November elections, Earl Browder, the secretary-general, was
questioned about Marcantonio and said bluntly that the party
"would be very stupid" not to support him.[10]

The exact nature of this support is difficult to determine at
this late date except in one particular. In mid-June 1936, less
than one month after Browder's statement, a group of Harlem
community organizations met at the Renaissance Casino in

Harlem and formed a new political organization, the All
People's party (APP). Behind this supposed grass-roots movement stood the monolithic structure of the Communist party.
While the APP platform carried a number of planks dealing
with strictly local problems, it also called for passage of the
Frazier-Lundeen Social Security Bill and the Marcantonio
program for relief measures, for continued opposition to war
and fascism, independence for Puerto Rico, freedom for all
political prisoners, and other measures characteristic of the
radical left. The new party gave its strongest endorsement to
Vito Marcantonio as its choice for the congressional seat from
the Twentieth Congressional District.[11]

In August 1936, Louis Sass, a lower-echelon Communist
party functionary and campaign manager of the All People's
party, addressed a meeting of Marxists in East Harlem and
made it clear that to him the future of the All People's party
and that of the Communist party were synonymous. Apparently there was little, if any, opposition to this view. There
were Communists who did not trust Marcantonio despite
Browder's assurance, and to that small body of waverers Sass
laid down the line. "The Party wants to elect Vito Marcantonio
to Congress," he explained. "You cannot guarantee for anybody, but right now we have confidence in Marcantonio."[12]

No matter how significant the Communists thought their
endorsement was, it was not nearly as important in East
Harlem as that of Fiorello La Guardia, which was given in
October. True, La Guardia's announcement was only a brief
message that since he lived in East Harlem he would cast his
vote for Vito Marcantonio, quite a comedown from the support he had given in 1934.[13] But it was welcome and possibly
unexpected support considering the verbal abuse Marcantonio
had been giving the city's chief executive on a variety of labor
and relief problems. There is no accounting for La Guardia's
extremely generous gesture except on the grounds of his possible paternal feelings for Marcantonio; Fiorello, with his
highly developed sense of the dramatic, liked the idea of playing the forgiving father to Vito, the erring son.

Marcantonio's Democratic opponent in the election of 1936 was James J. Lanzetta, whom he had defeated in 1934. While Marcantonio campaigned on his record compiled in and out of Congress during the previous two years, Lanzetta campaigned on the president's record: he was billed as "a loyal Democrat" and a "staunch supporter of President Franklin D. Roosevelt and the New Deal."[14] Trying to match Marcantonio, endorsement for endorsement, Lanzetta once again received the support of Antonio Barcelo, who urged Puerto Ricans in the Twentieth Congressional District to vote for Lanzetta as a sign of their approval of the Roosevelt administration.[15]

In the midst of all this normal political activity, the usual East Harlem in-fighting was also evident. On October 9, Marcantonio was indicted by a grand jury and charged with having instigated an attack on Solomon Silver, a Tammany poll watcher. The congressman was furious; he termed the charge "a cheap political trick—an attempt by Tammany to embarrass me."[16] He demanded an immediate trial to clear his name but the request was denied. Then, on October 27, Solomon Silver was arrested and charged with stabbing Felix Marquez, a Marcantonio supporter, on the same night that Silver had supposedly been attacked.[17] There may have been an attack on Silver, and Marquez may have been stabbed; the only firm evidence is that both charges were dropped after the election, an indication that there was more politics than blood in these comic-opera proceedings.[18]

Election day, Tuesday, November 3, was unseasonably mild with temperatures ranging into the high 70's, a beautiful day that provided no climatic impediment to the voting process in East Harlem. Congressman Marcantonio and his wife cast their ballots at the polling place on East 115th Street at ten minutes past eight in the morning, and the congressman spent the remainder of a busy day making the rounds of his district, apparently confident of victory. By late evening the not-yet thirty-four-year-old politician was an ex-congressman, beaten by more than 1,500 votes. The margin of victory was so large considering past elections in East Harlem that Marcantonio did not bother to charge Lanzetta with fraud.[19]

In retrospect, the election was by no means a repudiation of either Marcantonio or his program by the voters. Actually he increased his share of the vote from 13,099 in 1934 to 17,212 in 1936. But while Marcantonio's vote went up so did Lanzetta's: from 12,842 in 1934 to 18,772 in 1936.

Instead, the election was definitely an outpouring of votes in favor of Franklin Delano Roosevelt; it was undoubtedly Roosevelt, not Lanzetta, to whom Marcantonio lost in 1936. In his final speech to the Seventy-fourth Congress prior to the election, Marcantonio had declared, "No matter what is said and done, no matter how powerful the smoke screen of political propaganda . . . no matter how spell-binding the political oratory may be, the most important issue before the people is to put the unemployed back to work at a living wage."[20]

The voters of East Harlem turned out in unprecedented numbers on November 3 in support of the president and the party that were attempting to solve the problem Marcantonio had outlined so clearly. Few Republicans fared well in that landslide year of 1936. Even an "off-color" Republican like Marcantonio was handicapped by the Republican label since the ordinary voter could not be expected to be as perceptive as someone like William Bleakley. In defense of their president, the voters pulled down Democratic levers all along the line in the voting booths, giving to Roosevelt and the Democrats one of the greatest election victories awarded an incumbent president and party.[21]

For the moment then, Vito Marcantonio was as dead as was any politician without portfolio, only the body showed no signs of *rigor mortis*. Having severed relations with the Republican party, Marcantonio had to find prior to the next election a party under whose banner he could run. He still had control of the personal machine welded together during his years under La Guardia; but while this organization could be helpful, it was not a party with a place on the ballot. He also had to remain in the public eye, again no simple job for a politician out of office. But Marcantonio was apparently wedded to the idea of active political participation, and during the next two years he carried on an extended election campaign.

The task Marcantonio set for himself through all of 1937 and the early part of 1938 was by no means simple. It is a tribute to both his drive and ability that he managed to keep his name before the public despite the loss of his congressional seat.

While Roosevelt's court-packing measure threw the nation into a political frenzy and finally forced the Supreme Court to recognize the validity of much of the New Deal program, Marcantonio acted as counsel for numerous labor organizations including the very left-wing Workers Alliance, a union of the unemployed. Early in February 1937 he agreed to serve on the Legal Advisory Committee of the International Labor Defense (ILD), an organization later tabbed as a "red front" by the attorney general's office; within a matter of weeks he became president of the organization.[22] Marcantonio was not blind to the Communist control of the ILD, for he warned Anna Damon, the executive secretary of the organization, not to send anything from the office over his name or signature without first clearing it with him. He had no intention of being used as a personal front by anyone.[23] He committed himself to the International Labor Defense in much more than name alone; according to one reporter, there was no moment, "day or night, when he would not race from bedroom or dining room at the call of the distressed."[24]

As might be expected, he continued to defend the rights of the politically suspect, attacking the proposed deportation of the leftist labor leader Harry Bridges in February 1938[25] and later that same month defending the appointment of the Communist party official Simon Gerson as an aide to Manhattan's borough president.[26]

In the spring of 1938, while Congress struggled with the

momentous Fair Labor Standards Bill, the ex-congressman received nationwide publicity over an almost physically violent argument with the political machine run by Frank Hague in Jersey City, New Jersey.

As president of the International Labor Defense, Marcantonio announced a public meeting to be held in Hague's stronghold on May 7, 1938, to protest a long series of alleged violations of civil rights by the Hague administration. The protest was aimed particularly at the "deportation" the previous week of Norman Thomas, Socialist party leader, by Hague's police force.[27]

The Democratic boss of Jersey City countered Marcantonio's move by refusing the ILD a permit for a meeting and by threatening to arrest the scheduled speakers, Representatives Jerry O'Connell (Dem., Montana) and John Bernard (Farmer-Laborite, Minnesota). Hague's supporters threatened much more. Charles Brophy, senior vice-commander of the Catholic War Veterans of New Jersey, promised to meet any anti-Hague demonstrators with "800 uniformed men . . . each with 2 feet of rubber hose."[28]

At the scheduled time of the meeting there were between fifteen- and thirty-thousand people in and around Journal Square, the proposed meeting place. Most of the crowd were Hague supporters mustered in his defense by veterans' organizations, A. F. of L. unions, and the city administration. In the face of the massive and hostile crowd, Marcantonio canceled the meeting in order to prevent certain "blood-shed, violence and perhaps death at the hands of a mob incited to do violence by Mayor Hague." Bernard, and especially O'Connell whose father had been killed on a Montana picket line, were in favor of crossing the Hudson to Jersey City despite the mob and the predictable results; but Marcantonio's more realistic viewpoint prevailed.[29]

The incident itself is relatively unimportant except as a minor footnote to the history of civil rights in America; but the story was given prominence in the national press, and it served to keep Marcantonio's name before the public.

In a more private way he acted to prevent violence in his own East Harlem. Just prior to the elections of 1938, Marcantonio brought together a group of community leaders, including three Catholic priests and two Protestant clergymen, to deal with the problem of sporadic street fighting that had broken out in the neighborhood between gangs of young Puerto Ricans and their Italo-American counterparts.[30] This flare-up of enmity between old and new slum residents characterized many such areas of the city, but to Marcantonio such outbreaks were more than just a violent sociological phenomenon. They were politically dangerous since he depended on both national groups for political support. Swift community action kept the incidence of such conflict at a minimum.

By such means Marcantonio stayed out of that peculiar limbo reserved for defeated officeholders. By the early summer of 1938, when New York's political parties began preparations for the approaching election campaigns, Marcantonio was ready to make the fight for his old congressional seat. But first he had to solve a perplexing personal problem: he had severed relations with the Republican party organization, he had not the slightest chance of being nominated by Tammany and the Democratic party, and thus he found himself in the position of being a notoriously available candidate without a party. His only possible political alignment was with the American Labor party—which was newly organized in 1936, instrumental in the re-election of Mayor La Guardia in 1937, and ready to move into its first congressional election in 1938.

In terms of issues Marcantonio would have been more comfortable in the ranks of the ALP than in either of the major national parties. The American Labor party, organized by union leaders and left-oriented intellectuals, had the same radical viewpoint on many issues as he did. Like Marcantonio, the ALP supported the most progressive measures of the New Deal and called for the immediate extension of the welfare state. Unlike either of the major parties, it did not seem to have within its ranks broad collections of politically disparate groups. The consensus on major issues was undoubtedly greater within the American Labor party than it was in either the Democratic or Republican parties. The ALP's geographic restriction to New York State, and primarily to New York City, helped it to retain its unity and power in New York politics. In 1937, for example, when it was just one year old, the ALP virtually forced the Republican party to renominate La Guardia as its mayoral candidate, then delivered the half-million votes that enabled "The little Flower" to defeat his Tammany opponent.[31]

But whatever unity of purpose existed between Marcantonio and the ALP, he still had enemies high in the leadership of the party; for example, Antonini, to whom Marcantonio's pragmatic alliance with the Communists was anathema. Not surprisingly then, when Marcantonio announced in July 1938 that he was formally a candidate for the American Labor party designation as representative from the Twentieth Congressional District in the coming primary elections, he ran into a violent storm of opposition. The East Harlem ALP club characterized his declaration as a "further attempt by the Communist Party to dominate labor unions" and endorsed instead the candidacy of Joseph Piscitello, an organizer for Local 89 of the ILGWU.[32]

Six days later, with no intervening hint of reconciliation, Marcantonio was suddenly designated as the official ALP nominee in the primary election in a terse announcement issued by Alex Rose, who was head of the Milliners' Union, a member of the ALP State Executive Committee, and a firm anti-Communist.[33] The steps leading up to this alliance between the former Republican congressman and the political arm of the labor movement in the city are quite hazy. According to *The New York Times*, Marcantonio received the ALP nomination solely through the intervention of La Guardia. In light of the strange but strong relationship between the two Italo-Americans, and of La Guardia's political power as mayor in 1938, this supposition is credible.[34]

Two other factors, unexplored at the time, might also explain the unexpected decision by the leadership of the ALP.

The first was Marcantonio's undisputed power as a candidate. The American Labor party wanted to win, and there was no other candidate in sight who could have successfully contested the election with the Democratic incumbent. The very newness of the party and the fact that it had not yet had the time to develop public figures with the political attraction of Marcantonio acted in his favor. Second, and even less tangible, was Marcantonio's popularity among the rank and file of the American Labor party in his own district. Even if the state organization had opposed his projected candidacy, it was very likely that he could have won the primary election if he had been forced to fight it out with Piscitello. Thus the anti-Marcantonio faction in the ALP may have concluded that it was better to award him the prize than to have him take it away from their own candidate, an event that would have weakened their position in their own party.

Whether Marcantonio received the ALP nomination through La Guardia's influence alone or through a combination of factors, the fact remains that although it was welcome news it was not decisive. Marcantonio had no intention of entering the November election as a third-party candidate against a Republican and a Democrat. Not only would he have had no chance of winning, but he probably would have thrown the election into the hands of a Republican candidate. Thus, with the ALP nomination in his pocket, he still found it expedient to cast around for other means of gaining support; this he found in New York State's peculiar election laws.

By amassing sufficient names on petitions, a candidate could legally run as a contestant in the primary election of *any* party in New York State; he did not have to restrict himself to his own acknowledged organization. This system of "cross-filing" made it theoretically possible for the registered voters of each party to choose their own candidate, totally free from the dictates of the party bosses. The law was designed to prevent the political machines from forcing the voters to elect an unacceptable candidate. Usually the officially designated party choice had no difficulty since any independent candidate had to gather enough signatures to insure the passage of his petitions through the scrutiny of the Board of Election, and the board was controlled by the entrenched party organizations. Democratic in concept, the law was less than perfect in the light of political reality.[35]

Without any doubt, however, the law was almost tailormade for a person like Vito Marcantonio. He had a functioning personal machine capable of securing enough signatures to prevent the erection of any legal roadblock at the Board of Election. Deftly he squeezed through this slight gap in the bipartisan political door in 1938 and filed for the Republican nomination without any regard for the Republican county organization which quickly labeled him "an ultra-radical, unacceptable as a Republican candidate."[36] Marcantonio was willing to let the voters of the district settle the issue since he had virtual control of the Republican organization in East Harlem, where Republicans just were not like Republicans in other sections of the city, state, or nation.

This attempt at sneaking in the backdoor was quickly challenged by a political unknown, Samuel Kupferman, who had the backing of Kenneth Simpson, New York County Republican chairman, and other GOP bigwigs. Kupferman, insisting that the only campaign issue was "republicanism versus communism," announced that he had entered the campaign on the urging of "outraged Republican voters" throughout East Harlem.[37]

Lanzetta, Tammany's candidate in East Harlem since 1932, undoubtedly infuriated at what he must have considered a shabby political trick on Marcantonio's part, decided that he, too, could make use of a legal loophole and announced that he would run for the American Labor party nomination as well as that of his own Democratic party. Marcantonio then turned the contest in East Harlem into political confusion by filing a legal set of petitions for the Democratic nomination.[38] Lacking a party banner in the spring of 1938, Marcantonio managed by late summer to be in contention for the congressional nomination of every important party in New York City.

With opposition to his candidacy among the leadership of the American Labor party and among both the leadership and rank and file of the Republican party, Marcantonio's chances for a political comeback looked bleak to *The New York Times*. That newspaper predicted he had no chance in either the Democratic or Republican primaries and might possibly beat Lanzetta in the ALP fight, but only "by a none too comfortable margin."[39]

The anonymous prognosticator overlooked two important facts. First, Marcantonio had La Guardia's backing; and with the Republican party dependency on La Guardia for whatever patronage he controlled as mayor of the city, it was certain that despite what the party leadership said in its press releases, it would not challenge with all its power La Guardia's choice in the Twentieth Congressional District. Although Kupferman talked of the outraged Republican electorate in East Harlem, such a group was not in evidence during the primary campaign itself. Second, and a positive factor, was the support of the Communist party. Whatever doubts the party had had about Marcantonio in 1936 had been dispelled by 1938. A witness before the Dies Committee testified that Marcantonio was the only "Republican" candidate supported by the Communists; while Dies Committee testimony must be carefully weighed, there is little reason to doubt this assertion.[40]

The particular form of assistance the party was capable of rendering became apparent late in August 1938 when the left-led Workers Alliance, the union of relief workers and unemployed, announced its intention of throwing "everything we've got into the election of men like Vito Marcantonio who, during his tenure in Congress, was in the forefront of the fight for the unemployed and WPA workers."[41]

Neither the Communist party nor the Workers Alliance had the financial strength of the two major political parties, but they did provide Marcantonio with the election workers who trudged up and down the five-story walk-up tenements of East Harlem making the door-to-door contacts so vital in a local election campaign. Tammany and the Republicans had no political weapon that could compare with this kind of personal assistance in a primary election where only a small percentage of the electorate actually uses its vote; the advantage was all with Marcantonio.

The single important issue upon which both Lanzetta and Kupferman built their campaigns—Marcantonio's alliance with the Communist party—had no appreciable effect on the voting results. It apparently was not the kind of issue that could galvanize the voters in one of the city's worst slums into political action in 1938. Yet one of Marcantonio's opponents was so committed to the issue of anti-communism that he had printed and distributed throughout East Harlem on the day before the primary election a spurious letter in which the Italian consul in New York accused Marcantonio of being a Communist party member.[42]

The attempted smear failed. When the results were in, Lanzetta kept the Democratic nomination, but Marcantonio swept both the Republican and American Labor party contests. He defeated Kupferman for the Republican designation by a vote of 2,296 to 199; and he beat Lanzetta in the American Labor party fight, 1,759 to 170. Surprisingly, the single struggle Marcantonio lost, the Democratic campaign, offered some hope for the future. The radical garnered almost thirty-one per cent of the Democratic vote in a contest in which he had the least opportunity for success according to almost all observers. His total vote, a possible indication of things to come, was 5,985 while his two opponents had attracted only 4,621 ballots.[43]

Three days after the primary election Marcantonio jubilantly opened his campaign headquarters at 1776 Lexington Avenue in a building decorated with an eighty-foot-wide red, white, and blue banner bearing the legend: "Mayor La Guardia says 'Harlem Needs Vito Marcantonio In Congress.'"[44]

With an eye on his surprisingly large Democratic support, and with some justification in view of his past voting record if not the spirit of his speeches, Marcantonio called "upon the progressives of New York City, regardless of party affiliation, to rally behind my candidacy. This is not only the fight of the people of Harlem, in my district, but the fight of every New Dealer in New York City."[45]

The November election campaign was almost anticlimactic after the hot primary battle. Both Lanzetta and Marcantonio posed as champions of the New Deal on the basis of past performance. Each pointed pridefully to his record in support of Puerto Rico, and both appealed to the Italian majority by way of a "liberal" record on immigration laws.

Lanzetta hurled charges of "communism" at Marcantonio who spat back the "red-baiting" label, and the expected East Harlem violence and interparty intrigue played a role. Marcantonio, the more dramatic campaigner, added humor to the campaign by employing a young, bright ventriloquist named Paul Winchell at his street meetings. Winchell used a dummy, supposedly a typical Tammany hack named Jerry Mahoney, to inform the voters of East Harlem about the powers behind Lanzetta.[46]

Both candidates sought the support of labor in predominantly working-class East Harlem; some forty-two different unions backed Marcantonio's candidacy while Lanzetta procured, and happily furnished the press with, a letter of endorsement signed by William Green, head of the powerful A. F. of L.[47]

Once again the intellectual left came to Marcantonio's aid despite the dubious value of such support in East Harlem. Heywood Broun issued the call to arms in a letter to the editor of the *New Republic* by referring to Marcantonio's records as "a brilliant one" and insisting that "against him are aligned the big guns of Tammany corruption and the formidable artillery of Republican anti-New Dealism." The subscription list of the *New Republic* was undoubtedly infinitesmal in East Harlem; however, the intent of the letter was not to convince the voters but to procure election workers for the hard-pressed radical candidate.[48]

Marcantonio's prime advantage over Lanzetta was Fiorello

La Guardia's third endorsement, this time praising Marcantonio's "progressive record in Congress" and declaring that he had made "a genuine contribution to the welfare of the country."[49] Even the slight rift between the two men that had been manifest in the 1936 election apparently had been patched up, for this time La Guardia backed his written endorsement with an appearance at Marcantonio's election-eve rally at the "Lucky Corner," 116th Street and Lexington Avenue. To a crowd of more than ten thousand persons, the fiery rotund mayor promised, "I know he will support the progressive, humane, economic and social welfare program of the President of the United States." The promise drew the most resounding applause of the evening, as much for the president as for the candidate. Marcantonio more ambiguously pledged himself "to fight the forces of reaction and align myself with the forces of democracy."[50]

The election itself, on November 8, was a complete turnabout of the 1936 campaign. Marcantonio defeated Lanzetta by a vote of 18,802 to 12,375. Lanzetta's vote was about the normal off-year Democratic turn-out in the Twentieth Congressional District and was almost identical with his total in the campaign of 1934. Marcantonio's Republican support dropped by almost 2,000 votes, but he offset the loss by winning almost 9,000 votes on the American Labor party line. Thus the new party proved instrumental in his election and made itself a significant third force in East Harlem.[51] It was the ALP vote that sent him to Congress in 1938; and while the newspapers counted him in the Republican line-up for the forthcoming Seventy-sixth Congress, Marcantonio insisted on being listed in the *Congressional Directory* as the sole representative of the ALP, the unique vanguard of what he confidently presumed would be the wave of the future.[52]

IV

Greasy Stains on the
Legislative Toga

Sitting in the ornate chamber of the House of Representatives on January 4, 1939, listening to Franklin Delano Roosevelt's message on the state of the Union, Vito Marcantonio might well have pondered over the peculiar political system that had allowed him to return to the nation's capital as the representative from New York's East Harlem district. Among the most radical of his congressional contemporaries, he had been re-elected to Congress the same year the nation had once again swung back toward a more conservative political viewpoint.

In the elections of 1938 the Republican party made its first appreciable political gains since Roosevelt had come to power in 1932. Eighty new Republicans sat in the House of Representatives; even many of the newly elected members of the president's own party had campaigned on programs which, if not definitely anti-New Deal, at least indicated disenchantment with the reformist aspects of Roosevelt's programs. The president himself, pragmatic as ever, took cognizance of the changing temper of the political times. "We have now passed the period of internal conflict in the launching of our program of social reform" the chief executive informed the Congress. "Our full energies may now be released to invigorate the processes of recovery in order to preserve our reforms."[1]

The president was true to his word for two related reasons. First, there was little in the way of meaningful reform legislation that had much hope of passing the new Congress.

66

Second, by the time the Seventy-sixth Congress convened in 1939, the rising specter of international conflict spawned by a decade of worldwide depression forced the president and his administration to turn more and more rapidly away from consideration of strictly national problems.

But to the radical mind of Vito Marcantonio, who had campaigned as a "fiery supporter of Mr. Roosevelt," the President's words were sheer apostasy.[2] In the congressman's restricted world, the Depression and Depression-caused conditions still existed; six years of the New Deal had not wiped away the blot. There were still the unemployed and the families dependent on them. There were still national problems the New Deal had touched only in the most timid fashion and others it had avoided entirely. The reconstruction of American society had gone neither far enough nor fast enough. While the president pulled back on the reins, Marcantonio tried to whip the horse. By the time the Seventy-sixth Congress neared the end of its two-year term, Marcantonio wrote with bitter vehemence, "Franklin Delano Roosevelt is the world's greatest betrayer of his own New Deal."[3]

In the spring of 1939, one long-time Washington observer saw the radical from East Harlem as the new leader of a reconstituted "liberal" bloc that might possibly wield the balance of power between congressional supporters of the president and the historic coalition of conservative Republicans and Southern Democrats.[4] But the observation was based more on wishful thinking than on reality. Many of Marcantonio's old congressional cronies were gone from the field of battle: Maverick, O'Connell, Bernard, Amlie, all had lost out to conservative opponents in 1938. While Marcantonio found others with whom he might unite upon a particular issue, his own words, "I am quite lonesome in Congress," best express the political reality of the times. His isolation and his minor party status were clearly expressed in his committee assignments. Immediately after election he had solicited the aid of the president in trying to regain his seat on the Labor Committee, and Roosevelt had written to Speaker of the House

Sam Rayburn endorsing Marcantonio's request: "I am inclined to think he will be with us more than against us."[5] Roosevelt's letter had no effect and Marcantonio found himself relegated to the congressional "minor leagues": Invalid Pensions, Mines and Mining, and Public Lands.[6] On a long list of domestic issues Marcantonio found himself in a well, walled off from the general temper of the times. He was in continually more bitter conflict with the vast majority of the House, fighting, not to extend, but simply to maintain the gains made since his first term in Washington.

As soon as Congress got down to business Marcantonio engaged in a fight over what he termed "grossly inadequate" congressional appropriations for the WPA. The president had requested a supplemental relief appropriation of $875,000,-000—a sum Marcantonio thought nowhere near enough to meet the needs of the unemployed. When Congressman Clifton Woodrum (Dem., Virginia), chairman of the House Appropriations Committee, whittled the figure down to $725,-000,000, Marcantonio fought against the committee's report and termed the reduction un-American. "As long as private industry fails to give the unemployed of this country an opportunity to work," he insisted, "then I say it is the solemn duty of the Government . . . to give them work at a decent wage, enough to support them in an American fashion during their period of unemployment."[7] His own amendment to increase rather than cut the appropriation for relief was rejected, and Congress accepted the lower figure.[8] The reduced appropriation, Marcantonio told a New York audience, resulted from a "ganging-up of the worst reactionary forces in America" motivated by a desire "to undermine the President and the New Deal."[9]

On February 7, 1939, Roosevelt sent Congress a special message asking that at least the $150,000,000 cut be restored. The president's request was bottled up in committee and nine days later Marcantonio announced his "intention to daily call to the attention of the country and to the Congress the fact that the Committee on Appropriations is not giving immediate consideration to this emergency."[10] True to his word, the congressman used every parliamentary opportunity to hack away at the Democratic leadership of the House, certain the measure could be forced to the floor of the House if only the party leaders acted as if they really wanted it to come up for debate and a vote. When Congressman Richard Kleberg (Dem., Texas) asked for $400,000 to fight the pink bollworm in his state, Marcantonio took the floor to observe that "1 week from today 400,000 pink slips will be delivered to WPA workers. How about the $150,000,000 appropriation for the unemployed?" The question remained unanswered.[11]

As Congress approached the more important question of the WPA appropriation for 1940, Marcantonio again championed the losing side in the congressional battle. The Appropriations Committee, under Woodrum's direction, slashed the amount requested by the administration, forbade any deficiency appropriation, limited WPA workers to eighteen months of employment, denied any employment to aliens in need of relief, and strictly forbade the use of WPA funds for the Federal Theatre Project which the Dies Committee on Un-American Activities had earlier charged was infiltrated with Communists.

There was not a single important section of the bill with which Marcantonio did not find fault. Along with the American Labor party he charged that the Relief Appropriations Bill for 1940 "would throw relief back to the days of Hooverism. . . . With this new appropriations bill the House . . . throws overboard practically every progressive step that has been taken since the inauguration of the Federal Works Program." Repeatedly Marcantonio rose from his seat in the House to object to provisions in the bill or to amendments that limited relief payments even more sharply than the original bill. Particularly obnoxious to Marcantonio was the amendment forbidding the use of federal relief funds by aliens. "It is not the fault of the alien that he is not a citizen," Marcantonio insisted, pointing out that the House itself had consistently refused to pave the alien's road to citizenship. More important, by thus singling out for punishment the non-citizen, the House also punished the alien's children who, in many instances, were native born. "This," he insisted, "is not patriotism, it is just plain rotten." But there was no turning back the conservative tide; the amendment carried 144 to 41.[12] Every extension of the relief program the congressman from East Harlem favored was voted down.[13]

The Relief Appropriations Bill for 1940 passed the House, not in the form the administration wanted, certainly not as Marcantonio wanted it, but as rewritten by Congressman Woodrum and his committee. Fighting a lonely battle, Marcantonio watched as the administration failed to put up any concerted fight for its own bill and thus failed to fight for the thousands of unemployed across the nation who would be affected by the sharp limitations insisted upon by the committee. With an oblique reference to that portion of the measure wiping out the Federal Theatre Project, Marcantonio rose on June 16, 1939, and payed homage to Woodrum and through him to the conservatives of the House. "I am not a drama critic," he modestly admitted, "but one does not have to be . . . to know that the gentleman from Virginia is a great dramatist. I congratulate him," he continued, for having written "the greatest American tragedy of 1939 when he wrote this bill."[14]

Defeat on the major question of relief for the unemployed was soon matched by defeat on even minor extensions of New Deal programs. Marcantonio's bill to include domestic servants under the Social Security Act was never reported out of committee, and he lost when he attempted to broaden the provisions of the Public Housing Act.[15]

Even after losing every battle, Marcantonio continued to attack. Early in 1940 he introduced a resolution calling for an American Youth Act designed to handle the problem of the "4,700,000 . . . young Americans . . . out of school and unemployed through no fault of their own."[16]

The proposal was not even seriously considered by the Congress, but it deserves more than passing notice here since it serves as an indication of Marcantonio's bold approach to pressing national problems. The National Youth Administration and the Civilian Conservation Corps, the two New Deal agencies established to work on youth problems, were good as far as they went; but they were, the congressman pointed out, only makeshifts. He sought a more permanent solution to what he saw as a possibly permanent national problem. To this end he called for the establishment of a revamped National Youth Administration to provide: (1) a WPA specifically for unemployed young people; (2) academic work projects for college students; (3) employment of counselors to provide free vocational and psychological advice and help to all young people; (4) stimulation of apprenticeship-training programs set according to local trade-union standards for such work; (5) federal scholarships for needy high school students; and (6) federal scholarships for needy students up to the amount required for them to continue their education at law, medicine, and other graduate and professional schools. To augment this auspicious program he called upon the Congress for an initial outlay of $500,000,000.[17]

The measure was drawn up by the American Youth Congress for presentation by Marcantonio. The debate in the House centered not around the provisions of the American Youth Act but around Communist control of the American Youth Congress itself.[18] Granting Communist party control of this depression-spawned youth movement, and there is no reason to believe the party did not control the Youth Congress, it is still difficult to see how the American Youth Act furthered the cause of the Communist party. Quite contrarily, the passage of such a bill would have destroyed what little support the Communists had among the nation's 4,000,000 unemployed young people.[19]

Exasperated at the direction of the debate, Marcantonio finally exploded. "This House is making one grand record. For four weeks we have been fighting the Communists, for four days the Youth Congress. . . . Are you going to eternally dodge the youth problem because the American Youth Congress refused to follow the example of this Congress of whittling away at the Bill of Rights?"[20] The question was purely rhetorical; he knew the answer even as the question was being asked.

But the possibility of success was never the touchstone by which Marcantonio measured the value of a proposal. Thus, in May 1940 he offered his "American Standards Work and Assistance Act" as an amendment to the relief appropriations bill for 1941. This measure, almost quixotic in the atmosphere of 1940, called for an appropriation of $2,500,000,000 to provide employment for not less than 3,000,000 persons on projects "which provide useful work of a permanent nature offering an opportunity for the utilization and preservation of the morale, skill, and training of the workers, and which are most socially useful to the various communities of the Nation." It eliminated any means of relief test as a prior qualification for employment, for Marcantonio felt that any such test was humiliating to the worker who "resorts to W.P.A. . . . because he has no other choice in the matter." The amendment also called for the establishment of a labor relations board within the WPA "to make quick and impartial settlements of all labor relations problems submitted to it." No discrimination "by reason of sex, race, color, religion, citizenship, length of residence . . . political opinion, or membership" in a political organization would be permitted.[21]

In defense of his program Marcantonio decried the lack of attention being given to the twin problems of relief and unemployment. He blamed this lack on the "war hysteria" fomented by the president himself, who had called for increased spending for defense in his speech to Congress the previous week. The radical from East Harlem implied that the administration was placing the not-so-subtle suggestion in the minds of the membership of the House that "the problem of the unemployed will be solved by giving the unemployed uniforms and getting rid of them as soldiers at the rate of $40 a month."[22]

Even in the most liberal period of the second New Deal either of Marcantonio's proposed measures would have had tough sledding. To the cost-cutting, budget-balancing, archly conservative Seventy-sixth Congress, the American Youth Act and the American Standards Work and Assistance Act were simply two more proposals to be either dismissed out of hand or bottled up in the Committee on Labor and Education. When the direct legislative approach failed, Marcantonio tried the personal approach. Before the members of the House visited the New York World's Fair in the spring of 1939, he invited them "to take some time off and visit our slums and tenements and to sit down and discuss the situation with those people who have received discharge notices from the W.P.A."[23] There is no record of any of his fellow legislators accepting the invitation.

Marcantonio's unrelenting battle for the unemployed and the underemployed, young and old, citizen and non-citizen, was but a continuation of his most consuming interest during his first term in office. The situation had not changed in the two years he was out of office; thus his approach remained essentially the same. The Depression to Marcantonio could be both palliated and ultimately cured only by attacking it in human terms: the mass of unemployed with whom he had constant contact on the streets of East Harlem. He assumed that the unemployed worker had an absolute right to a job at a living wage, and during both his first two terms that was one criterion by which Marcantonio judged each and every measure for relief. He voted for measures that promised the worker help regardless of how inadequate he considered the legislation, but he constantly fought to procure for the unemployed more in the way of relief than either the administration or the Congress was willing to grant. Three decades later his speeches still ring with that concern for human rights versus property rights that has motivated so many American radicals.

Another thread tying together Marcantonio's two congressional terms during the Depression was his interest in Puerto Rico, the homeland of a growing number of his constituents. He made repeated efforts to win a pardon for Pedro Albizu Campos, the leader of the Puerto Rican Nationalists who languished in the federal penitentiary at Atlanta, Georgia.[24] In strictly legislative matters he frequently played a more important role in matters concerning the island than did Santiago Iglesias or his successor, Bolívar Pagán, the nonvoting Puerto Rican representatives.

Besides reintroducing his bill calling for independence for Puerto Rico and massive reparations to compensate the islanders for the years of "American imperialism," Marcantonio pressed for more adequate relief appropriations and for the application of all provisions of the Fair Labor Standards Act to the island. Both proposals were, if anything, even more necessary in Puerto Rico than on the mainland. If the United States' economy was still depressed in 1939-1940, that of its nearest insular possession was almost totally flattened.

There were times when Marcantonio and the nonvoting Puerto Rican delegate to Congress worked together in the interests of the islanders. Both sought an amendment to the Second Deficiency Appropriations Act of 1939 that would grant $3,000,000 to the Puerto Rican Reconstruction Administration for direct relief and work relief on the island. After Iglesias offered the amendment, Marcantonio painted a grim picture of conditions in Puerto Rico: 250,000 unemployed in a total population of 1,700,000, with wages ranging from five dollars a week down to four cents an hour for women engaged in sewing piecework. Congressman Woodrum, in charge of the bill, agreed to the amendment provided that the sum was reduced to $1,000,000. In that reduced form the amendment carried and granted four dollars more per year for the relief of each of the Puerto Rican unemployed and the families dependent upon them.[25]

Cooperation between Marcantonio and the official Puerto Rican delegate was not the normal relationship. Iglesias, and Pagán who took over the job in 1940, were elected officials who spoke for the "establishment" on the island; and the "establishment" was a powerful one. The most important of the conflicts Marcantonio had with Iglesias in 1939 and again with Pagán in 1940 concerned the application of the minimum

wage provisions of the Fair Labor Standards Act to Puerto
Rican industry. Iglesias favored an amendment to the act that
would have exempted the sugar and needlework industries
from paying the minimum wage of twenty-five cents an hour,
despite the fact that at an earlier time in his life "he charged
the federal government with neglect [of the island] because
it had allowed Puerto Rico to develop into a sweatshop." The
ex-radical and labor union organizer put his argument in
human terms. "I am in favor of 25 cents and I would be in
favor of $1 per hour if it were possible to pay it; but if it is
not possible, then I do not want the people of Puerto Rico
to starve."[26]

This was sheer sophistry to Marcantonio. Considering the
salaries paid on the island, thirty to fifty dollars a year, anything
less than the minimum wage could not possibly stave off
starvation. He was interested in protecting the worker, not
the industry. Any business that could survive only by paying
its workers, men, women, and children as low as four cents
an hour, "has no right to live. It has no right to exist." The
Congress thought otherwise.[27]

As important as anything else in Marcantonio's fight for
Puerto Rico was his running battle with the American governor of the island, Blanton Winship. Appointed governor
early in 1934, Winship had earned Marcantonio's enmity by
his handling of the Albizu Campos trial; nothing that occurred between 1936 and 1939 changed the congressman's
view. Contrarily, fuel was added to the smoldering fire when
Winship, shortly after the election of 1938, appointed James J.
Lanzetta special agent to the government of Puerto Rico, assigned to assist the island's legislative representative in Washington, Santiago Iglesias. "The political effect of this," wrote
one reporter, "is that Mr. Lanzetta will be able to claim credit
for whatever is done by Congress for Puerto Ricans, . . . it will
enable him to build fences in anticipation of running against
Mr. Marcantonio in 1940."[28]

The congressman went gunning for the governor almost as
soon as Congress convened, carrying on his fight not just from

the floor of the House but in the office of the president. Whether Marcantonio's charges against Winship were a factor, or whether the president came to his conclusion on the basis of an independent appraisal, Roosevelt informed Secretary of Interior Harold Ickes that Winship "had been Governor of Puerto Rico long enough."[29] Ickes was of the same opinion. Therefore it should have been easy at that point to obtain the governor's resignation.

Differing attitudes on the part of the congressman, on the one hand, and the president and his cabinet officer, on the other, worked against the result they all desired: the rapid removal of Blanton Winship. For example, after one conference with the president, Marcantonio informed the press that Winship was on his way out. From the congressman's vantage point this was a reasonable tactic, for he had to connect himself with Winship's resignation or dismissal in order to prove his usefulness to his Puerto Rican constituents. But no administration openly favors kowtowing to legislative pressure. Governor Winship, flying to Washington, played this theme to Roosevelt, insisting that "for him to resign at this time would . . . add to the glory of Marcantonio."

On May 4, 1939, Roosevelt and Ickes discussed the problem. "The President said to me," Ickes wrote with characteristic candor, "that if I could get Marcantonio to keep his mouth shut for a few weeks, we could handle the Winship matter." This was no simple matter, but Ickes broached the suggestion to Marcantonio who was set to introduce a House Resolution calling for an investigation of Winship's administration. The congressman, more desirous of the governor's scalp than any personal publicity he might have derived from the matter, kept his peace.[30]

Ickes "definitely assured me," Marcantonio wrote on May 10, "that Winship is out. . . . He would not tell me who the successor is but told me that one had been appointed by the President."[31] Two days later Roosevelt announced to a press conference that he had appointed Admiral William Leahy as the new governor of Puerto Rico to succeed Blanton Winship.[32]

There was some argument on the floor of the House between Iglesias and Marcantonio, with the congressman insisting that his exposures had been instrumental in forcing the governor's resignation and with Iglesias insisting just as strongly that Winship had resigned for reasons of health.[33] Whatever the cause, and the evidence seems to buttress Marcantonio's view. His victory was sweeter for its uniqueness; his opposition to a politician was ordinarily a guarantee of long public life, while, conversely, his support for a public figure was occasionally the kiss-of-death. Indeed, he recognized this special power by once threatening to unseat a southern congressman up for re-election by going to his home district and *supporting* him.[34]

His usual role in Congress has been compared to that of a gadfly buzzing around the body politic, irritating it, occasionally interrupting its business, sometimes goading it to slap back, but basically having no more effect than a fly fighting an elephant.[35] Marcantonio would not have liked the comparison, for he thought of himself as the conscience of Congress; but he was certainly one of the most ignored such faculties in recent political history.

Never was Marcantonio's political isolation more amply demonstrated than in his frequent attempts to defend the civil liberties of the American left. This position was not, of course, new to him. He had taken an identical stand on civil rights during his first term of office. But the question of civil liberties came up for discussion and action much more frequently during the two-year term of the conservative Seventy-sixth Congress than it had in the earlier period.

It was not always a simple question of the political rights of the left. On occasion the issue was much, much broader. Thus Marcantonio joined with other congressmen in 1940 in a successful fight against amendments to the Hatch Act that would have made it illegal for recipients of relief aid or workers on government-financed projects to participate in politics beyond the mere exercise of their franchise. While the proposal was offered with the ostensible purpose of separating politics and the welfare program, it struck Marcantonio as being, in essence, fascistic, denying to a large mass of the people the right to participate in their own government simply because they were unemployed.[36]

Along with protecting the right of the unemployed to participate in politics, Marcantonio rose time and again to champion the rights of the immigrant. Himself the son of an immigrant mother, representing a constituency that was composed primarily of immigrants and their children, Marcantonio deeply resented any legislation that singled out the foreign-born and equated place of birth with national loyalty. Through his work with the International Labor Defense, Marcantonio knew how frequently prosecution of aliens merged with persecution of the politically unpopular.

Nowhere was his attitude more clearly expressed than in his opposition to H.R. 5138, the Alien Registration or Smith Act of 1940. Among other things, the bill gave the government the right to register and fingerprint all aliens and to deport those who advocated or who conspired to advocate the forcible overthrow of the government. Marcantonio based his opposition to the bill on the incongruity involved in a proposal to protect democracy that in itself tended "to destroy American liberty." It should be obvious to every member of the House, he insisted, "that in a period as trying as is this period, the test of a democracy lies in the ability of that democracy to maintain its liberties, to preserve those liberties, and to have more freedom rather than less freedom."[37]

Supporters of the measure skirted the issue Marcantonio raised. The bill was necessary to protect American democracy from spies and saboteurs; the innocent alien would in no way be inconvenienced by the proposal. Did not the congressman from New York "concede the right of democracy to protect itself," asked Congressman Joseph Gavagan (Dem., New York). "A democracy," Marcantonio replied, "has a perfect right to protect itself, but remember this: you are not protecting democracy by this legislation. Spies and saboteurs will not register nor submit to fingerprinting. . . . I believe that spies and saboteurs and anybody who engages in illegal activity should be immediately apprehended and severely punished. You do not accomplish that end by this bill. You only undermine American freedom."[38] There was existing legislation that could be used to apprehend spies and prevent sabotage, he noted, and the passage of another act was in no sense necessary. Thus, in his view the Smith Act was nothing more than an attempt at legislative intimidation of the politically unpopular, especially that *bête noire* of the Congress, the radical left.

Just how large the gulf was that separated Marcantonio from his congressional contemporaries can be seen in the vote over the Smith Act. Marcantonio was one of but four congressmen who voted against the measure; 382 congressmen supported the bill. Nothing illustrates the temper of the times more than that overwhelming defeat.[39]

When the question before the House involved not just the rights of aliens or labor or the politically unpopular but all of these, Marcantonio outdid himself and did, in fact, rise to act as the conscience of the House. Such was the strange case of Harry Bridges which occupied the Congress during the summer of 1940.

Bridges was the leader of the West Coast longshoremen's union, a principal figure in the San Francisco general strike of 1936, and a frequent ally of Communists if not a Communist himself. Arrested in 1939 and held for deportation, he was ultimately freed after extensive hearings before a special tribunal directed by Dean James McCauly Landis of the Harvard Law School. With no further recourse to law, Bridges' enemies, in and out of government, succeeded in having a special bill introduced into Congress directing the secretary of labor to deport Harry Bridges to his native Australia.[40]

Twice Marcantonio blocked consideration of the measure by timely application of House rules.[41] When the measure finally came up for debate, Marcantonio bitterly assailed the "Congress of the United States," which, "in all its dignified might," was carrying on what could only be termed a vendetta against Bridges. The labor union leader had never even been permitted the courtesy of testifying before the Committee on Immigration which had approved the bill calling for his deportation; and Marcantonio asked, at the very least, for unanimous consent to read a letter giving Bridges' side of the argument. There were several objections from the floor.

"Mr. Speaker," Marcantonio said, "now it becomes very, very obvious to every Member in this Chamber that you are asked to convict and sentence a man without giving him an opportunity" to be heard. Again he repeated his request for the necessary unanimous consent of the House, and again there were objections.

"All right," Marcantonio snapped. "Let us proceed with the legislative lynching."

Possibly goaded by this remark, one of the objectors reversed himself; and, after a brief and bitter verbal exchange between Marcantonio and some others, unanimous consent was granted.

The seven-page letter from Bridges that Marcantonio read into the record was a detailed answer to the charges against him. It had no effect on the temper of the House, which voted 330 to 42 in favor of the unique deportation.[42] Only the saner action of the Senate, which revamped this bill of attainder into an authorization for an investigation by the attorney general, prevented the leftist leader of the longshoremen from being shipped back to Australia.

To Vito Marcantonio the Bridges case, the registration of aliens, the attacks on radical political opinion, and the attempted Hatch Act amendments were all part of the general erosion of civil liberties in prewar America. Liberty, in his own frequently expressed view, was indivisible; and liberty applied to the Communist as well as to the Republican, the Democrat, or the apolitical person.

He fought all attempts at limiting the liberty of the left, even when the limitation was more a threat than an actuality. Late in 1939, J. Edgar Hoover announced that the Federal Bureau of Investigation was collecting dossiers on individuals and organizations engaged in subversive activities; Marcantonio viewed this as an "index-card menace" to American liberty. The law, as he saw it, clearly allowed the government to arrest those guilty of espionage or sabotage. "If, on the other hand, these people are not engaged in espionage . . . but their names are put down . . . because of the views they may entertain, . . . then I submit the preparation of these indices is most dangerous to the constitutional rights of the American people."[43]

If Hoover's FBI created an "index-card menace" to American liberty, the Congress itself through its Committee on Un-American Activities presented a "clear and present" danger to those same freedoms. At the opening of the first session of the Seventy-sixth Congress, Marcantonio joined forces with the liberals in the House to oppose the continuation of the committee then chaired by Martin Dies (Dem., Texas).

The Dies Committee was itself the personification of un-Americanism to the radical from East Harlem. Under the pretext of investigating illegal activities, it had sought to destroy the right to constitutional activity. The Dies Committee, he charged, had failed to recognize the "difference between mere subscription and application. I say that every dissident minority has the right to advocate, it has the right to organize, and it has the right to propagandize." The committee under Dies' direction had consistently failed to distinguish "between subversive and constitutional."

There is a difference, Marcantonio argued, between

espionage, sabotage and conspiracy on the one hand, and on the other hand the right to organize, advocate and propagandize. Until you establish that a person is guilty of conspiracy to violate laws or to engage in espionage or sabotage, I say that person has the right to advocate, and to do everything the Constitution gives him the right to say, publish, and do, whether he be a Communist, a Socialist, a Republican, a Democrat, or a Laborite. Once you tamper with this principle, no matter under what pretext, once you undermine it, you undermine the Constitution of the United States and deal a death blow to the fundamental principles upon which this country is based.

"Mr. Speaker," he concluded, "take away the rights of people whom you do not like, take away the constitutional rights of dissident minorities, and you yourselves are engaged in un-American activities."[44]

Marcantonio's attitude toward the Dies Committee was predicated on personal contact with the committee and its supporters as well as on the political or legal theory of civil rights. Testifying before the House Rules Committee in February 1939, in the first of many attempts to kill the Committee on Un-American Activities, Marcantonio had hardly launched into his opening statement when Representative Eugene Cox (Dem., Georgia), one of Dies' staunchest supporters, interrupted and cuttingly asked the congressman from New York if he were a Communist.

"I'm a member of the American Labor Party," Marcantonio shouted. "I'm not a Communist, and anyone who calls me a Communist lies."

"I'm not accusing you," Cox shouted back while elderly Congressman Adolph Sabath (Dem., Illinois) banged on the table and pleaded for order. It was precisely that kind of tactic, now used against himself, that Marcantonio saw as a danger in the committee.[45]

Later in the same year, voluntarily testifying before the Dies Committee as president of the International Labor Defense, Marcantonio readily admitted that seventeen of fifty-eight members of the organization's national board were Communists including Anna Damon, its executive secretary. But, he argued, the ILD was in no sense communistic. When Dies himself retorted that the ILD had taken a firm stand against fascism but had yet to defend a victim of "communist persecution," Marcantonio admitted only that the ILD had never been presented with such a case.[46]

Marcantonio's position on this vital question of civil liberties would have been stronger had he always acted as he spoke;

but like so many radicals, he weakened his own argument by seeing only one side of the question.

Although opposed to censorship when it affected groups or individuals with whom he agreed, he was completely capable of calling for a bit of "book-burning" when the occasion warranted. For example, when Marcantonio learned that "a bunch of rats were doing a job on the progressives" in an Italian translation of a WPA-produced volume on the Italian community in New York City, he immediately called the WPA administrator for the city and demanded that publication of the book be postponed. To James Kiernan, administrative assistant to Mayor La Guardia, Marcantonio wrote, "In other words, before the book is published, the Mayor or someone designated by him should first read the proofs or manuscript."[47]

There is no record of Marcantonio ever fighting for or even speaking in favor of freedom to propagandize for the Fascist, the anti-Semite, or the segregationist. The "indivisible liberty" he referred to so frequently in his speeches on civil liberty was clearly divisible as long as he drew the line. Not so strangely, Marcantonio was completely incapable of seeing the essential inconsistency in his position; had the contradiction ever been pointed out to him, he would have denied its existence.

To the congressman from East Harlem, fascism was a real and ever-present problem during the Depression years while the threat of communism was nothing more than a red herring. Reference to the communist threat, he once told his congressional colleagues, was simply the most convenient method "by which you wrap yourselves in the American flag in order to cover up some of the greasy stains on the legislative toga." In the frequently complex world of the Seventy-sixth Congress, Marcantonio was not entirely wrong. Thus it is not surprising that he won laughter in the House when he asked the rhetorical question, "What are you going to do when there is no more communism in this country?"[48]

The threat of fascism was, of course, no mere figment of the radical's imagination. Marcantonio's second term in office coincided with the Fascist assault on the nations of Western Europe. It was during this period that foreign affairs became ever more important to the Congress as questions of war or peace, neutrality or involvement, isolation or intervention replaced the urgency of the New Deal in the mind of the nation. Marcantonio was as vocal on questions relating to foreign affairs as he was on domestic issues. The two sides of national policy were frequently connected in his own mind, and both must be considered for an understanding of the radical politician.

V

The Divided Mind of the Left

Nothing in Vito Marcantonio's entire congressional career did him more damage politically, no other complex of factors linked him more closely with the radical left, than did the confused series of positions he assumed on the very complicated questions concerning American foreign policy in the period between his first term in Congress in 1935 and December 7, 1941. Starting with a violent hatred of war and warmongers during his first appearance on the national scene in 1935, he ended by urging that an American expeditionary force be sent to Europe, fully three months before the Japanese attack in the Pacific brought the United States into the war against the Axis powers. It thus becomes vital to delineate the twists and turns of his attitude toward foreign policy questions during the two-and-one-half congressional terms he served prior to the tragedy at Pearl Harbor.

From the very first, Marcantonio's position on foreign affairs was tied to his view of the domestic scene. Early in his first term, in March 1935, he told the House, "I believe we should not freely and carelessly authorize millions and millions of dollars for war purposes and then preach economy when it comes to appropriating money for a living wage to the unemployed of this nation." When Representative Melvin Maas (Rep., Minnesota) argued that the expenditure under consideration was for defense rather than war, Marcantonio voiced his disagreement: "Under the guise of defense you prepare for war, and when you prepare for war you are bound to have war."[1]

Five years later, with Armageddon right around the corner, the congressman from East Harlem still maintained that ex-

penditures for the military were immoral when the unemloyed
and the underemployed, the young and the old, all victims of
the Depression, were "being disregarded with brutal callousness."[2]

Time and time again Marcantonio reverted to this theme,
finding infinite variation in the basic line. When Congress was
asked to approve a special expenditure of $104,000,000 for two
additional capital ships in April 1936, he declared that "we are
burying the forgotten man under the keels of battleships." He
was not, he took pains to explain, a pacifist. "I would not hesitate to do my share of fighting in the defense of our country.
But why spend this amount of money when you cannot even
identify the enemy that will invade the United States? Can
anyone mention the enemy?"

Representative Blanton of Texas attempted to answer the
question, but Marcantonio interrupted, "I know what the gentleman is going to say. He is going to holler 'red!' He reads
'red,' he dreams 'red,' he sees 'red' all the time."

Blanton characteristically replied, "The speech the gentleman is making is a pretty good reason."

"How can anyone justify the expenditure," Marcantonio continued, ignoring Blanton, "while at the time time 700,000 men
in the United States of America are being kicked off the WPA?"[3]

Six years later, in May 1940, Marcantonio lashed out in
similar fashion, noting the lack of attention given to the twin
problems of relief and unemployment, blaming this lack on
"war hysteria," equating the preparedness drive of 1940 with
that of 1916, and predicting the same result: "The more dependent we become upon a war economy the closer we are
going to come to the brink of war."[4]

To this primary component of his antiwar stand, Marcantonio added the view that the businessman's drive for profit
was somehow a cause of war and that if the possibility of
profit could be removed from warfare, war itself would not
occur.

Having grown to maturity during the First World War, an
active political radical at least as early as 1919, he saw the

Great War as a struggle between conflicting imperialisms. Important in shaping his thinking on this issue were the works of the revisionist historians and publicists which lent credence to this anti-profit view and popularized it to an almost unbelievable extent.[5] The revelations of the Nye Committee in 1935 and 1936 added documentary "proof" to the commonly held belief.

On this issue at this time, Marcantonio was in step with great numbers of the American people and with a significant portion of the men with whom he served in Congress. The attitude was an almost natural concomitant of the letdown that followed American participation in the First World War. Marcantonio's adherence to this view was at one and the same time an indication of his radicalism and a clue to how much he was a creature of his time. When he informed the Congress that once having eliminated all profit from war "you will abolish 75 percent of the cause of war," he voiced an opinion held by Democrats as well as by Communists, by Republicans as well as by Socialists.[6]

Through his first term in Congress and the two-year period when he was out of office, Marcantonio generally favored all measures designed to keep the nation demilitarized and at peace. He voted in favor of both the First and Second Neutrality Acts in 1935 and 1936, respectively. In May 1936 the congressman from East Harlem led the floor fight against "the largest peacetime naval supply bill ever put forward" with the cry, "We are arming for an imperialistic war. . . . The burden must be borne by the workers of this country."[7]

He was as militant in his opposition to war while out of Congress as he was in the legislature. When a New York City high school principal suspended more than 150 students who had participated in an antiwar demonstration in April 1935, Marcantonio wrote his friend La Guardia, "Don't you think that you ought to step in and see to it that this stuffed shirt principal . . . should be made to see the light of day?" The students, he reminded the mayor, were being punished "for having ideals which are today the hope of the world."[8]

In September 1935 in a two-hour review of his record for several thousand of his East Harlem constituents, Marcantonio drew a thunderous ovation, the loudest of the evening, when he declared, "I am determined to oppose war. America had no business in the last war," and to avoid a repitition of that unhappy event there had to be "an honest-to-God policy of neutrality."[9]

On April 22, 1937, having been defeated at the polls, ex-congressman Marcantonio urged 3,500 students at New York's City College, meeting on Student Peace Day, to unite for peace, stating that a "militant pacifism makes for peace."[10]

Through the period of the Italian invasion of Ethiopia, the march of German troops into the Rhineland, the Sino-Japanese conflict, and the outbreak of the Spanish Civil War, Marcantonio maintained his antiwar position. There was neither sympathy for the aggressor nations implied in his attitude nor anything but hatred for the fascism that seemed to be sweeping over Europe. On this latter issue he was militant and consistent, working against it in every possible way even when, it will be remembered, his attitude cost him the friendship and political support of men like Luigi Antonini. Whatever support and respect Italian fascism had in East Harlem, he believed, came from misplaced feelings of patriotism and not from any basic belief or understanding of the issues involved. An attack on Mussolini, he explained to a Jewish questioner, was converted in the minds of his constituents to an attack on the Italian people. "If they understood the implications of fascism they would join the progressive forces of this city."[11]

When it came to German fascism, Marcantonio was much more forceful. In November 1938, after the elections of that year, he urged President Roosevelt to sever relations with Germany in retaliation for German persecution of the Jews.[12] In December of the same year, in letters to various individuals, he noted his deep concern "about the recent events in the fascist countries of Europe. I am especially concerned about the latest barbarous wave of anti-semitism and its repercussions" in the United States. Concern, in his case, was followed by action; he invited recipients of the letter to a conference "to decide on what means to adopt in the field of publicity and education to combat the unhealthy current of intolerance and race hatred coming from Europe."[13]

Publicity and education were the weapons of the moderate, but Marcantonio sometimes went beyond moderation when dealing with fascism. Toward the German-American Bund, the American arm of German fascism which had its center of strength in the city's Yorkville district just south of East Harlem, Marcantonio urged something beyond an intellectual approach, something closer to complete destruction by any and all means. He looked at the Bund and saw in it almost exactly what congressmen like Dies or Blanton saw in the American Communist party. "The Nazi Bund," Marcantonio wrote, oblivious to the irony in his language, "is a conspiracy to use any methods and means to destroy our democratic rights."[14]

This anti-Fascist component of Marcantonio's view of international affairs eventually had to conflict with his antiwar position. The necessary catalyst would be an international situation in which fascism created the possibility of general war; and the outbreak of the Spanish Civil War in July 1936 was the catalyst. It was over that civil war that Marcantonio, for the first time, equivocated in his antiwar position.

To the majority of Americans the conflict in Spain was a war that could possibly broaden into a general European conflict; thus our position was to avoid being drawn into the maelstrom. In January 1937, with almost no significant opposition, Congress extended the arms embargo embodied in the various Neutrality Acts to prevent shipments to either the Loyalists or the armies of General Francisco Franco. To Marcantonio and to the American radicals for whom he spoke, the issue was not that clear-cut.

As an anti-Fascist and a radical Marcantonio sympathized with the leftist Loyalist government of Spain in its struggle against the Fascists; therefore, in spite of his antiwar bias, he called for the "lifting of the unfortunate and inhuman embargo on Spain." The rationale behind this obvious contradiction consisted of maintaining that this was not a war between two national belligerents, but rather a civil conflict during which the United States was morally obligated to sell arms to the legally constituted Spanish government, the anti-Fascist Loyalists. While there is a certain amount of logic in this position, Marcantonio's stand was much more pragmatic than it was logical. It is not hard to imagine that if civil war had broken out in Nazi Germany at the same time, the congressman would have developed a "logical" set of reasons for selling arms to the rebels rather than to the legally recognized Nazi government.

No matter what position Marcantonio the logician and Marcantonio the radical might take, the Spanish Civil War created very real problems for Marcantonio the politician in East Harlem. His congressional district was overwhelmingly Catholic, and the Church tried to play a directing role in the political as well as in the religious and social lives of the congressman's constituents. Marcantonio was raised as a Catholic and as far as anyone knows never broke with the Church. All his adult life he wore a Catholic medallion around his neck, under his clothes where the voters could not be influenced by the religious symbolism. But believing in the Church as the repository of spiritual truth did not necessarily mean accepting the Church as the last word in political matters.

It would have been politically expedient, demagogic in fact, had Marcantonio gone along with the Catholic Church, which adamantly opposed the Loyalist government and played an active political role in keeping the United States in a neutral position during the conflict.[15] Yet when Father Sebastian Schaff, one of the leading Catholic prelates in East Harlem, wrote Marcantonio demanding that he oppose any lifting of the arms embargo to Spain, the congressman responded with nothing more than a politely worded brush-off. At the same time he promised anti-Fascist Spanish groups in the United

States that he would do everything in his power to get the embargo lifted.[16]

The conflict between the armies of Francisco Franco and the Loyalist government of Spain was among the first of the international issues upon which Marcantonio had to choose sides. Late in 1938, as Munich and the Sudetenland suddenly became household words to a geographically unsophisticated America, Marcantonio's reaction, immersed as he was in the elections of that year, remained unrecorded. From subsequent speeches, however, it is relatively easy to reconstruct his attitude. The Munich agreement hardened his antiwar views. He saw in the policy of appeasement a vindication of his opinion that the European conflict was nothing more than a battle between two competing imperialistic systems, an analysis that corresponded with his view of the First World War. Just as the United States should have remained aloof from that prior conflict, so too should it remain outside the coming war.

A much more significant silence followed the signing of the Hitler-Stalin Pact in August 1939—the occurrence in the field of foreign affairs most damaging to the unity of the American left.[17] Long after the event Marcantonio maintained that the pact was an expediency by which the Soviet Union bought time to arm against the Nazi menace; that it was a reaction to the Munich agreement, which had been an obvious attempt at turning the German war machine from West to East; and that, in any event, there could not have been any real collaboration between communism and fascism, two antithetical ideologies. But at the time Marcantonio maintained a complete silence, neither condemning nor supporting the pact. He did not publicly praise the agreement as did the Communist party, but neither did he break off relations with the Communists as did many other American radicals; quite contrarily, his agreement with the party seemed more complete than ever.

When, on September 1, 1939, Hitler ordered the *Wehrmacht* into Poland, precipitating the most destructive war of all time, Marcantonio blossomed forth as an almost frantic opponent of intervention. In October he turned down an offer of the New York County chairmanship of the American Labor party because it was more important for him to devote full time to his job in Washington. "At this time," he wrote, "it is necessary to bend every effort to keep America at peace, to safeguard us against involvement in the European conflict, which is in no wise the concern of the American Labor Party and the American people."[18]

Only once did he deviate from this line in the following months, but the deviation is an interesting one. Soon after the Nazi invasion of Poland, Roosevelt called a special session of Congress for the expressed purpose of repealing the arms embargo legislation that now prevented any aid to the Allied powers. After a bitter congressional battle between the isolationists and the administration, Roosevelt succeeded in getting the so-called Fourth Neutrality Act through by a narrow margin. It was the first real break in the isolationist pattern of prewar American thinking. The new law allowed the sale of arms to belligerents on a cash-and-carry basis and has generally been considered as advantageous to the British and French.[19]

The American Communist party, adamantly against intervention at this time, joined the American isolationists in opposing the passage of the Fourth Neutrality Act. In November 1939, when the bill squeaked through the Congress, the party's *Daily Worker* blasted the new legislation as an act "balking the will of the people for peace" and accused the legislators of passing the bill "in an atmosphere strongly tainted with war hysteria." The Communist organ considered this revision of neutrality legislation as one more "long step in the direction of war."[20]

Despite his fulminations against intervention in the preceding months, Marcantonio voted in favor of the Fourth Neutrality Act and even voted against every amendment designed to restrict or weaken the legislation.[21] There is no explanation for his action on this particular question; in the debate that raged around the proposal he asked no important questions and made no speeches. Certainly his vote indicates his own independence of mind, but in a more important way it mirrors the multiple confusions of a congressman whose thinking on foreign policy questions was much more frequently emotional than it was intellectual.

Whatever the reason, he assumed his previous position without apparent discomfort and without reference to his vote during the special session. As the war in Europe moved from its brief "phony" stage to the horror of the German blitzkrieg, Marcantonio returned to the fold of the radical left. He informed a nationwide radio audience in mid-July 1940:

> Americans today are faced with making the most fundamental and far-reaching decision in the history of our country—war or peace. . . . At this point let me say, that there is no moral, economic, or social justification for our entry into the war in Europe. It is an imperialistic war. While there may be a difference between the contending powers, that difference is one of degree and the degree is not big enough to warrant the loss of one American life. . . . If this were a war of ideologies, if it were truly a war on which the outcome of our American way of living depended, . . . I would unhesitatingly advocate our immediate entry into it, . . . I am not a pacifist, I am willing to fight for the defense of my country, and in any war in which the interests of our American people are involved.

"The present war," he continued, "is no such war." Referring to the spate of repressive legislation he had opposed in Congress, he insisted that in the name of national defense the government had engaged "in the hounding and persecuting of all those who dared raise their voices for peace" and in the suppression of minority groups and of aliens but had forgotten the social and economic rights of labor.[22]

He immersed himself in what he thought of as a fight against war. "Life is so hectic down here," he wrote Anna Damon of the International Labor Defense, "that even my own family never hear from me. They just assume I am still existing as they have not as yet received an obituary."[23]

As step by painful step the president brought the nation closer to the possibility of actual intervention, Marcantonio became more and more convinced that entrance into the war was the Democratic administration's final answer to the problem of unemployment that it had, through its own timidity, been unable to solve in peacetime. It was in this bitter context that Marcantonio wrote to artist Rockwell Kent, "Franklin Delano Roosevelt is the world's greatest betrayer of his own New Deal . . . and you may quote me."[24]

To those who tried to link him to the Communist party because of his antiwar stand, he replied that the nation's role was not intervention but regeneration through the solving of internal problems. "America has nothing to fear from any isms," he wrote one such critic, "if we take care of youth unemployment, general unemployment, and secure economic security for the American people. If this makes me a red, then I am sure that I cannot convince you or anyone else."[25]

During the summer of 1940 he backed up his strong language with his vote and never had he been in such utter isolation. He cast the only dissenting vote against the Naval Ship Construction Bill and the Aviation Expansion Bill (the votes were 400 to 1 and 402 to 1, respectively).[26] He not only voted against the Draft Bill, a measure he considered a poor excuse for his own American Youth Act, but he had what can only be considered the gall to immediately introduce a bill calling for the repeal of the Conscription Act. Accepting a position as vice-president of the American Peace Mobilization, he carried the fight to the people of the nation in radio addresses and in numerous public appearances. "Only pressure from the American people will help," he wrote despairingly.[27]

The pressure he hoped for should have come, in his home state of New York at least, from the American Labor party, the party he alone represented in Washington. But as the nation moved ever closer to involvement in the European conflict, the split between Marcantonio and the state leadership of the party, already evident in the election of 1938, grew wider. Two basic and related issues were involved: foreign policy questions and an attitude toward Communist participation in the councils of the ALP.

The dichotomy in viewpoint between Marcantonio and the men who had brought the ALP into existence—men like David Dubinsky, Alex Rose, and Luigi Antonini—had been implicit in their earliest relationship. Marcantonio was adamant in his desire to work with any group espousing a similar program, including, if necessary, the Communist party. The labor union leadership of the ALP, familiar with the Communists through labor struggles extending back over two decades, just as adamantly objected to the slightest collaboration with the Communists. The issue became thoroughly divisive as early as the primary election campaign of 1938. There can be little doubt that the party would probably have split over this question alone, but the process of fission was hastened after 1939 by the intrusion of disagreements over the position to be taken by the ALP toward American foreign policy. Within months the organization was divided into two warring factions, neither of which gave any quarter.

Disagreement over the Communist question came first, and some explanation of the relationship between the Communist and the American Labor parties is necessary here. In 1938 the Communist party in New York State was denied a place on the ballot because it had failed to poll a sufficient vote in the previous gubernatorial election. The Communists moved en masse into the ALP by the simple expedient of registering with the American Labor party during registration week. This perfectly legal procedure fitted in well with the current Communist "popular front" tactic, and, most important, it gave the Communists the right to help choose ALP candidates in the primary elections in 1938. Almost all observers agree that by the end of that year, at the very least the New York County organization of the ALP, under whose jurisdiction Marcantonio's district fell, had been taken over completely by the Communist party.[28] Certainly the political positions taken by the county organization were far to the left of those taken by the state organization which was still under the control of the labor union leaders.

For example, when Marcantonio, as a leading figure in the New York County organization, demanded that the state organization's leadership take a stand for or against the Dies Committee, the most he could get was a qualified condemnation in which the higher echelon of the ALP accepted the idea of an investigation into un-American activities—a stand far different from Marcantonio's own position. There could be no doubt that Martin Dies' hatred of the Communists was matched in degree, if not actually surpassed, by that of Rose of the Milliners' Union or Dubinsky and Antonini of the International Ladies Garment Workers Union.[29]

It was foreign policy that brought the split into the open in such fashion that reconciliation was impossible. The ALP had been formed originally to help Roosevelt in New York State in the 1936 campaign, and the party's statewide leadership was firmly committed to backing the president. As Roosevelt turned from the domestic scene to face the succession of crises emanating from the European conflict, the labor union leadership of the ALP turned with him in every single respect while the New York county organization and Vito Marcantonio hastened toward complete and unremitting opposition. Marcantonio's unique votes on May 28, 1940, against enormous appropriations for the Navy and for military aviation were completely repudiated by Alex Rose in his capacity as executive secretary of the ALP. Rose went even further and "demanded . . . that the Communist Party in the United States be outlawed" in order to save democracy in its critical period. Whereupon the left-wing county leadership turned around and repudiated Rose. The American Labor party obviously had a divided mind.[30]

There was no issue even remotely related to foreign policy

upon which the two wings of the party agreed. The state committee roundly condemned the Hitler-Stalin Pact of 1939 while the county organization fought against any discussion of the agreement, a discussion that was sure to bring dissension. Similarly, Rose and his followers immediately backed Roosevelt's lend-lease idea while the county leadership condemned it as a step toward American participation in the war.[31]

The conflict between the left and right wings of the ALP erupted during the primary election campaign of 1940. Marcantonio was right in the middle of the fight, racing back and forth between New York and Washington. Antonini, speaking for the state organization or right wing, blasted the congressman as a "stooge of the Communist Party" and threw his support to Joseph Piscitello of his own union for the ALP nomination in the Twentieth Congressional District.[32] The left-wing New York County organization backed Marcantonio with every available force. As in the election of 1938, nomination by a minority party was insufficient for election; thus Marcantonio again filed for the nomination on the Republican and Democratic tickets.

James J. Lanzetta, by now a familiar adversary, received the nod from Tammany Hall; but strangely, Marcantonio had no opposition in his race for the Republican nomination. This latter fact stemmed from two important factors: (1) Although in 1940 no one would have considered Marcantonio a Republican, he still had effective control of the party machinery in his own district. (2) Through his relationship with the New York County organization of the ALP, Marcantonio had acquired political power that went beyond the confines of his own district.

Using that power, Marcantonio inaugurated a technique in the 1940 campaign that was to be an important element in his own future political career. Since ALP members tended to vote Democratic where their own party was not a contending force, the ALP controlled to some extent the Democratic vote. Where the vote was known to be very close, the ALP at times had effective power of election. In 1940 the ALP chose to run its own candidate in the Seventeenth Congressional District, thus virtually insuring the election of Kenneth Simpson, a liberal Republican, by taking votes away from the Democratic nominee. There is reason to believe that the ALP ran its candidate in return for the Republican failure to nominate anyone to run against Marcantonio in his own Twentieth Congressional District.[33] Such political wheeling and dealing was not, of course, unique to the ALP congressman, but it certainly made his job in both the primary and the November elections that much easier.

Campaigning on the negativism of his antiwar stand and the positivism of his relief program, the fiery radical Marcantonio beat Piscitello badly. He received the Republican nomination by default. Surprisingly, Marcantonio came within 200 votes of taking the Democratic nomination away from Lanzetta, an omen for the future of the two-party system in East Harlem. Equally important was the election for control of the American Labor party apparatus in the state. The New York County machine ran its own slate headed by Morris Watson against the labor union leadership, and in Watson's own words he lost "by about 40 votes and 14 fist fights" in a bitter state convention. The leftwing was breathing hard on the necks of Rose, Dubinsky, and company.[34]

Despite this seriously weakened position, Antonini, state chairman of the ALP, hurled anathemas at the duly nominated candidate of the party in the Twentieth Congressional District. "Mr. Marcantonio," he told the press, "has shown that he is not in sympathy with the aims and principles of the Labor Party as they are understood by the vast majority of our members and enrolled voters," and therefore, "the party had repudiated" his candidacy as an American Laborite.[35]

If by "party" Antonini meant himself and his friends, his statement can be accepted as true; but surely the primary election returns in East Harlem indicated no repudiation of Marcantonio by the enrolled rank and file. In East Harlem it had been Antonini himself who had been rejected. But no matter how viewed, the statement was little more than pure political bravado, since even on a statewide basis neither side in the intra-party fight had received a clear mandate.

At any rate Marcantonio, running for re-election, had little time to dispute the meaning of the primary vote with Antonini. The election campaign itself gave the voters of East Harlem a clear choice between two candidates who were in absolute opposition over the single most important issue of the time: war or peace. Lanzetta, the Democrat, supported Roosevelt and the administration's foreign policy without qualification, while Marcantonio told his constituents, "My record is clear and my stand is well known. I voted against repeating 1917 all over again."[36]

For the fourth time in as many election campaigns, Marcantonio received Fiorello La Guardia's endorsement, despite the fact that La Guardia backed the right wing of the ALP and despite the fact that the mayor was an outspoken interventionist.[37] In every way it was a puzzling endorsement; in contrast to his position on Marcantonio, La Guardia advised ALP members not to support the party's candidate in a by-election early the following year because the left-wing candidate "has frankly and honestly stated that he is opposed to the lend-lease bill." The mayor urged the voters to elect Joseph Clark Baldwin, a Republican who was "unequivocally pledged . . . to aid England in the fight against the dictator countries." La Guardia's thinking had undergone no great changes between the November election of 1940 and the by-election in March 1941, yet three days before the critical 1940 campaign terminated he gave his unqualified support to Vito Marcantonio whose views on foreign policy questions were diametrically opposed to his own.[38]

Any attempt to account for La Guardia's action in that critical year founders in a welter of contradiction. From the sources available there is no completely satisfactory answer, only hints, guesses, and intuition.

For one thing, there was, of course, the deepest kind of affection between the two men, an affection extending back almost twenty years. Yet firm friendships have been split asunder on less vital political issues. To both La Guardia and Marcantonio this was a critical question of war and peace, against which affection alone would not normally serve as a shield. Along with personal regard, some writers have hinted that Marcantonio had a mysterious hold over La Guardia, but no evidence exists to support this view and, given "The Little Flower's" personality, it is hardly credible. It would be safe to say that La Guardia was almost pathologically independent.

Arthur Schutzer, a personal friend and long-time political associate of Marcantonio's in the American Labor party, felt that La Guardia, disagreeing with Marcantonio, had enough respect for the congressman's independence of mind and intellectual abilities to respect his view on this particular issue.[39] It is difficult to accept Schutzer's explanation as the sole answer to the problem; but if it is coupled with the almost familial relationship between Marcantonio and La Guardia, it might explain the mayor's vital endorsement of the left-wing congressman.

Whatever the cause of La Guardia's support, his endorsement played a part in the election campaign's closing days and undoubtedly won some votes for Marcantonio that he might not otherwise have garnered. But the results of the election in the Twentieth Congressional District in 1940 indicate that Vito Marcantonio, in his fourth congressional battle, was fully capable of winning on his own.

The thirty-eight-year-old radical defeated Jimmy Lanzetta by the lopsided majority of 25,136 to 14,898, the biggest vote differential in East Harlem in decades.[40] This time not even the pull of a presidential election saved the Tammany candidate. Lanzetta almost immediately appealed to the House Committee on Campaign Expenditures and accused Marcantonio of spending enormous sums of money in violation of the Corrupt Practices Act. Any hopes Lanzetta might have entertained were quickly squelched when William M. Whittington (Dem., Mississippi), chairman of the committee, replied to the complaint that the committee was "authorized to investigate complaints when complaints are made under oath, setting forth facts and not rumors or opinions."[41]

The major point of contention between Lanzetta and Marcantonio during the campaign had been intervention; thus the important question is: To what extent was Marcantonio's victory in 1940 a vindication of his noninterventionist stand? The question is infinitely easier to ask than to answer, and it is tempting to allow the figures to speak for themselves and the reader to arrive at his own conclusion. The factors leading up to the victory of any candidate in an election are almost always multiple and are not ordinarily amenable to separaration. Marcantonio's successful campaign in 1940 is no exception to the rule.

There is no doubt that the congressman ran on the record he had amassed during two terms in Congress and that the record was well-known in East Harlem. His militant support of public housing, public and presumably cheaper power, liberalized immigration and citizenship legislation, and a larger, better-paying WPA certainly helped him in the slum where he lived and campaigned. Marcantonio was ethnically attractive (admittedly, no more so than Lanzetta) to the Italian majority of his district, and the series of fights he had waged in behalf of Puerto Rico and the islanders cemented his ties to the Puerto Rican minority among his constituents. His status as the incumbent gave him other advantages over Lanzetta, not the least of which had been the ability to keep his name before the voters during the previous two years in a way that Lanzetta could not match.

By 1940, six years after his first race for Congress, Marcantonio had succeeded in constructing a superb personal political machine that cut across all party lines in East Harlem, embracing Republicans, Laborites, Democrats, and Communists. It was a machine that served the people of East Harlem in a thousand different ways as it operated daily from the congressman's headquarters on 116th Street. While the machine operated all year and not just at election time, it was augmented during the campaign by all of the physical resources of the Communist party and of the broader-based New York County ALP, each of which considered Marcantonio's re-election of paramount importance to its own cause. This assistance was rank-and-file support, doorbell-ringing and stair-climbing support of a kind many politicians dream about but few could match.

Yet it is equally true that Marcantonio pinned his campaign to the idea of nonintervention. From sound trucks along East Harlem's avenues and from the platforms at countless indoor meetings, Marcantonio and his supporters hammered away on the theme that ran through the campaign literature: the congressman had voted against "plunging our people into an imperialist war . . . against repeating 1917 all over again." No one can say to what extent this theme affected the voters. But it is true that the concept of nonintervention, of keeping America remote from the war in Europe, had enormous attraction to millions of Americans, the vast majority of whom, in East Harlem as elsewhere in the U. S., had no sympathy for Communists or leftists of any stripe. The idea had particular emotional strength among Italo-Americans who in many instances had personal reasons for wanting to keep America isolated from a world conflict in which it would have found itself at war with Italy. The strength of noninterventionist feeling can perhaps best be gauged by remembering that, although Roosevelt won the election of 1940, the margin of victory had considerably lessened and undoubtedly millions of people had voted against him because they feared the ultimate result of his interventionist ideas. Even Roosevelt found it expedient during the campaign to deny that American boys would be sent overseas.

Whether re-elected because of his position toward domestic and foreign affairs, his machine, his personality, or, as seems most likely, by a combination of these factors, Vito Marcantonio returned to Washington in January 1941 ready once again to take up the cudgels for peace, the only American Labor party representative in the new Seventy-seventh Congress.[42]

From the floor of Congress and at public meetings, racing between New York and Washington with a show of energy that constantly characterized the man, Marcantonio voted and spoke along the lines laid down during his campaign. He opposed both the naval expansion and army supply bills of 1941 and berated the administration for its lend-lease proposal which he and his party considered insulting. While Roosevelt called for all-out aid to Britain, the ALP explained, millions in America "are still unemployed, millions of our farm population are roaming the nation, disinherited, the youth are without opportunity, the aged and the unemployed are being disregarded with brutal callousness [and] the Negro population . . . is subject to the worst forms of discrimination and oppression and alien minorities are treated as pariahs in our midst."[43]

"The Yanks are not coming," Marcantonio thundered to New York audiences. He joined Senators Burton Wheeler (Dem., Montana) and Gerald Nye (Rep., North Dakota) at a rally against the Lend-Lease Bill and, in a period noted for its strange political combinations, won the plaudits of such diverse groups as the America First Committee, the Communist party, and the American Student Union.[44] The war, he wrote the journalist Luigi Criscuolo, was an "imperialist plot" directed by the "Rockefeller and Morgan interests who certainly do control the monopoly finances of this country, . . . these gentlemen and those dependent on them have been beating the war drums."[45] Remove the date from the letter and he might just as well have been opposing Wilson and World War I.

On March 19, 1941, while London suffered through the most devastating air raid of the war up to that point, Marcantonio warned "that if the United States became involved in the war the responsibility would rest with President Franklin D. Roosevelt,"[46] a responsibility the chief executive bore without the congressman's reminder. Three days later Marcantonio addressed a rally of 3,500 people gathered by the American Peace Mobilization. Before banners inscribed, "Keep the Yanks in Yankee Stadium" and "We Won't Fight for Wall Street," the ALP congressman thundered, "We are not appeasers. We want to defeat Hitler and we also want to defeat the other axis—the Wall Street-Downing Street axis." How Hitler's war machine and German fascism could be defeated in the face of Marcantonio's own refusal to vote for increased armaments or aid to the powers then struggling against fascism was a factor he chose not to discuss at a peace meeting.[47]

Three months later, on June 22, 1941, the German Army hurled itself across the Russian border and raced across the flat heartland of the Soviet Union in a three-pronged drive toward Leningrad, Kiev, and Moscow. This new element in the European war caused mixed reactions in numerous capitals throughout the world. In London, Winston Churchill gladly accepted the Soviet Union as a new ally in the brutal struggle against Germany. In Washington, Roosevelt and his advisers immediately sat down to tackle the knotty political problems involved in the possible extension of lend-lease aid to the Communist nation. And on the ninth floor of a gray-faced office building on New York's East 12th Street, the hierarchy of the Communist party of the United States promptly reversed the antiwar policy it had followed through June 21 and called for all-out aid to the Soviet Union, one of the most blatant political reversals in American history.

Those few writers who have dealt with the political career of Vito Marcantonio have presumed that on this major issue he immediately reversed himself along with the Communist party, thereby providing another vital link in the chain of intimate relationships connecting him and the American comrades. Since Marcantonio never hid the fact that on many issues he supported the Communists and accepted support from them, the need for the construction of such a chain is unclear. But the truth is that on this major issue the leftist congressman did not immediately reverse himself and follow the so-called "party line."

Marcantonio's immediate reaction was silence, an unusual silence considering the importance of the German invasion of Russia, an embarrassing silence considering his frequent pronouncements on foreign affairs. When Eugene Lyons, the militantly anti-Communist editor of the *American Mercury* wrote Marcantonio in obvious glee over what he presumed was the congressman's discomfiture and requested a statement on his present view of the war he had so recently opposed, Marcantonio angrily scribbled "Ignore" across the top of the letter.[48]

Immediately following the German invasion of Russia, Earl Browder's Communist party began racing in all directions at the same time, attempting to affect coalitions with labor and political groups, with anyone who favored intervention. Men who had been called warmongers up to June 21, 1941, suddenly found themselves embraced by the party; the *Daily Worker* spewed love on a mélange of American public figures who days before had been "jackals of imperialism."

For the disciplined party member who had survived the shock of the Moscow purge trials and the Hitler-Stalin Pact of 1939, this new change was relatively simple to make; for the congressman from East Harlem the switch was much more difficult. Two months and a day after the German attack in the east Marcantonio broke his self-imposed public silence for the first time. While the two million residents of Leningrad threw up barricades in the streets and vowed to fight the Nazis to the death, Marcantonio scotched a rumor of impending reconciliation between the right and left wings of the American Labor party, a reconciliation pushed by the Communists in line with their new policy of all-out intervention.

Characterizing the right-wing leadership as "political punks and Hitler labor racketeers," Marcantonio insisted that if any overtures for unity in the face of the changed world situation had been initiated by the left wing, such overtures had been made without his knowledge. Had he known of any such moves, he explained, he would have opposed them.[49] The Communists moved toward unity; Marcantonio, acting independently, maintained his previous position.

Then the outspoken leftist retreated into his uncharacteristic shell for another two months. When he did speak again, on October 15, 1941, four months after Hitler's move into Russia, it was with the voice of the sinner embracing religion—more fervent even than the minister himself. The man who cast the only vote in opposition to the president's Conscription Bill confessed at a conference held by the American Youth Congress in New York that he was "now ready to vote for war."[50]

The following day, as Congress debated a bill providing for the arming of merchant marine vessels, Vito Marcantonio delivered the most difficult speech of his career to that point, his noninterventionist swan song, breaking completely with Fish, Nye, Wheeler, and the other isolationist faithful.[51] Recounting his earlier position on foreign policy, he reiterated his belief that the European conflict from 1939 to June 21, 1941, was an imperialist war. "However," he maintained, "from the standpoint of defense of our Nation, the liberties, and the national interests of the people of the United States, the invasion of the Soviet Union by Hitler transformed that war which was predominantly imperialist into a war which is now essentially one of national defense." And for the national defense, he urged not just aid to the allies but direct American intervention in force.

Why had the character of the war changed? First, a conquered Soviet Union "would place a Nazi military bridgehead within rowboat distance of our own northwestern shores." Second, in the world situation of 1939, 1940, and the first half of 1941, Germany could not have successfully mounted a military offensive against the United States. "We were not in military danger as long as Hitler had on his eastern boundary a powerful, well-armed Soviet Union. The defense interests of the United States and the Soviet Union were interdependent. The existence of the Soviet Union depended on an unconquered United States. The existence of the United States depended on an unconquered Soviet Union. A Hitler conquest of either made a Hitler conquest of the other almost a certainty."

Marcantonio went on to charge the western European powers with trying to incite Hitler into a war against the Soviet Union rather than against the West. He defended the Stalin-Hitler nonaggression pact since it gave the Soviet Union time to build up its defenses against the expected onslaught by the Nazis. The conquest of the Soviet Union was not, he continued, on a par with the conquest by Hitler of any other nation, for it would give the Fascists the enormous industrial capacity and the wealth of natural resources to be found in the Soviet Union. America's only defense, therefore, lay in the military defeat of Nazi Germany. He said:

> I submit that in now supporting these very measures which I have opposed in the past, I am supporting them for the same reasons which motivated my opposition, namely defense of our Nation and its liberties, and opposition to imperialism and opposition to fascism, irrespective of their national character. The character of the war has changed and I have no other consistent course to follow but to support a war of defense as vigorously as I opposed a war of imperialist aggression.

As Marcantonio turned the last page of the lengthy speech, Representative Hugh Scott (Rep., Pennsylvania) pointedly asked if it were not "a fact that the gentleman's interest in the defense of America to the extent to which he has just stated it, dates from the day of the invasion of Soviet Russia by Germany?"

"My interest in the defense of America," Marcantonio replied, "has existed since December 10, 1902, the day I was born."[52]

The radical congressman from East Harlem had come full circle. He had entered Congress in 1935 firmly opposed to war and militarism. During his second term his anti-Fascist leanings and the anvil of the Spanish Civil War had modified his original viewpoint to the extent that he wanted to aid the Spanish Republican government. As the western European democracies and his own country failed to save the Loyalists from the Fascist onslaught, and as Munich and the sell-out of the Czechoslovak Republic indicated the ability of the West to compromise with fascism, Marcantonio again reshaped his thinking. To him the war in Europe became an imperialist conflict of much the same character as the First World War. In October 1941, four months after the German invasion of Russia and two months before the debacle at Pearl Harbor, the antiwar, antimilitarist Marcantonio called for America's immediate entrance into the European war.

In his final congressional speech of the prewar period relating to foreign policy, Marcantonio attempted to prove his own consistency of view. He tried to show that in now supporting war, he was moving along the same lines that previously had led him to support nonintervention. This can be dismissed as rationalization, for, if anything, his behavior mirrored confusion not consistency; and the four months of almost total silence, during which that last speech was worked out, indicate uncertainty rather than clarity of mind.

The uncertainty itself is reasonable. Millions of Americans at every level from national leaders down to the man in the street mirrored the confusion of the times. Those last years of the Depression were a time of disorientation during which the American people had to taste the bitter fruit of international conflict they had themselves brought to ripeness by their actions over the previous two decades. Marcantonio's view of the international scene was, of course, vastly different from that of the majority of the people. Up to 1941 he was both antiwar and anti-Fascist when it was truly impossible to hold both views and plead consistency. The destruction of fascism after September 1939 could only come through war, yet Marcantonio used what little power he had to prevent both aid to the Allied powers and the build-up of America's own military power in the period between the outbreak of the European war and October 1941.

If an explanation exists, it lies in the way the West reacted toward fascism before September 1939 and in the way in which the rising tide of war forced a change in the domestic policies of the Roosevelt administration. On the first matter there was little in the conduct of foreign relations between Britain, France, and the United States, on the one hand, and Nazi Germany, on the other, that indicated any great anti-Fascist motivation. To a mind such as Marcantonio's, Spain and Munich indicated quite the opposite. Tons of paper have been used to explain those two events, but at the time the American radical left tended to see in them nothing other than the perfidy of Western capitalism. In his last two terms in Congress Marcantonio heard the voice of the anti-Communist and the antiradical raised much more frequently than that of the anti-Fascist. As Hitler prepared to march into Poland, the American Congress ripped into the problem of left-wing infiltration of the WPA and destroyed the Federal Theatre Project because it was supposedly a hotbed of radicalism. In 1940, as the Nazi war machine ground up Western Europe, Marcantonio watched as the Congress tried by legislative edict to deport Harry Bridges and as the Dies Committee spent infinitely more time investigating the American left than the American Fascist movement.

The same president who urged aid to Britain and France after September 1939 also indicated that the reforming period of his administration was over. True to his word, Roosevelt sat back and allowed the basically conservative Congress to emasculate relief, unemployment, and public housing programs. Historians of the New Deal now insist that Roosevelt had no choice, that he had to compromise on domestic issues in order to gain a congressional majority for his foreign policies. But Marcantonio did not see it that way. He saw the administration attempting to bail out Britain and France while forgetting the plight of the American worker and farmer. Thus, Roosevelt became the betrayer of the New Deal, and rearmament and war became the New Deal's ultimate answer to the problem of unemployment. That was the view from the left, Marcantonio's view, a view that shaped his thoughts and which he in turn helped shape among the small but vocal group of American leftists.

But the thinking behind his final speech to Congress still eludes us. Marcantonio's own papers, full for many other events in that prewar period, are totally devoid of documentation for the period between June and October 1941, documentation that might have cleared up this problem. But we can guess, and the guess can be an educated one: If Marcantonio had taken any other view he would have found himself isolated from the political left for which he presumed to speak, from which he drew his closest friends and his ideology. Had he continued to follow the nonintervention path, his only political "playmates" would have been the primarily conservative isolationists with whom he had no common ground beyond nonintervention. In short, he would have found himself in a politically untenable position, practically the only American leftist still in league with the isolationists. By late summer 1941, every section of the left, from the labor leaders of the ALP to the Communist party, was supporting some form of intervention. It is not unreasonable that during the time Marcantonio took to make up his mind he cast an eye now and then on the election of 1942. If he stuck to his nonintervention stand, where would his support, physical and financial, have come from? It is in no sense denigrating to say that he was a politician, and like all such politicians he had to worry about maintaining his public position. It is true that the radical left needed him as a spokesman in Washington, but it is equally true that he needed the radical left in order to win re-election to Congress. His October 16 speech was a rationalization of all of these factors and probably more, a rationalization of both the inner and outer turmoil that surrounded him during those four months of public silence.

His enemies, and he had his full share by 1941, jumped on the speech almost immediately. In the hands of his critics, it indicated that he was either a Communist or a dupe of the Communists, for obviously that he was in total agreement with Browder, Foster, Dennis, and the rest of the American Communist party leadership. He never argued the point, which was immaterial to him. A curt "So what?" was the closest he would come to dignifying the question which haunted him until his death made it academic. He insisted always that his point of view was predicated upon the national interest of the people of the United States.

Marcantonio's reversal of opinion in October 1941 might have proved disastrous to him in the election of 1942, but the question never came up in any meaningful way. On December 7, 1941, Japanese planes screamed down on Pearl Harbor, and the war of national defense became a reality depending on no argument, sophistic or otherwise. "Everyone," wrote Eugene Connolly, one of the leaders of the New York County ALP, "is very excited about the developments in the Far East and our clubs are very anxious to get their members involved in all phases of the defense activities. . . . I set to work today and will get out directives so that it can be done in a really coordinated manner."[53]

VI

The All-Party Congressman

Through the years of the Depression, Vito Marcantonio had been a consistent critic of the New Deal. If he voted in favor of some of Franklin Roosevelt's most important programs, it was primarily because the New Deal happened to be the best deal the radical congressman from East Harlem could hope for at the time. He could masquerade as a New Dealer himself, as he did during the election campaign in 1940, on the basis of his voting record, but no one familiar with the speeches he delivered prior to casting his vote would have been misled by the label.

America's declaration of war on the Axis powers immediately created an entirely new set of conditions on the domestic scene. Marcantonio reacted to those new conditions by shedding the prewar stance of the political gadfly and emerging into public awareness as a wartime worker bee, ready, willing, and able to support the Democratic administration to the limits of a congressman's power. Winning the war became the touchstone against which every political act was tested.

In June 1942 the *New Republic,* justifying the call for Marcantonio's re-election that year despite his embarrassing record of consistently following the Communist party line, informed its readers, "We don't know how Mr. Marcantonio's name could be excluded" from any list of "those men who could be counted on, from now on, to vote in favor of the necessary war measures and to support liberal domestic legislation."[1]

Three months later, the same magazine complimented the congressman and patted itself on the back at the same time:

112

"Marcantonio has been the most zealous supporter of the war in all Congress."[2] A less-impassioned observer writing eighteen years later bears out the *New Republic's* opinion, noting that Marcantonio's record in support of the administration was as good as that of any member of the New York State Democratic contingent in Congress and better than ten of the eleven Democratic representatives from Georgia.[3]

The web of national unity shaped by the overwhelming importance of defeating the Fascist nations encompassed even radical leftists like the congressman from East Harlem. It was during the conflict that Marcantonio finally broke through the wall of isolation behind which he had previously operated and reached a level of acceptance and usefulness he was never to achieve again once the guns had been silenced. The new conditions created by the war created new issues that drew Marcantonio's fire or support; but not every issue was new, and some that seemed to be so had their roots deep in the changes that had been wrought in American society during the Depression years.

To the American left wing and to Marcantonio, who was frequently looked upon as its legislative spokesman, the war was more than a fight against fascism in Europe and in the Pacific; it was also a time to consolidate and, if possible, extend the gains in social legislation made during the Depression decade. On the other hand, American conservatives and reactionaries sometimes saw the war as an opportunity to roll back and destroy those same gains. The conflict was an old one and, while the terms of the argument were unique from 1942 through 1945, it should surprise no one that the argument still existed.

Typical of Marcantonio's domestic battles during the era of international conflict was his vehement condemnation of the so-called Smith Amendment to the War Powers Act of 1942, an attempt at negating the forty-hour workweek provision of the Fair Labor Standards Act of 1938. Supposedly a patriotic measure designed to increase industrial production during the war emergency, the Smith Amendment would have deleted that portion of the wages-and-hours law providing for time-and-a-half pay for all hours worked exceeding forty a week. In arguing against the amendment in Congress Marcantonio noted that the same congressmen who had opposed progressive labor legislation during peacetime were among the first to use the war as an excuse to wipe out labor's hard-won gains.

Appealing for support from the public, Marcantonio took to the radio to charge that labor's enemies had inundated the public with billions of words designed to give the impression that organized labor refused to cooperate in the war effort. "You have been urged," he told his listeners, "by false patriots, by reactionary politicians, by radio commentators, and by columns and editorials in your newspapers to write your Congressman asking that he vote for legislation which would destroy the wages-and-hours law," the Smith Amendment.[4]

This mass of verbiage, he continued, was designed to give the impression that the Fair Labor Standards Act of 1938 *restricted* American labor to a forty-hour week; simple patriotism indicated the necessity for modifying the law. That Marcantonio was not fighting a "paper tiger" can be seen by the fact that the Mississippi state legislature submitted a petition to the Congress supporting the Smith Amendment and exhibiting exactly this misconception of the law.[5]

"Labor in war industries," Marcantonio explained, "is now working 48 and more hours a week. What the law simply says is that when American labor works more than 40 hours a week the employer must pay time-and-a-half for the hours over 40. Therefore, what is really behind the lie that you have heard so often is an attempt to cut wages and increase profits by those with no interest in this war other than that of exploiting labor and increasing their profits."[6]

The patriotism inherent in backing increased war production, he said, was nothing more than a smoke screen raised to hide the real intent of the amendment. With the administration on the same side of the fence as Marcantonio, the amendment was voted down, 226 to 62. No subsequent attempt to accomplish the same end was any more successful.[7]

Marcantonio had less luck with another amendment to the War Powers Act. One section of the original bill provided that legally resident aliens of good character serving in the nation's armed forces could acquire United States citizenship upon simple application. Congressman Joe Starnes (Dem., Alabama) introduced an amendment eliminating this provision. Marcantonio immediately objected. It was, he declared, one more round in the same old game called "kick the foreign-born around." Reminding his colleagues in the House that the alien soldier had been allowed to become a citizen during the First World War, Marcantonio emotionally pleaded, "The bullets that are shot against us do not discriminate. They shoot down the man in uniform be he a citizen or a non-citizen." His effort was wasted as the House accepted the Starnes Amendment, perhaps because, as Marcantonio sarcastically charged, the alien had no vote with which to retaliate.[8]

In a less public manner the congressman worked to secure the right of aliens to contribute to the war effort on the home front. In the fall of 1942 Marcantonio wrote to the president and gave complete details on several cases in which government regulations had made it difficult or even impossible for aliens with needed skills to hold or find jobs in war industries. It was not, he explained, a question of loyalty but rather of bias against the foreign-born. Many of his own constituents, born in Italy, which was then an enemy power, were particularly ill-treated. Marcantonio had always opposed such nativism, but his indignation was multiplied because the prejudice hurt the war effort.[9]

In another congressional battle during the first year of the war, Marcantonio attempted to convince the House of the importance of raising the legislative appropriation for the WPA which had been cut to $28,000,000 in the projected 1942–1943 budget. Arguing that, in his own city at least, war production had by no means absorbed the unemployed, that there was and would continue to be an employment lag affecting millions of workers, and that the WPA was vital to cushion the changeover from peacetime to wartime production, Marcantonio called for at minimum the 1941 appropriation for the agency: $875,000,000. The congressional tide engulfed the East Harlem radical. The appropriation remained at the lower level. In fact, the following year the WPA, the Civilian Conservation Corps, and the National Youth Administration were eliminated completely from national life as though a more conservative Congress wished to exorcise the remnants of the New Deal while it was possible.[10]

With such peripheral war legislation as the Smith and Starnes amendments or the WPA appropriation, Marcantonio fought hard for his viewpoint and voted as he argued. But with more direct war legislation, the congressman placed his own radical view on record and then voted for the measure under consideration even when he saw serious weaknesses in it. When the Revenue Act of 1942, a first step in paying for the war at hand, was considered by Congress, Marcantonio predictably favored the imposition of staggering rates on high individual incomes and on corporate profits. This was the course he had favored in a war against poverty, and he hewed to the same line in the battle against fascism. The administration bill, he charged, "continues to allow special privileges, . . . fails to recapture undue profits, . . . places the burden upon the poor rather than upon those who are able to pay." In his view the revenue act lent credibility to the charge "that Congress does not yet have that singleness of purpose which we must have to smash the Axis."

But the bill came up for debate under a House rule permitting no amendment from the floor and Marcantonio demonstrated his own singleness of purpose, the quality that led the *New Republic* to call for his re-election, by reminding his colleagues that the choice was between the bill at hand or no bill at all. "Obviously the latter alternative is not even to be considered in times such as this." The Revenue Act of 1942 passed by the overwhelming vote of 395 to 2.[11]

The biggest legislative gun that Marcantonio added to his range of armaments during the war years was a relatively new-found interest in Negro rights legislation. During the Depression years the fight for such civil rights laws, at least among white groups and including the American left, had been implicit in the battle waged against general poverty. The organization of nondiscriminating industrial unions under the banner of the CIO, or the legislation providing that the WPA hire without regard to race, illustrate the approximate limits of white America's interest in one of its oldest continuing problems. For Marcantonio personally, the introduction of legislation designed to include domestic servants under the social security laws or migrant workers under the wage and hours law implied an interest in the Negro as well as in his own predominantly white constituents.

Not until 1941, when the issue of the day was peace or war rather than recovery or depression, did Marcantonio begin to emerge as one of the leading congressional spokesmen for the Negro portion of the nation. In March of that year, when he was still noninterventionist and when his motives could have been to embarrass the administration as well as to further the cause of civil rights, he introduced a measure designed to prohibit discrimination because of race, color, or creed by any agency supported by government funds.[12] Just as he had been prematurely anti-Fascist, he was in 1941 prematurely anti-Jim Crow; and the bill languished in committee.

The coming of the war catapulted the question of civil rights into public consciousness for the first time in many years; it was difficult to reconcile a worldwide battle against fascism with the staggering array of anti-Negro legislation on the statute books of most southern states and with the psychic apparatus of racism still in the minds of many Americans in all sections of the nation. Another less intellectual and more utilitarian reason for the emergence of the civil rights question was the obvious fact that Negro manpower was as vital to the war effort as was white manpower; yet there existed a tenuous, unformed, but prevalent and disconcerting attitude among some Negroes that this was a "white man's war."

Both of these factors were important to the political being that was Vito Marcantonio, but he had perhaps even greater interest in the question than most congressmen because so many of his implacable congressional foes—Dies, Blanton, Woodrum, Smith, and others—came from southern states where they were usually elected and re-elected by comparatively small percentages of white, and only white, voters. For a variety of reasons then, it would be reasonable to assume that when the question of civil rights came up in Congress in 1942 and later, Marcantonio would take part in the legislative battle. What could not be anticipated was the commitment the congressman made to this "new" issue.

Early in 1942 Marcantonio reintroduced the above-mentioned measure banning discrimination by government-supported agencies. In June he joined Paul McNutt, chairman of the War Labor Board, at a Harlem rally honoring Dorrie Miller, a young Negro sailor who had won the Navy Cross for heroism at Pearl Harbor. Marcantonio told a cheering audience that those who wanted to attain victory "must see to it that every available man, Negro or white, is employed whether in the military forces or in industry."[13]

While the battle for equal economic rights was to occupy much of Marcantonio's time during the war years, he emerged as a leader of the pro-civil rights group in the House during the fight over that peculiar southern institution, the poll tax, which took up a great deal of time in the last session of the Seventy-seventh Congress.

Representative Lee Geyer (Dem., California) had dropped a bill abolishing the poll tax into the legislative hopper early in 1942; but the measure fell under the jurisdiction of the Judiciary Committee whose chairman, Representative Hatton Sumners (Dem.) of Texas, a poll-tax state, looked askance at all such "democratic" efforts. When Geyer died in mid-year, Marcantonio took charge of a campaign to accumulate enough signatures on a discharge petition to force the bill from committee to the floor of the House, where the members of Congress would at least have the opportunity to debate and vote on the measure.

Slowly, patiently, relentlessly, Marcantonio stalked his colleagues, and congressman after congressman added his name to the list. By August the liberal *New Republic* editorialized, "Once deemed an impossible task by the weak in spirit, abolition of the poll tax as a prerequisite to voting in a federal election now seems quite possible."[14]

In October the necessary two-hundred-and-eighteenth name was added to Marcantonio's petition, and the House embarked on one of the bitterest verbal battles of recent times. There can be little doubt that the responsibility for forcing the debate in the House was Marcantonio's. Certainly none of the southern representatives doubted it or failed to appreciate his role, and the congressman from East Harlem earned their unremitting hatred, in public at least.

"I salute you, Sir," said Eugene Cox of Georgia to his radical colleague. "I salute you for having at last attained that burning ambition which you carry in your soul of becoming for one moment of your life the master of this House. You bring it to you, Sir, on its knee, and again I congratulate you."[15]

Marcantonio accepted the Georgian's congratulations "with a great deal of apprehension," operating under the general thesis that one should "beware of poll taxers bearing gifts." Moreover, it was not he who was deserving of congratulations, Marcantonio said, but the 218 members of the House who had signed the discharge petition.[16] Turning to a more serious vein, he deftly pinned down the basic issues involved in the legislative conflict before the Congress: (1) whether to restrict or extend democracy; and (2) whether to win or lose the war. On the first issue, Marcantonio insisted that the poll tax "restricts and destroys democracy in those States" where it was operative. Its abolition would thus extend "democracy to the disenfranchised Negroes and whites" and serve to restore democracy throughout the South. On the second, he explained, "The continuance of the poll tax is discrimination and makes for disunity [while] abolition of the poll tax abolishes this form of discrimination and makes for unity that is vital to victory."[17]

As more than one congressman pointed out, the angry debate on the floor of the House was a sham. Everyone knew that the supporters of the Geyer Bill had enough strength to override the southern objections to the measure, and in October 1942 the anti-poll-tax bill was approved by the House. But with Congress soon to adjourn, with elections only one month away, and with the threat of a protracted filibuster in the Senate that would impede the passage of other vital war legislation, the anti-poll-tax measure died quietly despite the action of the House.

As supporters of the measure analyzed their stunning victory and the defeat that rapidly followed, it became apparent that the fight had been started too late in the legislative session. Marcantonio announced that the first order of business for the new House convening in January 1943 would be the fight against the poll tax, and he smilingly expressed confidence that, if necessary, he would again force it from committee to the floor of the House through the device of the discharge petition.[18]

While taxes, labor, and the rights of the foreign-born and the Negro were important issues to Marcantonio in the first months of the first wartime Congress, his spleen filled to overflowing when House Resolution 420, continuing the Committee on Un-American Activities, was introduced. Martin Dies, the red-hunting Texan who chaired the committee, was the very personification of the fascistic enemy to Marcantonio, and he could hardly have been more vituperative had Hitler himself been the chosen representative from Orange County in the Lone Star State.

As with other issues upon which Marcantonio spoke in the House, his fight against Dies and Dies' committee was a continuation of a long-standing battle, but the war made the battle more important than ever. To Marcantonio and others it was the height of paradox for the Congress to lead a fight against fascism and yet to support a congressional committee that was itself less than democratic in method and intent. His basic charge against the Committee on Un-American Activities, amplified on numerous occasions in and out of Congress, centered on the fact that it had "failed to investigate the real enemy and in so failing it has tended to cause disunity, division, and disruption among those who are today joined in a collective effort to defeat fascism all over the world."[19]

In searching for support during the battle against continuing the Dies Committee, Marcantonio had earlier written to Roosevelt, on the theory that a word from the president, leader of the majority party in the House, would be helpful in the fight. The president had a better estimate of his power than did the congressman and refused to be drawn into the argument although his sentiments were clearly on Marcantonio's side. A word from him against the committee, Roosevelt wrote, "would probably cause many Congressmen to vote for the continuation of the Committee and I would be charged with executive interference!"[20]

Roosevelt was undoubtedly right in his estimate of the legislative situation; and, in truth, Marcantonio and the other congressmen who fought the resolution continuing the Committee on Un-American Activities needed no help in demolishing the committee to their own satisfaction. During the long and frequently acrimonious debate in the House Marcantonio had a verbal field day. A committee designated by the Congress to ferret out un-American activities was supported, he noted, by such fascistic groups as the Ku Klux Klan and the American Silver Shirts; Herr Doctor Goebbels, Hitler's propaganda chief, made frequent use of the committee's statements and reports in bolstering the German war effort.

Marcantonio took particular delight in dissecting in minute detail, in a speech that was long even by *Congressional Record* standards, a report of the committee upon which Dies had based his contention that he and the committee had had information that could have prevented the tragedy at Pearl Harbor.

This report, covering Japanese subversive activities in the United States, unfortunately was published after Pearl Harbor. In addition, Marcantonio showed it to be identical, almost word for word, including errors, with an article in a magazine that could be purchased on several Washington newsstands for ten cents. The crowning insult, he charged, was that the committee issued the report as its own work, brought together by its "incomparable staff" of researchers and experts.

But no matter how damaging his assertions may have been, Marcantonio was little more than an East Harlem Don Quixote ineffectually attempting to lance Dies. By 1942 the Committee on Un-American Activities had become a legislative sacred cow, unproductive but indestructible. Supported by some of the most influential mass organizations in the nation, such as the American Legion and the Veterans of Foreign Wars, the committee had little difficulty in winning House approval by a lopsided majority once the debate was closed. The Congress insisted on waging a two-pronged war: against fascism overseas and against a disparate assortment of home-grown reds, pinks, and leftists on the home front.[21]

Marcantonio, ever the urban maverick, insisted on going his own radical route. The nation had accepted as policy a view he held as principle: alliance with any group for a common end. Communist and capitalist were allied in a "holy" war against fascism; what was good for the nation could not be too bad to Marcantonio. In September 1942 the American Labor party's sole representative in Congress called for a "second front now" to a wildly cheering Communist party rally in New York.[22] Later the same month he became a contributing editor to the Communist-directed magazine, *New Masses*. Joseph North, the editor, even suggested a regular monthly column, a chore Marcantonio avoided by insisting that his congressional duties left little time for writing.[23]

Such action on Marcantonio's part did little to bridge the gulf that existed between him and the state leadership of his own party. The wartime national unity in no way extended to the right and left wings of the American Labor party. Attempts at reconciling the prewar split were angrily rebuffed by both sides, and by election time 1942 there was an open fight for power within the party between the two groups.

The right wing, led by Dubinsky, Antonini, and Rose, never forgave Marcantonio for his continuing ties to the Communists and his prewar opposition to intervention. By 1942 Marcantonio's defeat became an issue of paramount importance to the right-wing leadership. The question was not just one of personal enmity but really revolved around the issue of control of the party on a statewide basis. As long as Marcantonio, a leader of the left wing, remained the sole American Labor party emissary to Congress, his voice rather than the collective voice of the labor leaders would tend to speak for the party. Among the organization's rank and file, too, Marcantonio frequently had an influence that far surpassed that of Dubinsky or Rose, the titular heads of the party. Before the leaders of the garment unions could recast the ALP as a leftist but anti-Communist organization, Marcantonio had to be deposed. The primary election campaign of 1942, held in August, offered a logical opportunity.[24]

Two weeks before the election, the right wing received its severest setback when Fiorello La Guardia, ostensibly an opponent of the left wing, once again refused to remain in a pigeonhole and threw his unqualified endorsement to Marcantonio. "I have sentimental and personal affection for Marcantonio," he announced to the press. "I am going to support him in his candidacy for re-election." Concerning any other issue in the election, the mayor continued, "everyone knows I am lined up with the right-wing of the American Labor party."[25] The endorsement defies analysis; La Guardia thus stood with both feet to the right but with an arm around the leader of the left, a precarious position even for La Guardia. Only the personal relationship between the two men can possibly explain it.

Antonini immediately attacked the mayor, referring to the endorsement in Fiorello's own pet phrase as a "beaut of a mistake." La Guardia had told the right-wing leadership, Antonini alibied in a counter statement the same day, "that Marcantonio is a spoiled boy. But our stand is, and always has been, that Marcantonio is the world's biggest faker. He has been the man on the flying trapeze, like the Mayor himself. Only the Mayor swings with ease and pleases the people.

Marcantonio does it in a clumsy way and the people don't like it."[26]

The people were yet to have their say. Meanwhile it was all in the hands of the politicians. If by 1942 Marcantonio infuriated liberals like Antonini, he absolutely enraged Republicans like Thomas J. Curran, leader of the New York County organization. The Republican party, Curran insisted, had no "room for Communists," thus mincing no words in giving his opinion of Marcantonio. The party officially backed Charles Mucciolo in the primary election, and Curran expressed his confidence to Mucciolo that the voters would "rebuke your opportunistic and demagogic opponent who should be running on the Communist ticket alone."[27] So important was the defeat of Marcantonio to the ALP right-wing leadership that they threw their endorsement to Mucciolo as well, a bit of "trapeze swinging" that did not seem to disturb Antonini.[28]

The Democratic party in the Twentieth Congressional District finally passed over Lanzetta and nominated in his place Frank J. Ricca whose prominence in East Harlem approximated that of his Republican counterpart and whose major asset, again like the Republican, was his Italian last name. Ricca's candidacy might well have been sacrificial, indicating a deal of some sort between Tammany Hall and Marcantonio, a factor suggested at the time by reporters covering the campaign.[29]

Marcantonio himself seems to have gone into the primary election campaign full of confidence in his ability to beat the opposition. Unawed by the blasts from either Antonini or Curran, he took the fight to the enemy and, operating under the beneficient New York State electoral laws, filed for the nominations of all three parties as he had in 1940. The campaign was as bitter as in the previous primary but the result in 1942 differed in one important aspect: Marcantonio won all three nominations.

The American Labor party and Republican contests were almost comic opera in result. Mucciolo might have been better off had he entered a plea of *nolo contendere*. Marcantonio beat him as a Republican 2,784 to 291 and whipped him as decisively in the American Labor party contest, 2,049 to 234. In the race for the Democratic garland the result was even more startling; Marcantonio amassed 5,247 votes while Ricca, the official Democratic designee, received only 2,529.[30] *The New York Times* wryly commented that the election was singular proof, if Marcantonio wanted it, that the congressman was no Communist. Communism, the editorialist wrote, "insists on the one-party system, but Mr. Marcantonio can run on three party tickets, and very likely a lot more if there were any."[31] The victory was stunning and it appeared to the politically astute as if the radical congressman from East Harlem was in process of constructing an "all-party machine" that would make a reality of La Guardia's dictum, "I could run on a Chinese laundry ticket and get elected."

The only ray of sunshine left to the labor leadership of the American Labor party was the victory it had achieved in the contest for control of the party in the state despite a seriously depleted majority. But the failure to unseat Marcantonio was a major failing, especially since the right wing had brought every available big name into the campaign against Marcantonio in the Twentieth Congressional District, from Eleanor Roosevelt to the philosopher John Dewey.[32]

A study of the vote in the 1942 primary elections leads to several interesting speculations. Marcantonio's victory on the American Labor party line was predictable; with the New York County machine completely behind him even Mucciolo's 234 votes can be considered somewhat surprising. The congressman's easy victory on the Republican line is equally explicable if perhaps more shocking. East Harlem's Republicans were a breed apart from the remainder of their party and had a long record of sending liberal or progressive Republicans to Congress. Equally important was the fact that Marcantonio's personal machine had Republican antecedents in the Fiorello H. La Guardia Political Association. Marcantonio undoubtedly had better contacts among the Republican voters in the neighborhood than did, say, Thomas J. Curran. And, of course, La Guardia's endorsement in no way hurt Marcantonio's campaign.

None of the foregoing, however, explains Marcantonio's vital victory over Ricca in the fight for the Democratic nomination. While there is no available documentary evidence, the vote itself points to the conclusion that a political deal had been effectuated earlier that year. It is inconceivable that Tammany could not have turned out the vote against Marcantonio had it been seriously trying. The question remains: Why was the deal made?

Many of Marcantonio's critics insist that his ability to win the Democratic nomination in 1942 hinged on the patronage power he enjoyed as a congressman and as La Guardia's "fairhaired boy." Warren Moscow, a seasoned observer of local and state politics for *The New York Times,* wrote of Marcantonio, "He built up a patronage machine unequaled in the city, and working for him were many who were actually district leaders and district captains in both major parties."[33]

The problem with this charge of patronage power is that there is little evidence to support it. Moscow insists that "during the La Guardia administration [Marcantonio] was given privileges by the Mayor that The Little Flower would never have dreamed of permitting elsewhere." But the critical reader is entitled to ask "What privileges?" and to note that Moscow never enumerates. There is evidence that La Guardia did not hesitate to uphold his own Emergency Relief Bureau when it ruled against Marcantonio's constituents and that "The Little Flower" had no compunctions against throwing his protégé into the police "cooler" when necessary; odd privileges for a "fair-haired boy."

Yet it would be naive to presume that patronage played no role in explaining Marcantonio's political power. At one point, he indignantly telegraphed La Guardia from Washington, complaining that "one of my boys" was being discharged from a position as corporation inspector, one of the city's patronage plums, and asking La Guardia to put a stop to such "chicanery."[34] In 1940 the Roosevelt administration gave Marcantonio patronage in the form of several census enumerator positions; these were promptly awarded to needy La Guardia faithful through Stanley Howe, the mayor's secretary.[35] At almost the same time, however, Marcantonio complained that in cases he was fighting before the city's Welfare Bureau, "All I get from your Commissioner Mahatma Gandhi Hodson is passive resistance."[36] There is tantalizing, if less explicit evidence, in some letters in the Marcantonio Papers. For example, Harlem Democratic leader J. Raymond Jones wrote, "No one has ever given such prompt and courteous treatment to a request for a favor." Since major political leaders do not normally waste letters on trivia, it can be assumed that the matter under discussion was of some import.[37]

So far no picture emerges from the record of Vito Marcantonio wielding enormous patronage powers. There is the negative argument, of course, that patronage deals would not show up in the written record of a congressman's career. While this is undoubtedly true, it would be unfair to jump from that negative knowledge to the presumption that, therefore, such deals were made. It is probably closer to the truth to presume instead that Marcantonio had control of the normal patronage accruing to any member of Congress, limited by his adherence to a minor, left-wing party and augmented to some degree by his relationship to La Guardia.

A second factor raised by Marcantonio's critics to explain what was obviously a Tammany/Marcantonio deal in 1942 is much more solidly based than any argument founded on patronage power. It involves Marcantonio's power as leader of the New York County ALP to bestow his party's nomination on either a Democrat, a Republican, or an American Laborite. As has been pointed out in the previous chapter, in the numerous Manhattan congressional districts where the third party vote of the American Labor party was pivotal, the congressman from East Harlem could virtually elect the candidate of his choice. Since ALP votes almost always came from among otherwise Democratic voters, Marcantonio's influence in the county's Democratic machine was great. As but one example during this general period, it was American Labor party support of Democrat Adam Clayton Powell in the 1944 election campaign that was instrumental in the Harlem minister's first election to Congress. A close associate of Powell's wrote to extend thanks, adding, "Adam will be happy to serve with [Marcantonio] in the next Congress. And boy, what a team!"[38]

At least once in the 1940 campaign Marcantonio had entered an ALP candidate, thus insuring the election of a Republican candidate. In 1942, the same year Marcantonio won the Democratic nomination in his district, the ALP backed several important Tammany candidates and helped give them their margin of victory. He justified his action on the grounds that the Democratic candidates were more liberal than their Republican opponents, never having been antilabor or anticivil rights.[39]

That an astute politician like Marcantonio would not have used this peculiar power to insure as much as possible his own re-election would be almost unthinkable; nothing could possibly be less effective than a radical congressman without portfolio. If one couples knowledge of this power with the known facts that Tammany Hall had never exhibited an aversion to political deals and that Frank Ricca was not the strongest Democratic candidate who could have been run against Marcantonio in 1942, one has circumstantial evidence for presuming that a deal was made.

There are two other factors that must be considered in any attempt to account for Marcantonio's stunning victory in 1942. First is the simple proposition that Marcantonio worked "harder for his constituents than perhaps any other legislator in either house."[40] Second is the fact that a large number of the voters in East Harlem agreed with his legislative record on many issues. His consistent stand in support of labor, in defense of the foreign-born, in support of the war program, in defense of Puerto Rico and Puerto Ricans in East Harlem, all these and more struck responsive chords in the Twentieth Congressional District. Conversely, the charge hurled about by both his American Labor party and Republican opposition, that he was a Communist or an ally of the Communists, "hurt him little in an area where capitalism showed so few of its own virtues."[41]

The reasons behind his victory in the primary elections of 1942 were less important than the result to Marcantonio. He returned to Washington after the campaign without any worries about the coming November election. He had won all three primaries and his name would be the only one to appear on the ballot for the congressional seat from East Harlem. He could devote his full energy to the pressing problems facing the Congress.

VII

The Leftish Phenomenon

Vito Marcantonio's fourth term as a member of the House of Representatives spanned the mid-years of the war against fascism. It was the war itself that consumed the largest part of the energies of the American people. These years witnessed the invasions of North Africa, Italy, and Normandy; the turning of the Nazi tide at Stalingrad; and the bloody battles for rocky islands in the Pacific. But while the military conflict indisputably held the center stage, there was still much political activity going on in the wings of the national theater. The unity created by the war by no means covered the multiple domestic conflicts that plagued the nation. Roosevelt's Democratic party maintained its control in the Seventy-eighth Congress with 222 seats; but 208 Republicans, a larger number than at any time since the Depression began, were there to challenge the majority. Marcantonio again served as the solitary congressional representative of the American Labor party.[1]

It was around Marcantonio himself that the first major conflict of the new Congress raged. True to his promise the radical congressman's first act after the House convened was to reintroduce the bill to abolish the poll tax. Southern Democrats in the House immediately voiced the hope that the bill would be allowed to die quietly; any action on the bill, they warned, might turn the slim Democratic majority into a minority. Ignoring the threat, Marcantonio expressed confidence in his ability to guide the measure through the House, if necessary through the use of the discharge petition, the same parliamentary device used the previous year.[2]

Marcantonio thus laid down the gauntlet before his southern and conservative enemies and the stage was set for a repeat of 1942. What followed was completely unexpected and turned the congressman into a national *cause célèbre*. On January 15, 1943, the Democratic leadership of the House of Representatives designated the radical from East Harlem for membership on the House Judiciary Committee, one of the most powerful of the standing committees of the Congress.[3]

The southern wing of the Democratic party literally rose in revolt, and House Speaker Sam Rayburn's office became a seething mass of outraged Democratic delegations from Dixie. "Designation of Representative Vito Marcantonio . . . for membership on the House Committee on the Judiciary," wrote *The New York Times* on its front page, "has stirred up a storm which threatens . . . to develop into a major Democratic revolt."

Representative Sumner of Texas, Chairman of the Judiciary Committee, Sam Hobbs (Dem.) of Alabama, and Cox of Georgia "promised to exert every effort to defeat" their own party on the question of Marcantonio's appointment. Congressman Charles McKenzie (Dem., Louisiana), noting that it was Marcantonio who had sponsored anti-poll-tax and anti-lynching legislation in the previous session, insisted that the appointment of the radical congressman to the Judiciary Committee was "just another New Deal effort to sabotage the white people of the South. . . ."

Marcantonio himself stayed in the background during the bitter intra-party fight that rapidly developed over this issue. His own opinion concerning the surprising appointment was almost majestic in its simplicity. "On the basis of my service," he explained to reporters who questioned him, "I think that I am entitled to an assignment on a decent Committee."[4]

The hundreds of letters that poured into Marcantonio's Washington and New York offices were mostly laudatory, and many credited his committee nomination to his statesmanlike action in favor of civil rights. There were some correspondents who opposed his appointment, and most of these accused Marcantonio of favoring civil rights legislation primarily as a way of winning the Negro vote.[5] But there were few Negroes in East Harlem, probably fewer than three per cent of the total electorate, and Marcantonio stood to lose as many votes among the white majority in his district as he stood to gain among any racial minority by his espousal of civil rights legislation.[6]

Whatever the effect among the voters in East Harlem, Marcantonio's position on civil rights obviously hurt the possibility of his nomination to the Judiciary Committee being approved. Yet, with real power in his grasp for the first time since his election to Congress in 1934, Marcantonio refused to moderate his view and made no effort to placate the southern Democrats.

In retrospect, the admittedly unusual assignment of a minor-party congressman to a major House committee was neither a reward to Marcantonio for long, honorable, and statesman-like service in the House nor a part of a New Deal plot against the white South. More likely, it was tacit recognition by the administration of the growing power of Marcantonio's American Labor party in New York City. ALP support of Democrats in the city during the preceding November elections had provided victory for more than one member of Roosevelt's party, thus helping the Democrats to retain control of the House by a narrow margin.

Paradoxically, however, it was that same narrow margin of congressional control that undoubtedly motivated the Democratic Caucus, which met on January 19, 1943, in a session marked by shouted speeches, implied threats, and a well-organized revolt against party leadership, to reject Marcantonio's assignment to the Judiciary Committee. Had the southerners bolted the party over this issue, as they threatened to do, they could have thrown control of the House to the Republicans.[7]

The intensity of the southern revolt apparently caused some concern among administration leaders and made it unlikely, in Marcantonio's view, that Roosevelt would move to force

Marcantonio defending Mervyn Rathbone (left),
president of the CIO American Communication
Association, before the Dies Committee [Acme]

With Joseph Curran (left), national vice president of
the CIO, and Mayor La Guardia at a labor rally [UPI]

With Puerto Rican picket line [Wide World]

Congratulating Leo Isaacson, ALP candidate, on his decisive victory over three opponents [Wide World]

At the Progressive party's first convention [Wide World]

With Representatives Adam C. Powell (center) and Franklin D. Roosevelt, Jr. (right), supporters of the FEPC Bill [Wide World]

With 1948 presidential candidate Henry Wallace
on election eve at "Lucky Corner" [Acme]

With Henry Wallace and Paul Robeson before
ALP rally in 1949 to "Make Marc Mayor" [Acme]

civil rights legislation through the Congress.[8] His opinion was supported by the Washington correspondent, I. F. Stone, who wrote, "The White House has passed the word along to soft-pedal the fight against the poll tax." The Fair Employment Practices Committee (FEPC), established by Roosevelt's Executive Order in 1942, and the general "fight against racial discrimination are being elbowed to one side" in order to hold southern support for other aspects of the president's wartime program.[9]

Whatever path the leadership of the Democratic party took, Marcantonio, ever his own man, followed a steady route. In addition to the anti-poll-tax measure he had already placed on the legislative assembly line, the congressman introduced early in February a bill designed to give broader powers to the president's Fair Employment Practices Committee. Attempting to establish the "repudiation and prohibition of all forms of employment discrimination by any agency of the federal government" as firm public policy, Marcantonio's proposal would have given the FEPC the power to assess fines, to issue cease-and-desist orders, and to compel, after proper hearings, the hiring of individuals found to have been discriminated against.[10]

The mere introduction of proposed legislation, important in itself, was a comparatively passive action. Marcantonio soon moved into high gear and again attempted to force the anti-poll-tax bill from the Judiciary Committee through the discharge petition process. He was determined that the will of the majority would not be thwarted again by lack of time. His commitment to the task was heightened by his personal feelings concerning the manner in which he had been denied a seat on that committee.

Late in February, in a nationally broadcasted radio speech, he urged "the American people who hear me tonight to let their Congressmen know that they wish them to sign this petition. It is up to you who hear me to give your support to this effort to bring democracy to our whole people."[11] The support of the public was an important adjunct to Marcantonio's own tireless efforts on behalf of the bill to outlaw the poll tax.

Marcantonio cornered his colleagues one after another, and finally on May 6, 1943, he jubilantly delivered to the speaker's desk a petition bearing the necessary 218 names.[12] Having completed the spadework, the radical from East Harlem sat back and let others handle the debate which took place on May 24 and May 25. The vocal southern opposition pulled out all stops in a frantic effort to either amend the bill into worthlessness or have it recommited for further study. The sanctity of states' rights and of the Constitution, the death of the Democratic party, and the horrors of communism were all trundled out in an effort to convince the House that the poll tax was as necessary as the air itself in those eight southern states where the tax was still a prerequisite for voting.[13]

The debate was momentarily interrupted on the final day when a young, uniformed sailor, infuriated at the proceedings on the floor, leaped from his seat and shouted down from the visitors' gallery, "I came here to see how a democracy works and find them fighting the Civil War all over again." Collared almost immediately by the efficient Capitol police, the young gentleman was not a spectator as the North won again by a vote of 265 to 110.[14] "A great victory for democracy," commented The Nation, "the first to be registered in Congress in a long while."[15]

The victory was incomplete since the bill still had to pass the more powerful guardians of southern civilization in the Senate who were prepared to filibuster the measure to death if necessary. Senator James Eastland (Dem., Mississippi) declared that if a filibuster failed, he personally had approximately one thousand amendments to offer on the bill, each of them highly debatable.[16]

Of course, other measures drew Marcantonio's attention besides civil rights bills. As the spokesman for an urban, working-class community, Marcantonio consistently favored and worked to strengthen the price-control and rationing laws introduced by the administration to prevent runaway inflation during the war years. Early in 1943 he joined a group of representatives in forming the very unofficial Congressional Committee for the Protection of the Consumer. This rump group kept a watchful eye on congressional legislation affecting price control, rent control, and rationing; and when necessary, it exerted congressional influence to assure that government administrators worked in the best interests of the consumer.[17]

Of at least as much importance to Marcantonio as any of the civil rights bills was the battle he waged against the Smith-Connally Strike and Labor Control Bill during 1943. Agitation in and out of Congress for legislative action prohibiting strikes or at least modifying labor's right to strike during the war became particularly active when some 400,000 coal miners led by John L. Lewis struck in the spring of that year. Marcantonio's record on the issue of the coal strike itself was clear and outspoken. He could not reconcile a strike of such magnitude, hitting at the very heart of the nation's effort at war production, with the necessity to win the war; and victory over the Axis powers came first. He wrote the state leadership of the American Labor party, speaking both for himself and for the New York County organization, "We strongly urge that the State Executive Committee take a position squarely against Mr. Lewis and his . . . tragic disruption of the war effort.[18] Nevertheless, Marcantonio was not prepared to go as far as some of his more conservative colleagues in reacting to the coal strike. Understanding the necessity of limiting labor's right to strike in order to bring the war to a successful conclusion, he was by no means willing to wipe out the gains labor had made during the Depression era.

To Marcantonio, the Smith-Connally Bill, the congressional answer to Lewis' strike against the coal industry, was clearly motivated not by any desire to help the national war effort but by an antilabor attitude that had its roots far back in the American past. Besides giving the president authority to seize strike-bound plants and to regulate strikes by means of directed elections and cooling-off periods, it also amended the election laws to prohibit direct contributions by labor unions to political campaigns. This last provision, in particular, not only seemed far removed from "war" legislation but struck at one of the few important sources of financial aid Marcantonio himself found necessary in election campaigns.[19]

The House and Senate both passed the bill with heavy majorities and with the congressman from East Harlem among the most vocal of the opposition. When President Roosevelt vetoed the bill, for one reason because he felt it actually gave legislative sanction to strikes during wartime, Congress slashed back by overriding the veto with greater support "than there had been for the bill initially." Marcantonio sided with the administration against the majority.[20]

The Smith-Connally Act became law in the summer of 1943. Exhibiting the irony that frequently makes the study of American politics delightful, one immediate and unpredictable effect of the bill was the establishment by the CIO of its famous Political Action Committee under the direction of Sydney Hillman. The committee was a fire much worse than the frying pan to those antilabor congressmen who had voted for the Smith-Connally Act.[21]

From late 1943 into the spring of 1944, Marcantonio concerned himself with another major issue: the congressional struggle over the enactment of a bill that would have provided a federal rather than a state ballot for absentee voting by members of the armed forces. One section of the bill, of particular interest to Marcantonio, waived the requirement for a poll-tax payment as a prerequisite to voting, thus attempting to accomplish in a limited way what the anti-poll-tax measure pending in the Senate set out to make national policy. The bill finally passed by Congress was a victory for Marcantonio's opponents. An emasculated federal ballot was allowed, but only in certain limited cases and even then only with the permission of the state involved. The temper of the Seventy-eighth Congress was never more markedly conservative. The war was of an obviously democratic nature, Marcantonio pointed out in his speech on the soldier vote bill,[22] yet the Congress was unwilling, for a variety of political reasons, to extend the franchise in the United States itself.[23]

Senatorial inaction on the House version of the anti-poll-tax bill supports Marcantonio's contention. Favorably reported by the Senate Judiciary Committee in November 1943, the measure was studiously avoided by the Senate leadership in what Marcantonio referred to as the "silent filibuster," lending credence to rumors that the administration was trying to soft-pedal such civil rights legislation. The threat of a filibuster by the powerful southern bloc in the upper house, at a time when so much important legislation connected with the conduct of the war was before the Congress, undoubtedly led to hesitation on the part of the administration. When a senatorial petition to invoke the cloture rule, limiting debate over the poll-tax measure, failed to secure the required number of signatures, the bill itself was quietly buried for the second time in two years.[24]

Marcantonio's only complete success in the field of civil rights legislation dealt with the appropriation in 1944 for the president's Fair Employment Practices Committee, which faced continuous sniping by southern members of the House. When some of the southerners accused the FEPC of trying to cause a revolution in the South, Marcantonio hurled the charge back in their teeth. "The record," he said, "will show that insurrectionary language was used by the opponents of FEPC. One member threatened that Negroes would walk the streets jobless if FEPC were continued. Another opponent of FEPC had the temerity to stand in the well of this House and say that if the ballots failed they would resort to bullets. Just what is revolutionary? FEPC or its enemies?" As far as he was concerned the president's committee was a "continuation of the Emancipation Proclamation, . . . democracy in action, the democracy for which men are fighting and dying everywhere in this world."[25]

Presuming that a coalition of northern Republicans and southern Democrats would combine to defeat any appropriation for the committee in 1944, Marcantonio resorted to a parliamentary tactic to include the FEPC among eighteen other war agencies in a supply appropriations bill. With the help of the House leadership, the bill was taken to the floor under a unanimous agreement by which the measure could not be divided, thus preventing the FEPC appropriation from being thrown out on a point of order or some other device. "For once," the liberal periodical *The Nation* exulted, "the agile Southern parliamentarians were beaten at their own game."[26] The total appropriation for the FEPC was only one-half million dollars, hardly enough for the committee to do a real enforcement job; yet "meager though the amount may be it must be considered a major political victory for the advocates of racial justice."[27]

While struggling with his congressional colleagues on a variety of broad national questions, Marcantonio did not neglect those issues of more immediate concern to the voters in his own East Harlem. He continued to champion the question of some form of independence for Puerto Rico and at the same time urged the House to do something, almost anything, to alleviate conditions in Puerto Rico which had been worsened by the war. "Puerto Rico's plight," Marcantonio reminded the Congress, "is not the fault of the Puerto Rican people. We are responsible for it, and we must accept our responsibility as a true democratic people."[28] He pointed out that ships normally carrying foodstuffs to the island were now engaged in carrying war materiel to the armed forces in Europe and in the Pacific, thus leaving many Puerto Ricans in a state close to starvation. His lengthy analysis of the island's problems was undoubtedly correct, but it failed to move his congressional colleagues. As one magazine writer noted at the time, "His fight to abolish poll taxes, to strengthen the Fair Employment Practices Committee, . . . has made him so many enemies that almost any legislation he proposes starts with two strikes on it, however necessary to the general welfare it may be."[29] Fortunately for Marcantonio's political career, most Puerto Ricans in East Harlem failed to understand that their greatest congressional champion was also one of their more serious liabilities.

Speaking for the Italian majority in East Harlem, and for himself, Marcantonio slashed out at those nativists "who malign the loyalty and dispute the patriotism of Americans of Italian descent, by discriminating against them in industry, by denying them equal opportunity with other loyal Americans, and by regarding them with suspicion because of the sound of their names."[30] With other Italo-Americans he hailed the fall of the Mussolini government in July 1943; and like his friend and mentor La Guardia, he became increasingly bitter as the Allies failed to keep their promises to the Italians after the signing of the armistice.[31] In February 1944, Marcantonio noted that it was almost impossible for some of his constituents to get mail to or from Italy.

In June he pleaded for a greater amount of relief to the wartorn nation; and in September, in a long speech to the House, he denounced the treatment of the Italians by the American military government. "Hunger," he explained, "has already reached the stage of famine in Italy. Children are dying. . . . 4,000 girls of adolescent age have been treated for venereal disease." The failure of the military government set up by the United States "will go down in history as a gross example of arrogant neglect." He proposed an alternative policy: that Italy be recognized immediately as an ally, be extended massive aid, and be allowed to arm so as to help the Allied powers in the fight against the "common enemy." There is no reason to doubt the depth of Marcantonio's feelings on this issue. Nor can the accuracy of his factual statements, his descriptions of Italy under Allied occupation, be questioned.[32] But the practicality of his proposals was extremely debatable. Nevertheless, the proposals certainly did nothing to lower his standing in the eyes of the Italo-Americans in East Harlem.[33]

On June 6, 1944, while Allied forces smashed across the English Channel and landed on the beaches of Normandy, Marcantonio wrote to the president urging him to direct the establishment in the United States of a rescue camp for the "tens of thousands of Jewish war refugees from every section of Europe who have hitherto been ruthlessly uprooted" from their homes. "In this hour of the liberation of the continent," he said, "it is my fervent prayer that our first act of mercy in liberated Europe may be extended to the Jewish people: first victims of Hitlerite slavery."[34]

By the time the beachhead at Normandy was secure, Marcantonio was already deep into the election campaign of 1944, a campaign that differed markedly from his five previous efforts. During the two years he had been fighting in Washington to make the nation more democratic in the midst of a war for democracy, the basic conditions upon which he had built his political power had undergone rapid and confusing change.

The year Franklin Delano Roosevelt ran for his fourth consecutive term as president, Vito Marcantonio tried for a fourth consecutive congressional victory. Three factors combined to make his campaign in 1944 the most difficult of his political career up to that point: first, the American Labor party split early in the year; second, Marcantonio faced strong opposition in the primary elections, the kind of opposition he had been spared in 1942 when he had won the nomination of all three parties; third, and undoubtedly the most significant factor, Marcantonio's geographic stronghold, East Harlem, no longer coincided with his congressional district.

In a general reapportionment and redrawing of district lines, the Twentieth Congressional District disappeared and a new political entity, the Eighteenth Congressional District, was created by the Republican-controlled state legislature. The Eighteenth Congressional District was vastly larger than the Twentieth. Instead of stopping at 99th Street, it extended down the east side of Manhattan as far south as 59th Street, just short of the luxury district known as Sutton Place. It was bounded on the east by the river. Its western boundary was a confused zigzag line and its northern limits were substantially those of the old Twentieth Congressional District.

But as important as the change in physical area of the congressional district was the shift in social, cultural, ethnic, and economic make-up. Going south across 96th Street was almost like stepping across the border between two disparate nations. The disintegrating slum of East Harlem gave way to a less economically depressed area which in pockets here and there reached a level of luxurious living. While the area to the south also was composed primarily of four-, five-, and even six-flight walk-up tenements, most of them were in a better state of repair than the buildings in East Harlem; and the area gave the impression, on the surface at least, not of a slum but of a somewhat seedy, if perfectly respectable, section of the metropolis. Along the three wide east-west thoroughfares that cut through the area—86th Street, 79th Street and 72nd Street—were row after row of comparatively modern structures, serviced by elevators, doormen, and separate tradesmen's entrances. These were the homes of, if not the rich, at least the obviously well-to-do. Spotted here and there throughout the neighborhood, similar multistoried apartment buildings towered over the ancient tenements, giving the neighborhood an economic mixture totally unlike East Harlem.

Historically known as Yorkville, the area south of 96th Street was home to a confusing welter of ethnic groups. To the average New Yorker, Yorkville was synonymous with "Germantown" or, more bitterly, "Nazitown," for the area was home base to the German American Bund before the war. The blocks immediately north and south of 86th Street were a colorful mixture of German bakeries, gift shops, *Bier-stuber*, book and music stores that catered to a German clientele, and German restaurants like the Cafe Geiger, the Brauhaus, Hans Jaeger's, and the Rheinland. In truth, however, German influence in Yorkville was more apparent than real, and the Germans failed both in number and in power to dominate the area the way the Italo-Americans dominated East Harlem.

Germans in the east 80's gave way to Czechs, Slovaks, and Magyars in the east 70's, each with their own restaurants and stores. Shops along First and Second Avenues catered to every national taste, from Hungarian paprika establishments to stores specializing in Greek olive oil. Along Third Avenue, under the rattling "El," bar followed bar with paralyzing regularity, rivaled for numerical superiority only by antique shops which catered to the wealthy community living between Third Avenue and Central Park. Throughout the entire geographic area, but lacking any center of concentration, were heavy pockets of Irish who lived in comparative peace with smaller numbers of Italians, Jews, Poles, a scattering of Negroes, and at least one of every other race or nationality. Any ethnic breakdown of the new Eighteenth Congressional District in 1944 would probably have indicated that the three major nationalities represented were the Italians, the Germans, and the Irish.[35]

The one indisputable fact about the new congressional district in which Marcantonio was forced to operate in 1944 was the enormous economic and social contrasts to be found within its confines, from the miserable hovels of the Puerto Rican *barrio* to the luxurious, upper-class American apartment buildings fronting Carl Shurz Park and the East River.

Along with the gerrymandered district, Marcantonio encountered a strong political opponent, Martin J. Kennedy, the very able politician who had formerly represented Yorkville before its amalgamation with East Harlem. Kennedy had a long public career: chairman of the New York City School Board from 1918 to 1924, state senator from 1924 to 1930, and since 1930 a member of the House of Representatives for six consecutive terms.[36]

But even before facing Kennedy in the primary or in the general election in November, Marcantonio had to face the battle in his own political establishment. It was clear by 1944 that the dichotomy between left- and right-wing factions in the American Labor party was too great to ignore and too wide to breach.

The lines of battle had been forming since 1938 when the Communist party in New York moved into the ALP in force. Issue after issue divided the leftist but anti-Communist labor leaders and intellectuals who had formed the ALP from those leaders like Marcantonio who worked closely with the Communists for common goals. The Communists within the ALP naturally threw their support behind Marcantonio; but, in reality, there were many non-Communists among the rank and file of the organization who also agreed with the party's best-known member. Only the fact that neither the left nor the right wing had a clear majority kept this two-headed political monster operating between 1938 and 1944. In that final year both sides built up strength for a show of force in April in a special election to select delegates to the party's state convention.

Marcantonio and the left wing gained important support from Sydney Hillman, head of the Amalgamated Clothing Workers Union and chairman of the CIO Political Action Committee. Both sides invoked the politically powerful name of Franklin Delano Roosevelt, and each insisted that a vote for the opposition would be politically embarrassing to the president. Both left- and right-wing factions pledged wholehearted support to the Democratic administration.

While Dr. George S. Counts, one of the leading spokesmen for the right wing, hurled the charge of Communist domination at the left wing, Marcantonio dismissed it as nothing more than liberal red-bating. "There is only one issue [in the campaign]," he asserted, "and that is whether the ALP is to continue to be the property of a small group of labor fakers or whether it is to belong to the common voters who enroll in the party. And no red herring can disguise that issue."[37]

The April election itself was a complete rout of the old-line labor leadership of the American Labor party, the same men who had breathed life into the organization in 1936. The left wing elected 600 of the 750 delegates to the state convention in an election in which 87,000 members of the party, out of a total of 180,000 enrolled, went to the polls. The election served as a fair judgment of the relative strength of the contending factions. "Neither major party," *The New York Times* reported, "has ever approached such a percentage" of voters in a primary election.[38] Marcantonio was obviously a better judge of the temper of his own party than was George Counts.

The victorious left wing immediately held out an olive branch to the opposition, and just as rapidly the right wing refused it. Dubinsky, Rose, Antonini, Counts, and their numerous followers could not remain in an organization they considered merely an adjunct of the Communist party. They announced their withdrawal from the American Labor party as soon as the election returns were in and declared their intention to organize another group, progressive but anti-Communist. Within the year they organized a fourth important party in New York, the Liberal party.[39]

Firmly in control of his own party, not just in New York County but throughout the state, and with Sydney Hillman as state chairman, Marcantonio now turned to the primary election campaign in the new Eighteenth Congressional District. Despite his ties to and supposed hold on the New York County Democratic organization, Marcantonio was powerless to prevent Tammany Hall from nominating Martin Kennedy as the official Democratic candidate. The internal struggle among Tammany leaders was apparently fierce; and one long-time Marcantonio supporter, James Pemberton, held out to the bitter end, refusing to make Kennedy's nomination unanimous.[40]

Having previously won the Democratic nomination in a primary fight and with apparent disregard for the new boundaries of the congressional district, Marcantonio immediately announced his intention to buck the machine. "The voters of New York," announced Eugene Connolly, Marcantonio's spokesman, "want a pro-Roosevelt, win-the-war and all-People's representative. They'll vote for Marcantonio and not Kennedy."[41]

The leadership of the Republican party chose as its official designee Lt. Robert C. Palmer, who unfortunately remained an absentee candidate throughout the campaign since he was then on active duty with the Navy. His campaign was managed by John Shedd McCook, a former president of the New York Young Republican Club. Both Palmer and McCook came from the high-rent, luxury district on East 86th Street, part of the new area added to Marcantonio's old district.[42] Marcantonio filed against Palmer for the Republican nomination and became involved in a two-sided primary campaign.

Martin Kennedy also received the endorsement of the newly formed Liberal party (Dean Alfange, state vice-chairman, called on the voters to come out and vote—*for* anyone, but *against* Marcantonio).[43] But the obvious dissension within Tammany indicated that Kennedy's support from the party machine might not be as intensive as he had a right to expect. The local Democratic leaders, especially those in the northern end of the district, Marcantonio's old bailiwick, were not happy with Kennedy's candidacy. Either they did not throw their full support into his campaign or, as was charged at the time, they pushed Marcantonio rather than the organization's man.

McCook, campaigning for Palmer, pulled out all stops. His campaign broadsides referred to Palmer as being "opposed by Hillman, Browder, and the Communists' Congressman." Just a few days before the election he released to the press a letter from fifteen leaders of the American Legion who pleaded for Marcantonio's defeat, referring to him as a Communist. The letter asked "all patriotic men and women, irrespective of partisan politics," to vote *for* anyone, but *against* Marcantonio; it was probably one of the few times the American Legion and the Liberal party found themselves supporting identical policies. "We feel," the Legionnaires continued, "that the best interests of the United States . . . demand that Mr. Marcantonio be eliminated from representing American citizens in Congress."[44] The major New York City newspapers made their positions clear. The Hearst-owned *Daily Mirror*, in an election eve editorial, characterized Marcantonio as "utterly no good, a liability to the city of New York, a disgrace to the nation's Congress and an enemy of everything that American democracy should stand for."[45]

The newspaper, like the Legionnaires, studiously avoided any mention of Marcantonio's record, a deficiency that the congressman and his supporters corrected in their door-to-door and block-by-block election campaign. Moving into the area south of East Harlem for the first time, Marcantonio opened a full-time office over a Woolworth's store on First Avenue near 78th Street. From this new office and the old one on East 116th Street, more than 1,200 part-time voluntary campaign workers fanned out through the tenements, up and down the steep flights, getting the congressman's record to the voting public.[46]

While running against Kennedy and Palmer, Marcantonio also had to contend with Woodrow Wilson! Posters bearing the congressman's picture and the date of the primary election, August 1, were soon surrounded by other posters bearing the similar legend, "Wilson, August 1st." The latter were advertisements for a movie biography of the former president starring Alexander Knox, as Marcantionio supporters had to explain patiently to confused voters who asked, "Who in the hell is this guy Wilson running against Marcantonio?"[47]

By election eve Marcantonio felt confident of victory on at least the Democratic line. He had, he insisted, signed pledges of support from about 12,000 of the 36,000 enrolled Democrats in the Eighteenth Congressional District. He made no prediction about the outcome of the contest between himself and Palmer.[48]

Early in the morning of August 2 the vote was in and the left-wing radical from East Harlem had once again won the nomination of all three major political parties. Marcantonio beat Kennedy 10,311 to 7,761 for the Democratic nomination and he just managed to squeak past Palmer by less than 200 votes out of a total of more than 5,000 ballots cast by enrolled Republicans. The exultant winner of the political "triple crown" told a wildly exuberant crowd awaiting the results at his headquarters, "We've done it again. . . . political parties do not belong to the bosses but to the people."[49]

Life, referring to Marcantonio as a "leftish phenomenon," ascribed his victory to the machinations of Hillman's Political Action Committee. Further along the political spectrum, *The Nation* analyzed his stunning three-party victory and attributed it to his consistent support of the president and the administration's program.[50] *The New York Times*, eschewing cause, concentrated on effect. The result of Marcantonio's primary victories, the paper stated,

> poses a serious political problem. In November there will be no one to vote for in his district but Mr. Marcantonio. The voters who troubled to turn out for the primaries settled the results of the election for the voters of the whole district. Mr. Marcantonio and his friends knew how to get out that vote. Thus Mr. Marcantonio has succeeded in making a mockery of the political parties in his district.

The editors apparently felt that somehow, if the free, open primary election led to the selection of leftists like Marcantonio, there was something undemocratic about the process. "The episode," the editors concluded, "once more raises the question of the wisdom of allowing candidates to run in the primaries of more than one party," an idea that eventually was to bear fruit with disastrous results for Vito Marcantonio.[51]

Kennedy and McCook were more interested in cause than in effect. Both immediately screamed "fraud," charging Marcantonio with wholesale vote stealing, intimidation, and illegal use of funds. Two weeks after the election Police Commissioner Lewis J. Valentine reported that an investigation conducted by the police failed to find any substantiation for charges of irregularities in the Eighteenth Congressional District primary elections. District Attorney Frank Hogan came to the same conclusion two months later.[52]

McCook and the Republicans refused to give up and tried to run Palmer as an independent candidate under the banner of the Victory party. An ascertainable election irregularity now did turn up when the Election Board checked the necessary nominating petitions for Palmer and found only 1,461 valid signatures, less than half the number necessary to get a name on the ballot.[53]

Marcantonio was again spared the necessity of conducting an expensive November campaign. Running unopposed, he garnered more than 66,000 votes in the new congressional district he would represent for the first time in the Seventy-ninth Congress.

The war itself, during which Marcantonio had played perhaps his most constructive and most successful legislative role, was rapidly coming to a close. In the West the American, British, and Russian armies hammered at the gates of Hitler's Fortress Europa; in the East the Japanese junior partner in the Axis had lost control of the oceanic empire it had wrested from the Allies after December 7, 1941, and was soon to be the sacrificial victim heralding a new age of destructive power.

The Seventy-ninth Congress in which Vito Marcantonio took his place in January 1945 spanned the old war and the new peace. Old problems continued to gnaw at the congressman from East Harlem; but a new question, concerning the nation's place in the postwar world, began to take prominence in his thinking as it did in the thought processes of countless Americans. In a relatively short time Marcantonio's attitude toward American foreign policy became of infinitely greater significance to his career as a politician than his stand on the multitude of domestic issues that simultaneously faced the nation. More important, his position on foreign policy became the anvil upon which his enemies ultimately forged the weapon that completely destroyed the political edifice the left-wing radical had so successfully built since the early days of the great Depression.

VIII

Consistency in a
Changing World

The first half of that ten-year period Eric Goldman termed *The Crucial Decade*[1] witnessed the precipitous decline and fall of Vito Marcantonio as a congressman and as a political power in New York City. In many ways he was much more consistent than many of the members of the House of Representatives who managed to survive the rapid and unexpected changes in national policy that occurred during those years, and perhaps it was his very consistency in a changing world that led to his political demise. He continued his fight for civil rights for Negroes; he vehemently opposed antilabor legislation; he stood squarely behind the progressive social legislation that had come to characterize the New Deal; and he fought for the protection of the alien and the radical, thus duplicating the prewar and wartime stands that had convinced his constituents to return him to Congress four times in succession, five times in all.

Consistency on domestic issues was matched by consistency on questions relating to foreign policy. Since late 1941 he had believed in collaboration for peace between the three major world powers: Britain, the Soviet Union, and the United States. When the "cold war" began and the international temperature dropped lower and lower, finally disappearing at the bottom of the thermometer at the end of the decade in the Korean War, Marcantonio maintained his war-born belief in an internationalist policy of peace and friendship with the Soviet Union, even when it cost him an enormous proportion of the limited support he had once enjoyed. By 1950 a one-time ardent Marcantonio supporter, Robert S. Allen, referred to the congressman as "malevolent and despicable . . . a ruthless obstructionist, and it will be a happy day when he is eliminated from the House."[2]

At the first meeting of the Seventy-ninth Congress in January 1945, again with the Democrats in control and as the only representative of the American Labor party, Marcantonio dropped his anti-poll-tax bill into the legislative hopper.[3] As if he and his colleagues were following a well-rehearsed script for a morality play, the bill was immediately bottled up in the Judiciary Committee; Marcantonio went on his busy rounds accumulating signatures on a discharge petition; the 218 names were collected;[4] the bill was acrimoniously debated; and on June 12 it was passed by a vote of 251 to 105.[5] The senators knew their roles too, and when the Congress adjourned in 1946, the poll-tax bedrock of "Southern Civilization" remained undisturbed by any action on the part of the federal government.

In the continuing fight to preserve the president's Fair Employment Practices Committee, Marcantonio and others were only slightly more successful. The legislative battle for the FEPC took place just prior to the Japanese surrender in August 1945. The war was obviously drawing to a victorious close, and the necessity for a nondiscriminatory employment policy was no longer a vital factor to many congressmen. As far as Marcantonio was concerned, neither the Democratic administration guided by its still new leader Harry Truman nor the Republican opposition in Congress gave the FEPC the support it needed. Both major parties, Marcantonio charged, were guilty "of double-crossing and double-dealing from beginning to end."[6] After prodding from a liberal minority, the House finally passed a minimum appropriation of $250,000 for the FEPC. Every attempt by Marcantonio or others to enact a permanent government commission with enforcement powers was rebuffed by the powerful southern bloc and its allies.[7] By 1946, FEPC was nothing more than a set of initials, ready only for a place in the history books and possible resurrection at a more advantageous time.

Marcantonio moved in at least two other directions in his attempts to get the Congress to make democracy a reality for America's Negroes. In April 1945 he introduced a House resolution directing the secretary of Commerce to investigate the employment policies of major league baseball clubs to determine if they discriminated against Negroes. Since not a single Negro was then under contract to any of the sixteen clubs in question, it is safe to assume that Marcantonio was more interested in frightening organized baseball into action than he was in any inquiry. It would be misleading to say that Marcantonio thus started the chain of tangled events that led to the hiring of Jackie Robinson by the Brooklyn Dodgers; other men were thinking along similar lines at the same time. But it would be equally misleading to ignore the role the congressman played in breaking the color bar in the national sport.[8]

A year later Marcantonio threw his rapidly diminishing congressional power behind an amendment offered by Congressman Adam Clayton Powell to the District of Columbia Appropriations Bill for 1947. The amendment would have desegregated the nation's capital.[9] Is it asking too much, Marcantonio rhetorically queried the House, "that here in the District of Columbia we practice the fundamental precepts of democracy that we are asking all of the world to practice at this time." The southern opposition answered that the Powell Amendment would lead to race riots, an argument Marcantonio dismissed with contempt. It was one he had heard many times before when he had fought for his anti-poll-tax bill and when the Congress attempted to enact legislation that guaranteed employment without discrimination. "Now we hear the same cry . . . in respect to a simple request that this Congress rise up to the dignity of the nation—the dignity that the world expects us to rise up to, of practicing the fundamental precepts of Democracy for which men died both black and white." For Marcantonio the legislative conflict was almost a continuation of the war. "This is Washington," he patiently explained, "which many would make the Capital of the world. Are we going to hesitate to remove from the Capital of the United States the blot of discrimination and segregation?"[10]

The answer from the House was a resounding "yes" as it hesitated not at all in rejecting the Powell Amendment. A decade later the United States would be ready to democratize its capital, but in 1946 Vito Marcantonio was clearly a premature integrationist. The nation would soon be asked by the Republican party if it had "Had enough?" On the issue of Negro rights, temporarily at least, white America clearly had.

On the issue of labor legislation, the pendulum of public opinion moved inexorably in one direction while the congressman stood firmly rooted in his past opinions. Only once did Marcantonio deviate from his pro-labor position; this concerned the attempt to enact compulsory work-or-fight laws, measures designed to mobilize the nation's manpower in the period just prior to the surrender of Germany and Japan. An amendment to the proposed National Service Act, debated by the Congress early in 1945, provided that individuals assigned to employment under the law need not join any labor union or similar organization as a condition of employment. To Marcantonio this was antilabor legislation of the worst sort, tending to nullify the closed shop for which labor had fought so long. The amendment was a precursor of the "right to work" laws which would soon sweep through many of the states. Yet the end encompassed by the bill, the mobilization of labor in defense of the nation, was a goal Marcantonio ardently favored. In this conflict between his position on labor questions and his desire for victory over fascism, it was the latter goal that emerged victorious. After he voiced his objections to the amendment and put them in the *Congressional Record*, he prepared to vote for the National Service

Act. His quandary was resolved when the amendment itself was defeated, and any other qualms he might have had about the bill became needless as the legislation faded away with the closing of the war.[11]

No matter how necessary the National Service Act seemed, it carried the seeds of an antilabor attitude that blossomed into bitter fruit within months of the Japanese surrender. With the end of the war the administration, pressured by business and by a clearly conservative Congress, began loosening the price and rationing restrictions that had served to restrict inflation during the war. Almost immediately prices began moving up. As prices rose, organized labor, held in check during the war, became restive. First a trickle, then a river of work stoppages flowed through the nation; 1946 was a record year for workdays lost due to strikes.

Time and time again, from mid-1945 on, Marcantonio rose in the House in attempts to protect the gains organized labor had made in the past fifteen years. He argued that it was not labor causing industrial unrest but rather a malign, intransigent management. His comments in the paralyzing coal strike of April–May 1946 were typical. During the war Marcantonio had urged the suppression of the coal strike of 1943; now he stood squarely behind the strikers. While most of the press fulminated against the supposedly "dictatorial" John L. Lewis and public opinion turned against the miners and unionized labor in general, Marcantonio blasted the owners of the mines who were carrying out a "conspiracy against labor and against the interests of the American people." A misinformed people, Marcantonio insisted, were aiming at the wrong target. It was, he explained, the owners "who provoked the strike," the owners "who are obstinate in their refusal" to arbitrate, the owners who "are interested only in profits and not in the welfare of the Nation. Pressure them, not the coal miners . . . and the strike will be settled without delay."[12]

While the memory of the coal strike was still vivid, another labor specter materialized to haunt the nation as the major railroad unions threatened a walkout. In the face of crisis, the president and Congress were prepared to enact sweeping legislation, even calling for the drafting of railroad workers who refused to work. Again Marcantonio shouted into the wind. "Yes," he agreed, the country "faces a crisis." However, it was caused "not by labor but by selfish and unpatriotic railroad corporations. You would think that the operators did not exist—not a word of condemnation of them in the press, not a single proposal advanced to curb them."[13]

The threatened railroad tie-up was averted at the last minute, but the provoked Congress moved ahead with legislation designed to curb the power of unions. Marcantonio considered the resulting Case Bill, H.R. 4908, "the most vicious anti-labor bill we have ever had before the House or that has ever been introduced in this Congress." Among its provisions it limited the right to strike, especially in industries involving public health, safety, or security.[14]

To Vito Marcantonio, who grew up in the slums, who still lived there, and who by his own admission looked at life through working-class eyes, any limitation on the right to strike, any weakening of labor's most potent weapon, was an absolute horror, a throwback to the days of Hoover and before. "Men do not . . . strike for the fun of it," he explained to his colleagues in the House. A strike is a worker's last resort, "provoked by the scheming, uncompromising, unreasoning tactics of profit-bloated, tax-benefited corporations." It was the corporations that provoked the strikes and it was the same corporations that controlled the organs of propaganda, the press and the radio, that then started "beating the drums against American workers in order to intimidate Congress to pass anti-labor legislation . . . . under the guise of an emergency created not by labor but by these [same] corporations who now ask you to pass this Case Bill."[15]

Ironically, just as Martin Dies, from the vantage point of the political right, looked at labor unrest and saw a Communist plot, similarly, Vito Marcantonio, rooted in the political left, looked at the identical problem and saw only a conspiracy of capitalists. Rarely was he more alone in his thinking. Both houses of Congress passed the Case Bill with heavy majorities and only a strongly worded presidential veto save organized labor, temporarily at least, from being flattened by the swinging pendulum of public opinion.

Coupled with Marcantonio's fight for labor was his fight for the consumer, the two being identical in his mind. As industry after industry converted from the production of war materiel to the production of consumer goods, manufacturers called for the removal of price restrictions. The Seventy-ninth Congress reacted by passing new price-control legislation in the summer of 1946, legislation that opened the floodgates to increased prices in almost every important industry. It was a new kind of "legalized inflation" to the congressman from the Eighteenth Congressional District.[16]

Once again going against a clear trend, Marcantonio favored not the relaxation of price controls but a stronger bill giving the Office of Price Administration more stringent powers. Anything less would take from labor whatever wage gains it had been able to wrest from management. As prices inched higher (thirty-three per cent above 1941 prices by the end of the year), Marcantonio's vision of a conspiracy of capitalists against the nation's working masses grew stronger.[17]

In the late summer and early fall of 1946, the meat industry attempted to eliminate the last vestiges of price control on meat products by withholding livestock from the market, thus creating what amounted to a comic opera throughout the nation. For example, New York City officials authorized the sale of horse meat, and women's page editors reminded their readers to use more onion and less carrot in cooking the rare flesh in order to compensate for its sweeter taste.

Marcantonio reacted by blasting the meat industry and calling upon the government to seize control of the plants. One irate citizen contrasted Marcantonio's proposal with the congressman's opposition to similar governmental action when the miners or railroad workers went on strike. "What a bunch of *baloney*," he wrote. "You sure are a *ham*." Undaunted,

Marcantonio scribbled across the top of the unsigned letter, "probably a butcher." Perhaps this was an indication of how widespread the "conspiracy" had become in his mind.[18]

The "plot" against labor "naturally" extended to the most militant sections of the political left itself. As early as May 1945, Marcantonio had to resort to the use of a parliamentary device to force the tabling of a bill that would have given the Immigration Service the right to make arrests without first securing warrants in certain cases involving "subversive" aliens.[19] "Hey, Sam," he wrote Congressman Samuel Dickstein (Dem., New York) of the House Immigration Committee, "you made the pants too long on this one." Dickstein, never an advocate of repressive measures, shot back, "I had nothing to do with either the fitting or the measuring of the pants." No matter who had tailored it, the bill was stopped. Abner Green, executive secretary of the leftist-controlled American Committee for the Protection of the Foreign Born, who had first brought the bill to Marcantonio's attention, thanked the congressman for his assistance.[20]

With much less success Marcantonio frequently protested against the use of the contempt citation by the House Committee on Un-American Activities as a weapon against radicals and sometimes the not-so-radical leftists. In March 1946, joined by only three other congressmen, he voted against a contempt citation for the national leadership of the Joint Anti-Fascist Refugee Committee, an organization originally formed to help individuals fleeing from Franco's Spain.[21] Two months later he showed his own scorn for the Committee on Un-American Activities by delivering another lengthy, detailed attack against both its aims and its methods.[22] In June he bitterly protested a contempt citation issued to Corliss Lamont, the leftist millionaire who was a leading figure in the National Council of American-Soviet Friendship. Again, Marcantonio was one of a very small minority that, if anything, was dwindling.[23]

The nation was moving away from Marcantonio. His leftist viewpoint had never been widely popular; but during the war, at least, his path and that of the majority of the public, as measured by the actions of its representatives in Congress, had run roughly parallel routes. Now, with the ink barely dry on the documents of surrender, the two paths began to diverge once again, the angle becoming more and more obtuse with each passing month. Nowhere was this cleavage more noticeable than over issues relating to foreign affairs.

Marcantonio and his American Labor party had clearly enunciated their ideas on foreign policy as early as February 1945. The peace of the world, the ALP insisted, depended on the continued alliance, after the war, of the three great powers: Great Britain, the Soviet Union, and the United States. Anything tending to break up that "grand alliance" tended also to disturb the peace that was soon to come.[24]

Yet within months of the day Marcantonio inserted the ALP's position in the *Congressional Record,* something was disturbing the peace that had just been declared. Few Americans could put their fingers on just what it was. Fewer still had any interest in facing up to it, no matter what the "it" turned out to be, for the war was over and peace existed in the world for the first time since 1939. Then, in the spring of 1946 in a speech at Westminster College, Fulton, Missouri, with the president of the United States behind him on the platform, Winston Churchill spoke of "an iron curtain" descending across Europe, dividing East and West.[25] A year later, another elder statesman, Bernard Baruch, in a speech at Columbia, South Carolina, used the words "cold war" to describe the existing and deteriorating diplomatic relations between the Soviet Union and the United States.[26] Thus two of the most characteristic phrases of the postwar world were off-handedly thrown into the language; two catchwords suddenly appeared and that disturbing "something" suddenly sparkled with brilliant clarity.

In July 1946, when few men could have predicted exactly where the nation was headed in terms of foreign policy, Vito Marcantonio took the floor of the House of Representatives to speak in favor of a proposed three-billion-dollar loan to

Great Britain. The loan was opposed by the Communist party in the United States. "I support it," Marcantonio explained, "[because] we cannot support the policy of unity among the Big Three and at the same time refuse to implement that unity with economic aid." With quiet moderation he agreed that since the coming of the peace "the relationship among the Big Three has deteriorated," but to refuse to extend the loan to Britain would only aggravate, not ameliorate in any way, the deteriorating state of affairs. There was one factor in the congressional debate over the loan that disturbed him. "I cannot help but deplore," he said, "the appeals made for and against this resolution which are based on the contention that either defeat or passage of this loan will work to the advantage of the Soviet Union."[27]

Marcantonio made few other public announcements on foreign policy in the next two months. Then, in rather unexpected fashion, Secretary of Commerce Henry Wallace, in a speech at New York City's Madison Square Garden in September 1946, attacked the development of American foreign policy toward the Soviet Union. He indicated that he did not think the United States was making an honest effort to meet the Communist nation halfway and that if such overtures were made they would tend to insure the world peace. The speech was a forthright attack on the administration of Secretary of State James Byrnes made by a former secretary of Agriculture, a former vice-president, and a man who, one week later, could add former secretary of Commerce to his list of imposing titles. It was clear that Truman's firing of Henry Wallace also meant the total repudiation of the foreign policy views Wallace had expressed in the Madison Square Garden speech.

In New York one week later, Congressman Vito Marcantonio addressed a convention of the Transport Workers Union of America and informed the assembled trade unionists that the dismissal of Henry Agard Wallace from Truman's Cabinet "marks the beginning of the disintegration of the two American parties. I don't know which will go, he added "but the historic condition is present for the creation of a new party resolving the question of peace and progress on the side of the people." To the roaring approval of the trade unionists, Marcantonio hurled anathemas at the Republican and Democratic parties, condemning both for trying to destroy organized labor and the accomplishments of the New Deal, for trying to suppress civil liberties, and for attempting to promote an imperialist war against the Soviet Union.[28]

Whether or not Henry Wallace wanted him, the intense little man from East Harlem was on Wallace's side in the fight for peace through collaboration with the Soviet Union. As far as Marcantonio was concerned, collaboration was the only method through which peace was attainable in the postwar world.

Neither Wallace nor Marcantonio ever spelled out the exact kind of collaboration they envisioned. Both seemed to assume that since collaboration had worked during the war it could work in peacetime as well and that if it was not working the fault lay with the foreign policy of the United States. Neither questioned the assumption that the Soviet Union under Joseph Stalin wanted collaboration for peace with the capitalist nations of the world. This seemed to be a question for the future if it were a question at all.

If Wallace intended to base a fight to return to the political arena on a New Deal view of domestic problems and a collaborative view of Soviet-American foreign relations, Marcantonio would clearly be with him. First, however, Marcantonio had a private battle to fight: the congressional election of 1946.

After nearly fifteen years of Democratic control of both the executive and legislative branches of the federal government, it looked as though the Republican party would begin its comeback in 1946. Even before the congressional election campaigns began, political analysts were predicting a sweeping Republican victory. Every vote was vital to the Democratic party, and the ballots Vito Marcantonio could deliver through his American Labor party were never more important to the leadership of Tammany Hall. Realizing his own strength Marcantonio used it to advantage, and this time there was not even the formality of official opposition. The left-wing congressman received the nomination for Congress in the Eighteenth Congressional District from the Democratic party.[29]

Those Democrats who lacked Tammany's realistic view of New York City politics, who could not or did not want to see the existing political situation, were incensed at the idea of a man they considered a Communist receiving the Democratic party's official support. As opposition mounted, Patrick J. Hannigan, former naval officer and former policeman, announced that he would run against Marcantonio in the Democratic primary election. Hannigan a young Irish-American neophyte politician who was unknown outside his own neighborhood at the south end of the Eighteenth Congressional District, received backing from a variety of Democratic factions in revolt against Tammany.[30]

When Marcantonio filed another petition for the Republican party nomination, the thunder from the GOP at all levels was almost deafening. There was talk of importing the popular war hero Lt. General Jimmy Doolittle into the district and running him against "the darling of the Communist Party," but Doolittle was unavailable.[31] By mid-May 1946 the Republicans had found their man and officially nominated Frederick van Pelt Bryan, who was a lawyer, former assistant corporation counsel for the city, and who had served with distinction as a colonel in the Army Air Force during the war.[32] Unlike Palmer during the election of 1944, Bryan indicated his ability and desire to fight the campaign personally; thus Marcantonio was under attack from two sides. Only the ALP nomination was safe, but even there he had to contend with the Liberal party which attempted to draw off the membership of the American Labor party by providing any uncertain leftists with a more respectable haven.

Frederick Bryan opened his campaign on July 11 with what was possibly the understatement of the year: he accused Marcantonio of "masquerading as a Republican."[33] It was an accusation Marcantonio might have denied vehemently, for nobody listening to his campaign speeches in 1946 could possibly have mistaken him for a Republican. In fact, as he slashed out at the vacillating president and the administration, at the Democrats as well as at the Republicans in Congress, it must have been difficult for his listeners in the streets of Yorkville or East Harlem to understand what he was doing running as a Democrat.[34]

Pat Hannigan, the Democratic opponent, described Marcantonio as being neither a Democrat nor a Republican. "He's a doctrinaire," said Hannigan, "reciting the phrases of Marx and a lead-off man for the party line, who plays politics, . . . with all the skill and tricks that can be found in the bag of any big city political boss." Then Hannigan hurled at the congressman the charge made repeatedly in the postwar period, "Not only in theory but on his actual voting record Mr. Marcantonio paralleled 100 per cent the *Daily Worker* and the Communist Party."[35]

Publicly, Bryan's campaign also hinged on connecting Marcantonio with the Communist party, implying that there was something unpatriotic about the congressman. Privately, however, Bryan admitted that it was hardly "possible to completely identify Marcantonio with the Communist Party," in part because Marcantonio had recently voted for the loan to Great Britain while the Communist party vociferously opposed the measure.[36] Such moderation never showed up in Bryan's public appearances. His campaign manager, F. Trowbridge vom Bauer, insisted, "The issue here is very clear. Do the voters of the district want Vito Marcantonio, the man who has consistently followed the Communist Party line, or do they want Frederick Bryan, a real Republican?"[37] Throughout the campaign Marcantonio insisted on talking about the issues—war or peace, rising prices, rent control, public housing, the protection of labor—while his two opponents and their supporters concentrated on the Communist issue.

Through the two hot months of the primary campaign, Marcantonio reiterated one theme to the street-corner audiences, a theme he delivered in English, Italian, or Spanish depending on the ethnic make-up of the neighborhood: the issue was not party labels but rather his record over the years as a member of the House of Representatives.[38] It was smart politics; while the opposition worked from a negative position, Marcantonio and his supporters were able to stress the positive aspects of the congressman's long tenure in office. The hundreds of ALP members, trade unionists, Communists, and members of left-wing youth groups, who campaigned for Marcantonio on a day-to-day basis, pointed to the new high school in the district or the publicly financed low-rent housing projects or the congressman's stand on price and rent controls and ignored the Communist tag.

The campaign was an intensely personal one. No major organ of propaganda supported Marcantonio's candidacy; and he was under constant attack in the city's newspapers, especially so by the two popular morning tabloids, the *Daily News* and the *Daily Mirror*. Prior to the primary election, the Hearst-owned *Daily Mirror* ran a two-week series of feature articles on Marcantonio in which accusations ranged from Marcantonio's supposed support of Communism, Mussolini, and fascism to his consorting with prostitutes and gangsters.[39]

The 1946 primary was a ferociously fought campaign, with physical disturbances committed by partisans for all three parties, with as much legal harassment as the three candidates could manage, and with all three men bringing in every ounce of support available. The vote was heavy for a primary election in New York and agonizingly close. In the Republican race Bryan beat Marcantonio 3,641 to 2,760, while Marcantonio, running as a Democrat, squeaked past Hannigan, 9,778 to 9,216.[40]

The closeness of the vote defies any meaningful analysis. Marcantonio was beaten in the south end of the district but was victorious in East Harlem. The difference between the candidates in the Democratic vote, a bare 562 ballots, can lead to several presumptions: that Marcantonio did not have firm control of the Democratic machine in his congressional district as was so often charged; that he controlled the machine but not the voters; or, more simply, that Patrick Hannigan was a popular young man. But how can one explain the fact that Marcantonio lost to Bryan by only 881 votes of the more than 6,000 cast by Republicans?

Marcantonio and Bryan had barely enough time to catch their breath let alone analyze the figures. For the first time since 1940, Marcantonio had to follow a primary election campaign with an effort in October and November, an effort made more difficult when Hannigan threw his support behind Bryan.[41]

The general election campaign of 1946 in the Eighteenth Congressional District was a more concentrated version of the primary. Bryan accused Marcantonio of placing "the interests of the Communist Party above the interest of this country,"[42] a charge to which Marcantonio replied by enumerating his legislative position on the "bread and butter" issues that meant so much to the average resident of the neighborhood. In speech after speech Marcantonio reviewed his record for the voters, from Depression days and his fight for WPA and the unemployed to the present and prices, rents, labor, civil rights, and civil liberties. He omitted "extraneous" items such as his noninterventionist stand between 1939 and 1941, issues he undoubtedly was convinced would only serve to "becloud" the issues of the 1946 campaign.

The New York Times, in its only congressional endorsement of the year, came out for Frederick Bryan. It devoted three-quarters of its editorial column to a recitation of Marcantonio's noninterventionist position prior to October 1941 and completely omitted any mention of the remainder of the congressman's record, exactly the reverse of Marcantonio's own speeches.[43]

The hard-pressed incumbent picked up valuable support when Fiorello La Guardia, no longer mayor of the city but still an important figure as director of the United Nations Relief and Rehabilitation Administration, publicly endorsed Marcantonio once again. Speaking to an enthusiastic audience of left wingers at Madison Square Garden just prior to the election, La Guardia announced that he was supporting all "real New Dealers" and all incumbents "whose voting records, attendance, and acts show they are serving the people." Then after pausing with typical La Guardia feeling for the dramatic, he added, "and that includes Vito Marcantonio."[44]

The partisan audience went wild and began chanting, "We want Vito! We want Vito!" Marcantonio, not a scheduled speaker, walked on stage and stole the show. Quieting the audience by holding up a bandaged hand, he explained that it had become infected from "playing around with the Republican lever" on a practice voting machine. He waited until the laughter died down then hurled out the single sentence, "There is only one issue in this campaign—collaboration of this nation with the Soviet Union for peace, and for the defeat of domestic fascism." The little man "with the baleful black eyes, hunched shoulders and the face of an erudite ferret" stalked off-stage to a thunderous ovation.[45]

On November 4, election eve, a crowd of more than ten thousand people turned out for Marcantonio's traditional "Lucky Corner" rally. There were the usual warm-up speeches. Then the congressman took the platform and delivered a furious, breathless attack on Bryan, the trusts, and the reactionary press.[46]

The morning after the election *The New York Times* announced that the 1946 congressional elections had "swung this nation sharply right in a left-veering world," everywhere except in New York's Eighteenth Congressional District; there Vito Marcantonio defeated Frederick Bryan by 6,500 votes out of approximately 78,000 cast.[47] In the year the Republican party regained control of Congress for the first time since 1930, Marcantonio "was one of the few, and certainly the most extreme, of the radical Congressmen who survived the national trend."[48]

At his headquarters on election night Marcantonio had stood on a desk, ready to announce victory to the assembled mob, and smilingly prefaced his statement with the order,

"No stamping of feet . . . the Fire Department might evict us."[49] In his brief victory speech he ignored the fact that only 15,000 of his 42,000 vote total came on the American Labor party line and that in terms of the party he really represented in Congress he was a minority representative.

Further downtown Fred Bryan, speaking to an audience of "fashionably dressed men and women," had said, "It's tough to lose, but we've got two years to work in before the next time."[50]

Even further downtown, in a New York City hospital, a young Italo-American named Joseph Scottoriggio lay on a bed fighting for his life, and almost managed to blow the lid off politics in the Eighteenth Congressional District.

IX

The Tide Turns

On election morning 1946, Joseph Scottoriggio was one of the thousands of anonymous residents of East Harlem. The only known fact that set him apart was his active commitment to the political cause of Frederick van Pelt Bryan, Vito Marcantonio's political opponent. By the end of that same week Scottoriggio's name had been spread across the front page of every newspaper in New York City and was featured in more than one magazine with a national circulation.

He left his East Harlem apartment on election morning, on his way to serve as a "watcher" at the polls; he had walked no further than across the street when four men jumped him and brutally beat him. Six days later Scottoriggio died. In the interim the New York City press and several anti-Marcantonio politicians delivered a verbal beating to the re-elected congressman that matched in violence the physical one given Scottoriggio.[1]

The tone of the furious assault on Marcantonio was set by New York's Governor Thomas E. Dewey, one of the leading Republicans in the nation, in a statement given to the press while Scottoriggio was still fighting for his life. "This savage, brutal beating by left-wingers," Dewey insisted without qualification and with no evidence at hand, "was done to intimidate others working for a free election."[2]

Within a few days of Scottoriggio's death, rewards totaling $13,500 were posted for any information leading to the arrest of the killers.[3] Every possible law enforcement agency in the city and state was put on the case. A special committee of the House of Representatives announced its intention to investigate the murder, and John Rankin (Dem., Mississippi)

166

drew up a House resolution aimed at depriving Vito Marcantonio of his hard-won congressional seat. "Who Killed Scottoriggio?" New York's *Daily Mirror* headlined a story that left no doubt in the reader's mind that the *Daily Mirror* knew and so did everyone else: Marcantonio and his machine.[4]

The general line of reasoning followed by Marcantonio's enemies had been laid down by Dewey in his statement concerning the "savage, brutal beating by left-wingers . . . done to intimidate others working for a free election." Scottoriggio had actively campaigned for Bryan and against Marcantonio. He had, according to one account, convinced sixty-three people to vote Republican. In sum, that was the evidence against the radical congressman. Even as circumstantial evidence it lacked soundness. If the beating was intended to intimidate others, why administer it on election day when it could not be reported in the press until late afternoon? Who would be intimidated? Certainly it would not intimidate the voters going into the polls to pull down levers behind closed curtains. Neither would it intimidate Republican campaign workers, most of whom would hear about Scottoriggio only after the polls closed. The Eighteenth Congressional District was a difficult political subdivision in which to intimidate anyone on election day. Because the campaign had been so hard-fought and because there had been sporadic violence emanating from both sides, Police Commissioner Arthur Wallander had doubled the normal police guard at the polls in the area.

One individual who had nothing to gain from a political murder in East Harlem was Vito Marcantonio, who already had enough people fighting him for enough different reasons. A beating administered to one unimportant election worker could hardly have swung the election one way or the other.

While almost everyone of any importance connected with Marcantonio's organization in East Harlem was questioned, only Dominick Petrone, an ALP district captain, was held by the police for any length of time. Petrone was released "completely and unconditionally," without even a summons to appear before the Grand Jury investigating the murder.[5]

Marcantonio himself, sick from the effort put forth during the two election campaigns since July, voluntarily waived all immunity and testified at length before both the Grand Jury and the congressional committee set up to investigate any possible irregularity in his election victory.[6]

Marcantonio's own defense to his congressional colleagues, both on Scottoriggio's murder and on political intimidation in East Harlem, was that, first of all, there were no specific charges of any kind to which he could reply. On the general question of intimidation of voters he informed the congressional committee that a greater percentage of voters had turned out in his district than anywhere else in the city, that the polling places were more heavily policed than at any other locale in New York, and that no one had charged him or his organization with intimidation of voters, other than some of the newspapers which did so by implication.

On the specific question of crime in his district, which the *Daily Mirror* in particular played up after Scottoriggio's death, Marcantonio insisted that he was in no way responsible for the crime that existed in East Harlem, anymore than any congressman was responsible for such a situation. On the other hand, he explained, his whole congressional career had been directed, in a way, toward fighting crime: "I have done more as a member of Congress to try to eliminate crime in my community than any other Congressman because other Congressmen feel that that particular problem is a problem for the District Attorney and for the Police Commissioner. I feel that crime is due to conditions, economic and social, and I have done everything in my power to try to alleviate those conditions." No newspaper man and no individual anywhere in the nation, he added, "is able to charge that I have ever, at any time, protected any racket; that I have received a penny from any racket; and that I have at any time asked the police to look the other way from any crime or racket that went on either in my district or elsewhere in the city of New York or in the United States of America."[7]

The city's press made much of the fact that Marcantonio

supposedly consorted with criminals. The congressman told an interviewer for the *Saturday Evening Post* at about the time of the Scottoriggio killing, "I was born and raised in this district, and there are men with criminal records here who are my supporters. And I'm not going to turn my back on anybody. But I've never had anything to do with a racket or with protecting rackets."[8] A close political associate of Marcantonio said some years later: "He knew some criminals the same way he knew, and was good friends with, some stockbrokers, some conservatives, some grocery store owners. Gangsters existed in the neighborhood and he was too much a human being to ignore them. Crime, he felt, came from the environment and it was the environment he wanted to change. He hated the slums, not their produce."[9]

The Scottoriggio killing continued to take up space in the newspapers through 1947 and well into 1948, but it had no palpable effect on Marcantonio. The congressional investigation found nothing to censure and no reason to deprive Marcantonio of the House seat he had won in the election of 1946. The Grand Jury returned no charge in the case. The murder remains unsolved in New York Police Department records.

On January 4, 1947, Vito Marcantonio, still sick, still tired, took his seat as the sole American Labor party member in a Republican-dominated House of Representatives at a time when the people of the United States turned sharply away from the views he espoused.

The Eightieth Congress, the first Congress elected after the Second World War, dramatically reversed the general direction of American public policy both on foreign and domestic questions. "This Congress," wrote a columnist in *The New Republic*, "brought back an atmosphere you had forgotten or never thought possible."[10] Rigidly controlled by a working combination of conservative Republicans and southern Democrats, the new Congress attempted to roll back or contain the progressive accomplishments of the New Deal era.

While liberal Americans shuddered at the domestic policy laid down by the Eightieth Congress, a policy that led President Truman to refer to that legislature as the worst Congress in American history, those same liberals joined a broad spectrum of the American people in applauding the Congress for its powerful anti-Communist stand in the area of foreign policy. Although the new Congress was conservative, it also destroyed any hope that the United States might return to its prewar isolationist stance. Along with the Truman administration, the Eightieth Congress laid down the basic lines of American policy in the era of cold war and the iron curtain.

Unique in the House by virtue of his political position, Vito Marcantonio was never more isolated at any time in his career. He buzzed angrily around the fringes of the body politic like an angry flea attacking an elephant and a thick-skinned donkey, periodically washed away by a tide of disinfectant conservatism. Sometimes indignant, occasionally shaking his head sadly, sometimes pleading, periodically exasperated by the actions of his colleagues, he had his stand recorded so that, as he frequently said, history could be the judge.

Three factors sufficiently illustrate the depth of the separation between himself and the remainder of the House. First, he failed to secure a committee assignment until the second session of the Congress was well under way in 1948; then he was assigned to the politically impotent Committee on House Administration, a housekeeping detail.[11] Second, he reintroduced his now-famous bill to abolish the poll tax, again designated H.R. 7; this time he never even came close to easing it out of committee through the petition process.[12] Third, more and more during the congressional term, Marcantonio became important to his colleagues only as a gauge by which the patriotism of other congressmen could be measured. Thus, Helen Gahagan Douglas (Dem., California) was charged with being "soft" on communism because she had voted on the same side with Vito Marcantonio 354 times.[13]

Perhaps the bitterest fight of the Eightieth Congress occurred when the House considered the proposed Labor Management or Taft-Hartley Act of 1947. To conservatives this was one of the major accomplishments of the first postwar Congress, substantially altering the advantages given labor by the New Deal. To Marcantonio it was an absolute and unmitigated horror.

"What is your justification for this legislation?" he asked the House. There was no answer that would satisfy him. The bill purported to be a new "bill of rights" for the American worker, but to Marcantonio it only served to free the worker from his union, "his only defense against exploitation. . . . You are making him free—and impotent to defend himself against any attempt by industry to subject him to the same working conditions that existed in these United States 75 years ago. You are giving him the freedom to become enslaved to a system that has been repudiated in the past not only by Democrats but also by outstanding progressive-minded Republicans."

Ostensibly designed "to get rid of the Communists in the unions, to get rid of the racketeers," said Marcantonio, the Taft-Hartley Bill would destroy "the whole philosophy of industrial relationships based on equality of bargaining" between labor and management. "Under the guise of fighting communism," he concluded, "you are, with this legislation, advancing fascism on American labor."

When Marcantonio identified the "real" racketeers as the corporations and the monopolies that "robbed" profits from the pockets of the workers and consumers of the nation, Congressman Hugh Scott of Pennsylvania interrupted to say, "The gentleman knows what a racketeer is, and in his own district too," a not-too-subtle reference to the uproar over the Scottoriggio killing. "My district," Marcantonio retorted, "is just as good, if not better, than the gentleman's district. . . . You cannot meet the issues and you drag out a red herring."[14]

In retrospect, Marcantonio seems to have overstated his case against the bill. After passage and implementation, the Taft-Hartley Act did not destroy unions in the United States, it did not destroy or even substantially alter the philosophy of

industrial relationships based on equality of bargaining between labor and capital, and it certainly did not advance
fascism in American life. But in the framework of 1947 and
1948, given other legislation passed by the Congress and given
his left-orientation, Marcantonio saw the developing domestic
policy laid down by the Eightieth Congress as an upper-class
plot against the common people. His understanding of the
American past and of American society necessitated the acceptance of a "concerted conspiracy" of the ruling classes as
one of its basic assumptions. When pushed to the wall, as he
was in these years, this argument became the only way in
which he could rationalize his own lack of success and the
general failure of the American left. With the same faith in
the righteousness of the people exhibited by Jeffersonians,
Abolitionists, Populists, and Progressives before him, Marcantonio presumed that if only the people had the facts, if only
the truth could be revealed to them, they would rise up in
massive indignation and strike down the plotters.

The attitude was inherent in the battle Marcantonio waged
against approval of the Taft-Hartley Bill. Along with other
opponents of the bill, he knew he could not alter the attitude
of the House. The majority clearly wanted a revision of national labor policy and law. What he could do was to hold up
passage of the bill and give the American people the opportunity to flood the Congress with letters and petitions calling
for the defeat of the legislation. Convinced that the people
were on his side, Marcantonio hoped his delaying tactic would
bring forth their protests. Thus, when the final version of the
Taft-Hartley Bill came to a vote on June 4, 1947, Marcantonio
invoked a rarely used rule of procedure and demanded, according to the New York *Herald Tribune,* that "before the
vote is taken all sixty-nine pages of the bill's text, plus the
voluminous report of the committee explaining its provisions,
be read to the membership of the House of Representatives."

Ex-speaker of the House Sam Rayburn agreed with the
stand taken by the radical congressman. "Frankly," he told
reporters, "I have been around here a good while, and I would

like to know what is in this conference report before I vote upon it."[15]

The uprising that followed was not of the type Marcantonio had envisioned; conservatives immediately called for his head. The *Herald Tribune,* in an editorial that typified the reaction, accused Marcantonio of "deliberately or unconsciously seeking to ridicule the democratic system" for the sake of his standing in the American Labor party.[16] The newspaper was totally wrong in the motives it ascribed to the congressman. He had no worries about his standing in the ALP, and he was bent on neither obstruction nor ridicule. He was after time—time in which to raise public opposition to the bill.

Protesting the *Herald Tribune's* position, Marcantonio informed the editors that the final version of the Taft-Hartley Bill had been agreed upon in a Senate-House Conference Committee on May 27 and that the report of that committee was not made available to the membership of the House until June 4, the very day the vote was to be taken. "My insistence," he wrote, "on the full reading of the bill was, therefore, merely an attempt to familiarize the members of the House with the provisions of the bill that obviously they had neither the opportunity to study or read. Unless I am greatly mistaken," he concluded, "the democratic system requires that Congress be fully informed of the provisions of legislation before it votes on it."[17]

Marcantonio's attempt to arouse the public failed. The opposition was neither massive enough nor broad enough to change the mind of the Republican-controlled Congress, and the Taft-Hartley Bill became law. All that labor and the American left could do was to attack it, rename it the "Slave Labor Act of 1947," and prepare to use it as an issue in the coming presidential election.

While the Congress acted conservatively on the question of labor, it conservatively refused to act on the question of Negro rights. Marcantonio's failure to move his anti-poll-tax bill has already been indicated. He raised the question of civil rights again during the debate over the Taft-Hartley Bill.

Throughout the legislative argument, Representative Fred Hartley (Rep., New Jersey) insisted on referring to the bill he authored jointly with Senator Robert Taft (Rep., Ohio) as a new "bill of rights" for labor. Accepting the definition at face value, Marcantonio asked Hartley if he would accept an amendment to the bill that would incorporate "the principles of fair employment practices," making it illegal for an employer to discriminate against Negroes in hiring policy. Hartley replied, "I will say to the gentleman that as far as that issue is concerned, I am opposed to injecting that argument into this bill." The reply proved to Marcantonio's satisfaction that the new "bill of rights" had rather sharp limitations.[18]

The attempt to attach Negro rights legislation to other bills was a tactic Marcantonio and other congressmen used throughout the Eightieth Congress. Adam Clayton Powell, the Democratic congressman from New York's Harlem district, offered an amendment to the Army-Navy Nurses Act of 1947 that would have prohibited the appointment of nurses in the armed forces or the Public Health Service on the basis of race, creed, color, national origin, or ancestry. Marcantonio supported the amendment, but it was not in agreement with the philosophy of the majority of the House. The measure was defeated, 187 to 47.[19] In 1948 Marcantonio offered an amendment to the Department of Labor Appropriations Bill that would bar grants of funds to states or educational institutions practicing discrimination. As with all other civil rights attempts, this amendment was voted down, 119 to 40.[20]

Labor and Negro rights were only two of the points on which Marcantonio disagreed with the majority of the House. On almost every important domestic measure considered by the Eightieth Congress, Marcantonio ineffectively tried to stop the flood tide of conservatism. Early in 1947 the House took up legislation designed to reduce the high wartime tax schedule. During the debate on the income tax provisions of the Republican-sponsored bill, Marcantonio developed the point that the measure, if passed, would increase the take-home pay of a married man by 3.8 per cent if his income were $5,000 yearly and by 70.7 per cent if his income were $500,000 a year. Obviously, he insisted, the Congress was considering legislation benefiting the rich alone.[21] The American Labor party had its own idea of what constituted a rational revision of the nation's tax structure, and Marcantonio placed that program in the *Congressional Record.* The ALP proposals called for a revision in the personal exemption for an individual from $500 to $1,500, including a maximum $2,500 exemption for a married couple without children; the repeal of all excise taxes on necessities; and the retention of a high excess-profits tax on corporations.[22] It is almost unnecessary to add that the Republican-sponsored measure easily passed in the House with only modest revision.

Marcantonio once again moved against the temper of the times by fighting to retain the Office of Price Administration. The war-born agency, he felt, had to be continued into the postwar period to prevent runaway inflation. But the House appropriated just enough money so that the OPA could liquidate itself by June 30, 1947. The congressman's only satisfaction came when he pointed out that elimination of the OPA also meant an end to national rent controls, the rules for which were established by the OPA. Only then did Representative Clarence Cannon (Dem., Missouri), speaking for the House committee responsible for the OPA appropriation, explain that the committee definitely intended to bring in a separate bill for continuing rent controls, a measure of paramount importance to Marcantonio's constituents.[23]

On the Taft-Ellender-Wagner Bill for public housing construction, an issue related to rent controls, Marcantonio termed the proposed legislation wholly inadequate in providing necessary low-cost housing. But since the bill was a "better-than-nothing" proposition, he voted "yes" until assured of its passage and then changed his vote to "present."[24]

In yet another field, seemingly strange to the congressman from the city's slums, Marcantonio objected to consideration on the unanimous consent calendar in July 1947 of a bill that would have returned the Jackson Hole National Monument to state control and thereby effectively blocked passage of the measure.[25] Momentarily a hero to conservationists, Marcantonio saw his parliamentary maneuver pay off three years later when the Jackson Hole area was incorporated into Grand Teton National Park and thus protected from state or private incursion.

No single measure introduced in the House stirred Marcantonio as much or brought out the fighter in him more than the myriad legislative proposals introduced during the Eightieth Congress that were related to the internal Communist menace. These proposals were based on the necessity, real or imagined, to stamp out "reds," "pinks," and "fellow travelers."

In February and again in April of 1947, Marcantonio cast the only vote against contempt of Congress citations for Gerhardt Eisler, Eugene Dennis, and Leon Josephson, all officials of the Communist party. The citations stemmed from their refusal to answer the questions of the House Committee on Un-American Activities during an investigation that Marcantonio felt was illegal. The power to investigate that is central to the legislative function, Marcantonio insisted in explaining his vote, becomes the power to destroy "when the objective is to destroy." In his view, the Congress did not have the constitutional power to outlaw the Communist party and "the objective, . . . being clearly unconstitutional, this proceeding [the citing of Eisler, Dennis, and Josephson for contempt] is unconstitutional." Reaching back into American history for examples, he compared his own times to the era of the French Revolution when the contemporary word for "Communist" was "Jacobin" or "Republican" and recommended Claude Bowers' *Jefferson and Hamilton* as required reading for the members of the House.

Opposing the contempt citations against the so-called Hollywood Ten later in the year, he took exactly the same position. The spectacle of a legislative body in a democratic nation trying to outlaw Communists through intimidation was, in his opinion, a sad "repetition of history." The same method had been used in Hitler's Germany and in Mussolini's Italy, said Marcantonio, and, "If I have to be alone again in this Congress, I will cast my vote against it ever happening in the United States of America."[26]

After December 1947, when Henry Agard Wallace announced his intention to run for the presidency on a third party ticket,[27] Marcantonio gained yet another insight into the anti-Communist movement in the United States. On March 8, 1948, he noted the recent arrest of five trade-union leaders, all left wingers, all supporters of Wallace, and all suddenly slated for deportation as dangerous subversives. "If these men are subversive, as the government charges," Marcantonio asked bitterly, "what has the government done about it in the past years? Why is it that all of a sudden, after the 29th day of December, the day Mr. Wallace announced his candidacy," and only after that announcement, "did the government finally make its move against these several dangerous individuals?"[28]

The actions taken against the three Communist party officials, five left-wing trade unionists, and ten Hollywood screenwriters did not constitute a concerted public policy against the suspected internal Communist menace. President Truman's Executive Order 9835 establishing procedures for determining the loyalty of government employees and the Republican-sponsored Mundt Subversive Activities Control Bill together constituted just such a policy aimed at the destruction of the radical left in America. Both the president's order and the bill outraged Marcantonio's principles, and he reacted by accusing Democrats and Republicans of running in a contest to "determine which is going to excel in the field of red-baiting." The executive and legislative actions tended to "make out of a Federal employee a person with a static mind, whose soul will be filled with fear."[29]

The Mundt Bill in particular, which the Congress debated in the late spring of 1948, horrified the radical congressman. Its wording was so broad, including in the general category of "subversive" even those who had "sympathetic association" with organizations to be listed as "Communist fronts" by the attorney general at some future date, that Marcantonio saw the bill as a potential weapon for completely stifling freedoms guaranteed by the Bill of Rights. The congressman fought his usual verbal battle, knowing that he and the minority for which he spoke were lost. His appeal was not to his listeners in the House, for he could not expect to change his colleagues' minds in view of their votes on related issues; he spoke instead to the future generations:

> I know many will succumb to hysteria and others will give us the usual flag-waving and red-baiting, but let us look back in retrospect: 1798–1948, 150 years. The men who opposed the Alien and Sedition Acts—Livingston, Madison, Jefferson— they constitute the bright constellations in the democratic firmament of this Nation; but those who imposed on the American people those tyrannies of which this bill is a monstrous lineal descendant have been cast into oblivion, relegated there where mankind always relegates puny creatures that would destroy mankind's freedom.[30]

Confident that history was on his side, knowing in his heart that eventually the people would right these current wrongs, Marcantonio indulged his sense of humor during the debate over the Mundt Subversive Activities Control Bill. When Congressman John Taber (Rep., New York), chairman of the Committee on Appropriations, complained that the Library of Congress had just acquired four hundred different volumes written in the Russian language, Marcantonio applauded Taber's detective work and dryly suggested that Taber's committee appropriate "a reasonable amount of money to provide for the burning of the books."[31] Neither the history lesson nor the humor served to stop the tide of anti-communism, and the Mundt Bill passed in the House by an overwhelming majority.

Rolling back the achievements of the New Deal and repressing the politically unpopular were but two components of what was, to Vito Marcantonio, the reactionary plot against the freedom of the American people. The third and perhaps the most vital ingredient was the new look in the nation's foreign policy. On March 12, 1947, President Truman went before the Congress and laid down the essentials of what became known popularly as the Truman Doctrine. At that time Vito Marcantonio, who had supported much of the nation's foreign policy for the previous five years, moved into the camp of the opposition and within a short period of time became almost the only congressional opponent of the rapidly developing bipartisan coalition united around the cry, "Stop Communism!"

Marcantonio's refusal to support Truman's program of economic and military aid to Greece and Turkey was based on three major points: the Truman Doctrine was essentially imperialistic; it would aid fascist regimes in those two countries rather than lead to the establishment of democratic governments; and, most important, Truman's policy bypassed the United Nations. Marcantonio did not oppose the granting of relief to wartorn European nations. To a group of college students who questioned his stand, he wrote, "I do favor giving relief to people who need it and believe that the best manner in which to handle it is through the United Nations."[32]

It was no secret that Marcantonio's position was essentially the same as that taken by the American Communist party and by the Communist parties of all nations. It would be foolish to presume that Marcantonio came to this view concerning the Truman Doctrine simply on the basis of internal reflection. A good portion of both his thought and his language by 1947 came from the Communists with whom he maintained close contact. But it is also important to indicate that there were others in Marcantonio's political circle, non-Communists, who arrived at the same conclusions. Before the war, the congressman and Fiorello La Guardia had been poles apart concerning foreign policy questions. There is no question concerning La Guardia's anti-Communist attitudes. Yet before the older man died in 1947, he and Marcantonio had again come to a similar position on what they saw as the correct path for America in international affairs.

La Guardia felt that the only way to meet the needs of the wartorn European nations was through the creation of "an international authority operating under the control of the United Nations and meeting the relief need, without any consideration of race, creed, or political belief, being guided only by the existence of true need." This he termed "the new way of the United Nations," although he also pointed out that it had ancient ancestry for it was "a way brought to this world nearly 2,000 years ago in the teachings of the Prince of Peace. And a wicked world has, to date, refused to learn the lesson."[33]

It is safe to assume that, given Marcantonio's left-wing view of life and society, his position on the Truman Doctrine would have been essentially the same without the urging of the Communist party. In his eyes, the same men who slashed at labor, who ignored the needs of the Negro, who failed to protect the consumer, and who suppressed radical thought on the home front were the architects of the bipartisan foreign policy. That alone, by 1947, was sufficient to make him view the policy with suspicion. Previously he had supported the loan to Great Britain because he believed that the continued collaboration of Great Britain, the Soviet Union, and the United States was the only realistic road to world peace. He wanted to continue that collaboration through the United Nations, while the president and the Congress moved in the direction of unilateral action on the part of the United States.

The promulgation of the Truman Doctrine marked a turning point in the conduct of American foreign policy. There is no question that the American people accepted the new foreign policy and everything that necessarily followed from it, from the policy of containment to the possible consequences of massive retaliation. The reconstruction of Europe through the United Nations was rejected, and in 1948 the nation accepted Secretary of State George C. Marshall's European Recovery Plan. That same year marked the high point of the radical left's attempt to defeat the idea of a foreign policy based on the principle of anti-communism.

With words that sound strangely prophetic almost two decades later, Marcantonio said, during the debate over the Marshall Plan:

> I have consistently voted against this war program. I shall continue to vote against it, for in so doing I am defending Americans. . . . I believe I am exercising a patriotic duty which is incumbent today more than ever before upon men of courage. Now is the time for men to stand up and fight for peace. Tomorrow will be too late. Now is the time to stand up and make the fight; for tomorrow, if peace is lost, all will be lost, for nobody will win the next war.[34]

"How long," asked Marcantonio's old congressional enemy, Eugene Cox of Georgia, "must members of this body sit here and hear assaulted the government we love . . . by people . . . who would run down the flag of the stars and stripes . . . and run up in its stead the flag of the hammer and sickle?"

"We are not," Marcantonio replied, "going to be deterred by any vituperation that may come from any tobacco patriot, or from any cotton king, or from any corn and corny orator, or from any arrogant Jim Crow flag-waver, who brazenly talks of democracy here, but personally refuses to apply it in the communities that he represents."[35]

Marcantonio lost the fight against the Marshall Plan as he had lost the fight against the Truman Doctrine. "We have been told to go back to the country that we love. We take that advice. We are going back to the country we love—we are going back to the election precincts of our cherished United States, and we are going to take this fight to the American people."[36] The opportunity to do so existed in 1948, not only for Marcantonio in his Eighteenth Congressional District where he faced another battle for his seat in the House, but throughout the nation where the radical left girded up for battle behind Henry Wallace in an attempt to turn the tide of conservatism in that presidential election year.

X

In Victory Lies Defeat

The idea of a third national party was not new to Vito Marcantonio. He had flirted with at least one such movement in the 1930's, had hoped that a Farmer-Labor party would be ready for competition with Republicans and Democrats in the election campaign of 1940, and in 1946 had surveyed the American scene and announced that historic conditions were ripe for the creation of a new political organization. His own successful career in politics depended on the existence of a local third party in New York, the American Labor party. He knew from experience that a modicum of power could be gained with something less than total victory. If a new third party gained sufficient strength, it could wield the balance of power in the nation as the ALP sometimes did in New York City.

But more important than the political possibilities were the political necessities. By 1947–1948, Marcantonio, in company with many on the left wing of the American political spectrum, saw no palpable difference between the Democratic and Republican parties. On the domestic front a coalition of members from both major parties prevented the extension of New Deal social legislation and in several instances had managed to roll back the times. In the field of foreign policy there existed a working bipartisan agreement between Democrats and Republicans, thus offering the voters no real choice. While the Democratic party was generally considered the more liberal of the two major parties, national victory for the Democrats brought into positions of legislative power a large number of southerners who were, if anything, more conservative on many issues than were their Republican counterparts. Whatever other observers might conclude, there existed a monolithic union between the two ruling parties as far as Marcantonio could see.

He felt that somehow, in some way, a new party had to act to give the American people a real choice and a different political story: that the social accomplishments of the New Deal were just the beginning, that equal rights for Negroes could become a reality in American life, that Communists were not about to take over the country, and that the United States could successfully collaborate with the Soviet Union in the interests of world peace.

Months before Henry Wallace made clear his intention to organize and lead just such a party, Marcantonio appealed for its formation. In March and again in August of 1947, speaking before New York City audiences, the congressman emphasized the need for organizating a third party prior to the presidential elections of 1948.[1] In July he queried the Legislative Reference Service at the Library of Congress on "procedures followed by a candidate for President or Vice-President in getting his name on the ballot."[2]

In December 1947, as soon as Wallace announced that he would make an independent run for the presidency, having "assembled a Gideon's Army, small in number, powerful in conviction, ready for action," Marcantonio became a leading member of the inner councils of the new political organization known nationally as the Progressive party.[3]

There were numerous obstacles in the way of success. Marcantonio, as the only radical able to maintain his seat in Congress for any length of time, was peculiarly conscious of them. For example, early in 1948 he recognized the fact that the Progressive party and Wallace's candidacy would be "handicapped by lack of a press."[4] Considering his own political career, he had no illusions about the way in which American newspapers and magazines would handle the Progressive party and its candidates. There were several tentative attempts at starting a pro-Wallace newspaper on a national scale, but the financial involvement was too great for a party with limited funds.

Even without newspaper support, however, it seemed possible for the new party to win a significant popular vote in the 1948 election. Political analysts generally accepted the thesis that if the Progressives could win five million or more votes around the country, the new party would have both permanence and leverage on the national scene. Time was short and the road difficult. Marcantonio knew from experience that political parties are built slowly; but, conscious of history, he also knew that the Republican party had not won on its first try either.

The way to win votes, the congressman insisted, was for the Wallace movement to stress the day-to-day issues: housing, high cost of living, veterans' care. These issues were important to the ordinary people around the country who had basically the same needs and worries as those he had served for so long in East Harlem. Against the "party strategists who talk in generalities and abstractions," Marcantonio hit back "with harsh singleness of purpose."[5]

In January 1948, Marcantonio was elected state chairman of the American Labor party, the New York State arm of Wallace's "Gideon's Army." He immediately put his ideas about political campaigns into effect. Whatever doubts the public or the professional politicians had about the potential strength of the new movement were brushed aside in February 1948. An unknown American Labor party candidate, running in a Bronx County, New York, special congressional election to fill a vacated seat in the House, decisively defeated his Democratic, Republican, and Liberal party opposition. Young Leo Isaacson catapulted into national prominence by garnering fifty-six per cent of the total vote and winning more than 10,000 votes over his Democratic rival in a normally Democratic district. For the first time in the party's history, an ALP candidate had received a majority of the votes, an achievement Marcantonio himself never matched.[6]

Overnight the American Labor party had doubled its congressional delegation and Marcantonio was doubly jubilant. For the first time in his career as an ALP congressman since 1938, he would have a caucus mate. He felt Isaacson's victory was tangible proof, in the form of votes from a majority of the voters, that the nation hungered for the Wallace and Marcantonio brand of domestic and foreign policy. "Mr. Isaacson never had been considered to have a chance to win," wrote Warren Moscow in *The New York Times,* "but the percentage of the votes given to the third party forces was to be regarded as an indication of the potential Wallace strength in November."[7]

In addition to helping to establish the Progressive party and giving it the benefit of his political sagacity, Marcantonio played a minor role in Wallace's race for the presidency in 1948. He made several speeches for the former vice-president and served as chairman of the new party's Rules Committee, which drew up the general organizational plan approved at the party's July convention in Philadelphia.[8] His participation undoubtedly would have been greater had he not been involved in a congressional campaign that taxed his every resource. Throughout the nation 1948 was a strange election year, but nowhere was it stranger than in the Eighteenth Congressional District.[9]

For the first time since his election in 1934 Marcantonio was spared the physical and financial drain of a primary campaign; it was not a gift but a punishment. Early in 1947 the New York State Legislature passed the Wilson-Pakula Act, broad in scope but aimed directly at the radical from East Harlem and at the party he controlled. The Wilson-Pakula Act limited a candidate to the primary of the party in which he was enrolled and to that primary alone. He could cross-file for another party's nomination only with the consent of the second party's county committee or machine. The Wilson-Pakula Act made Marcantonio's double or even triple candidacy almost impossible. When the New York State Court of Appeals upheld the validity of the new law, there were rumors that Marcantonio might circumvent the act by enrolling in the Democratic party, the majority party in his district. But he soon announced that he would run on the American Labor party line alone.[10]

Statistically the congressman's chances looked poor. In the 1946 congressional election, the vote in the Eighteenth Congressional District, broken down into parties, indicated clearly the new problem posed for Marcantonio by the passage of the Wilson-Pakula Act. The Republicans had garnered 35,625 votes; the Democrats, 27,162 votes; and the American Labor party, only 14,963 votes. In his entire political career, Marcantonio had never won an election without the support, in name at least, of at least one of the major parties.[11]

There were persistent rumors throughout the first part of the year that Marcantonio's political wizardry would still manage to pull off some kind of deal with Tammany Hall. Murray Baron, New York County chairman of the Liberal party, charged that in return for the American Labor party's endorsement of a Tammany candidate for an important judgeship, "Democratic district leaders in the 18th Congressional District are expected to wage a vigorous campaign aimed at discouraging as many Democratic voters as possible from voting for their own Congressional nominee, . . . thus seeking to insure Marcantonio's re-election."[12] Apparently Baron's thinking was slightly askew, for Democratic district leaders would have had to do more than discourage the voters from voting Democratic. The only way Marcantonio could have won was for those same Democratic district leaders to positively push his candidacy. In the political climate of 1948 it was unlikely that ward heelers would take such a risk; by so doing, they would be urging the election of a man popularly accepted as a Communist. Marcantonio himself proved Baron's charge false when the ALP nominated O. J. Rogge, a leading Wallace supporter, for the judgeship Baron had in mind, thus practically insuring the defeat of Tammany's candidate.[13]

The rumors of an impending deal persisted despite the evidence and although it should have been obvious that by

1948 Marcantonio had little bargaining power. Certainly he had no influence with William O'Dwyer, the Democratic mayor who had replaced La Guardia in 1945. As early as 1946 O'Dwyer began cutting any patronage ties the ALP had with City Hall. By the fall of 1948 Marcantonio complained bitterly that a hospital he had been assured would be built in East Harlem was now rescheduled for a location further downtown, a change he ascribed to "O'Dwyer and his gang."[14] The following year a reporter writing in *Time* explained that Marcantonio's radical political position on both domestic and foreign affairs had cost him patronage power at all levels.[15]

In part, at least, the rumors about a political deal found their origin in the Democrats choice of a candidate to run against Marcantonio in 1948. John P. Morrisey, Tammany's choice, was not the kind of candidate who instilled confidence in the electorate. Throughout the campaign Marcantonio referred to him as *testa di cappuccio* or "cabbage head," while the Democratic Mayor O'Dwyer dismissed Morrisey as a "dumbhead." Morrisey, an electrical contractor by profession, added nothing to his stature as a politician when he boasted to reporters that he had "a far-fetched knowledge of electricity." According to newspaper accounts his campaign headquarters on East 86th Street remained closed most of the time. He is known to have made only three speeches during the election furor.[16] Morrisey's inactivity fueled the rumors of a deal with Tammany.

Another explanation for the Democrats' inaction, however, might have been that Tammany did not think it would win in a year that looked like a Republican landslide year all over the nation; thus it was more likely to put its resources into other districts where the chances to win seemed better. One could also argue that the Democrats did not think Morrisey had to campaign in a three-way election to win, for there were many more registered Democrats in the district than there were either Republicans or American Laborites. And the insinuation that Democratic district leaders betrayed

Morrisey is not confirmed when the voting record is inspected.

The real fight in the election revolved around Marcantonio and his Republican rival, John Ellis. A navy veteran active in veterans' groups, a machine Republican, and a former vice-president of the city's Young Republican Club, Ellis waged a driving, fighting campaign, attacking Marcantonio at his weakest points. Ellis met all the qualifications the Republican machine set for a candidate, but he had his own vulnerable points, and Marcantonio was quick to point them out.

For one thing Ellis was a stockbroker by profession, the very personification of the Wall Street conspiracy to Marcantonio and certainly not a profession that ranked high with the average resident of the basically working-class Eighteenth Congressional District. Along with the handicap of the profession went the fact that Ellis was listed in the *Social Register*. Although these two facts were meaningless to those Republicans who selected Ellis, they were ammunition to Marcantonio who knew his voters. But the two aspects of Ellis' personal life that Marcantonio had the most fun with during the campaign were that the Republican candidate owned and lived in a fourteen-room apartment and that the apartment was not in the Eighteenth Congressional District. Imagine how must those fourteen rooms have looked to the young voters in the district, the veterans who could not find any kind of apartment during the housing shortage of 1948. By the time Marcantonio and his campaign workers were finished, the voters might not have known anything else about Ellis but everyone knew about those fourteen rooms.[17]

Ellis' attack on Marcantonio, as might be expected, hinged on pinning the Communist label on the congressman. The Republican opened his campaign in mid-July by referring to Marcantonio as "Moscow's mouthpiece" in America.[18]

Ellis counted on and received the support of some of the best-known Republicans in the city. Stanley Isaacs, the popular city councilman, Mrs. Wendell Willkie, Newbold Morris, Oren Root, Jr., and a host of GOP luminaries endorsed the young stockbroker and spoke for him in the district. Every newspaper in the city, with the exception of the *Daily Worker,* editorially called for the defeat of Vito Marcantonio. *The New York Times* devoted three editorials, on October 12, 14, and 15, to urging its readers to vote against the congressman who had "accepted, spoken for and voted the Communist line during the last decade." The *Times* went on to pose for the readers going to the polls on November 2 the question of "whether they are going to vote Russian or vote American."[19] The paper, making no mention of Marcantonio's position on domestic affairs during his long service in Congress, based its opposition on foreign policy considerations alone.

The name Joseph Scottoriggio loomed large in the election along with Marcantonio's supposed ties to Moscow. Just four days before the election the New York City Council discussed a resolution calling for intensified efforts to solve the two-year-old murder, a resolution with rather obvious political motivation.[20] Along with the implication of wrongdoing in the past, Marcantonio was accused by Ellis' organization of fraud, intimidation, and hooliganism during the campaign itself.[21] While nothing came of the charges in a legal sense, the Republicans hoped that the attendant publicity would have its effect on the voters.

Publicly Ellis stated that Marcantonio's strength came entirely from his support by Communists and the money they channeled into his election campaign, but in private the Republican candidate admitted "that Marcantonio's principal appeal and strength lies in his long and tireless record of personal service to the voters of the district."[22]

Marcantonio immersed himself in campaigning in 1948, on street corners, in school auditoriums, at club meetings, wherever he collected an audience. He blasted away at the issues of the day, at the reactionary record of the Eightieth Congress (Harry Truman was making the identical charge across the nation with startling effect), at the meaning of the Marshall Plan to Italy and to world peace, at the inaction by both major parties on questions of civil rights. He had an innate capacity to simplify complex political questions and to couch them in terms his audience understood and reacted to. For dramatic effect he used folk singers and, as he had done a decade earlier, a ventriloquist and dummy. This time the dummy was Ellis. Marcantonio would say, "I'm doing something no other candidate ever does. [Enter the dummy.] I'm introducing you to my opponent." He then mocked Ellis' occupation, his social position, and his multiroomed apartment.[23]

He met head-on the charge of being a Communist. To *The New York Times,* which had denounced him in its editorial, he wrote, "However much these views and actions of mine may resemble the 'Communist line' in the opinion of the *New York Times,* I nevertheless stand by them. I am confident that history and the final judgment of the people will support me in the future as they have so consistently in the past."[24]

The 1948 campaign was bitter and grueling. Ellis and Marcantonio fought right up to election eve. The following day, November 2, was cold and crisp. The voters flocked to the polling places in the largest outpouring of the electorate the Eighteenth Congressional District had ever witnessed. When the results were tallied Vito Marcantonio had won his seventh term in Congress, as the candidate of the American Labor party without help derived by having his name listed on the Republican or Democratic line. He more than doubled his previous high total as an American Laborite, winning nearly 36,000 votes to Ellis' 31,500 and Morrisey's 31,200.[25] Morrisey's total is significant, for it certainly does not indicate that Tammany had, in any way, thrown the election into Marcantonio's lap.

If ever there was an election Vito Marcantonio should have lost, 1948 was it. Opposed by all the organized power of anti-communism, running for re-election in an area where probably ninety-five per cent of the population was anti-Communist, the radical congressman from East Harlem should have been a lame duck. John Ellis, in private, had touched on the reason why Marcantonio was so difficult to dislodge from the House of Representatives.

In a very real sense Vito Marcantonio ran his re-election campaign "day in day out, six days a week, every week of the year, whether Congress is in session or out," without any consideration of whether or not it was an election year.[26] From his two offices, the old one on 116th Street in East Harlem and the newer branch office on First Avenue near 78th Street in the Yorkville section, Marcantonio provided his constituents with a combination social service/legal aid society/guidance clinic the likes of which had never been seen in American politics. On weekdays the work was left to assistants; Saturdays, Mondays, and sometimes on Sundays, Marcantonio returned to New York from Washington and directed the operation himself.[27]

The work itself was simple, in theory at least. People had problems: an intransigent landlord, a real or imagined conflict with civil service regulations, discrimination, unfair treatment by the city, state, or federal bureaucracy; and the congressman offered his services. In time a large proportion of the population of the Eighteenth Congressional District learned to take problems to "Marc." There was no political tie-in; no one was asked to become a member of the American Labor party or to contribute to the fund to re-elect Marcantonio. There were not even physical hints in the offices that donations would be appreciated. The services of Marcantonio and his staff were available for the asking. The congressman insisted "almost fanatically that no constituent, however lowly or troublesome, get the kiss-off."[28]

When one woman resident asked about legal fees, Marcantonio replied, "As your representative in Congress I am most pleased to do whatever is proper and possible in this matter without any fee." It was not his practice, he explained, to accept fees from constituents. The same rigorous standards were applicable to those lawyers who voluntarily assisted him.[29]

The bulk of the cases that came to Marcantonio from his constituents fell into two distinct categories. Before the war, they were all relief problems—WPA applications, and the

like. After the war, they were all rent control problems—
tenants fighting unwarranted rent increases or reporting violations of the law by landlords and asking Marcantonio's help
in bringing action. During the 1948 campaign a huge sign
covered the façade of his First Avenue headquarters, the
bold words reading: "Don't pay rent increases. If your landlord asks for a rent increase report here and I shall help you
fight the real estate trust. Your Congressman Vito Marcantonio." Literally thousands of such cases came to him in the
postwar period.[30]

Where possible and necessary, Marcantonio instituted legal
action on behalf of the constituent. In most cases, however,
his action was limited to the writing of a letter or a phone
call to the proper authorities. A war widow came to Marcantonio with a problem during the 1948 campaign; the government had just informed her that she was no longer entitled
to pension checks since she had remarried and that she owed
it $156. "Marc got right on the phone and called the Secret
Service—which was investigating the matter. He had it all
straightened out in a couple of minutes—the General Accounting Office, it seems, had slipped up somewhere."[31]

The correspondence between Marcantonio and La Guardia,
while the latter was mayor, illustrates the variety of cases that
poured through Marcantonio's office: a bridgekeeper for the
city asking reinstatement as a transportation inspector, a
druggist concerned about anti-Semitic outbreaks in Yorkville, a seventy-year-old civil service worker asking for the
right to work another six months. The picture of the powerful city boss drawn by Marcantonio's critics does not emerge
from the letters the congressman wrote to cover these cases.
Marcantonio's tone was always correct: "Will you please be
good enough to inform me if it is at all proper to reinstate
Mr. Donohue as a transportation inspector," or "The reason
I write . . . is because I believe that someone has violated
Civil Service and this is a complaint," or "If there is anything
that you can properly and possibly do . . . I shall greatly
appreciate it."[32]

There were times, as with the war widow above, when the congressman delivered handsomely. And there were times when his power seemed to be spectacular. During the war an Italian mother came in, obviously distraught over the equally obvious pregnancy of her unmarried young daughter. The guilty party was a British sailor; was there anything the congressman could do? Marcantonio called the British consulate in New York and perhaps because wartime amity dictated special services for members of the American legislature, the Royal Navy promptly delivered the embarrassed young seaman. In a short time the pregnant daughter was made an honest woman, with Marcantonio and his staff in attendance, while East Harlem buzzed with stories about how "Marc" had brought the British Lion to bay.[33]

With adults bringing him cases, it was only a matter of time until the children of his district got the idea that the congressman was the one to see in times of dire need. "The children around 82nd Street, between First and Second Avenues, are ganging up on me," he wrote La Guardia. "They complain that the playground in P. S. 190 is closed and they need it."[34]

Although pressed for time, he did not limit himself to his own constituents. When a group of Park Department engineers solicited Marcantonio's help in recovering back pay owed to them by the city, Marcantonio investigated the case and then supported the engineers' request in a letter to La Guardia. With typical humor he noted that "[Robert] Moses and I are in complete accord on this issue and when he and I see eye to eye how can you or anybody else be right?"[35]

There were, of course, those cases that verged on the ridiculous: the owner of an animal act then appearing on stage at the Roxy Theater asked Marcantonio's help in retrieving from the pound one of his dogs which had, in all innocence, taken a large chunk out of someone's leg. Reporting the facts in the case and asking if anything could be done, Marcantonio added the plaintive note in handwriting at the bottom of the typed letter, "Do I get cases?"[36]

There were times when the congressman, inundated by the great numbers of people who trooped through his office, failed to appreciate all the ramifications of a particular request. When one constituent had his permit to operate a vegetable stall in one of the city's public markets revoked, Marcantonio fired a blazing letter to La Guardia; the letter was filled with contempt for the highhanded bureaucracy that would grind the face of the poor into the dirt. With great delight, La Guardia wrote back that the vegetable seller in question had been guilty of violating established OPA prices and regulations and that the charges had first been brought to the city's attention "by the Honorable Vito Marcantonio." La Guardia concluded, "I am sure that you would not want the decision to be changed." There was no second letter from the congressman.[37]

Occasionally Marcantonio's constituents asked only for advice, as when an army veteran inquired how best to introduce his Czechoslovak bride "to American life and letters." The congressman took the time to reply, "I believe that the history of our country is so rich in democratic traditions that I would recommend to her . . . the writings of Jefferson, Paine, Lincoln, and Franklin Delano Roosevelt. Carl Sandburg's life of Lincoln would give her a thorough idea of the traditions and lives of the American people."[38]

Of course there were times when Marcantonio could do nothing to fill a request for assistance. During the heat of the 1948 campaign a woman left her infant son in a basket in front of a restaurant at 34th Street and Seventh Avenue with instructions that it be delivered to the childless Marcantonios and raised by them as their son.[39]

As research for an article, one conscientious reporter spent a day with Marcantonio in his office.

> "What do you make of it?" the Congressman asked us.
> We said that a couple of days like that would drive us nuts.
> "Well," said he, "it's what I get ten thousand a year for. It's their dough."

We also said that we were very grateful that we were not a member of Congress.

"You probably have something there," sighed Vito Marcantonio.[40]

Did it pay off? Did it mean anything at all in terms of winning elections?

An elderly gentleman, a registered Republican since the days of Theodore Roosevelt, wrote of Marcantonio:

He may be as pink as the red flag of Russia as far as I'm concerned, but I do know only this about him, . . . I do know that one can get to see him. . . . I do know that when people in this district were evicted, he gave them shelter; I didn't see Bill O'Dwyer take them into Gracie Mansion [the mayor's residence which was in Marcantonio's district].[41]

Leonard Covello, a long-time friend of the congressman, writing some years later, stated:

those who did not know him wondered at the terrific plurality he always managed to pile up, no matter what his political banner. These doubters never saw Marcantonio in his office, in shirt sleeves, the crowd consisting of neighbors he had helped or was about to help. They never saw him on a street corner making a speech or listened to the comments of the crowd. They never saw him walk along 116th Street, never heard the old and young greet him. If they had seen these things, they would not have wondered.[42]

Marcantonio's critics have always contented that the services rendered to his constituents were simply a cover, diverting "the attention of many voters from his views on public policy."[43] But his office on First Avenue was always piled high with literature putting forth his position on public questions. Marcantonio campaigned on the issues in 1948 and in preceding elections from sound trucks and public platforms, anywhere he could get an audience. Service to the community was essential, but no more so than promulgating the political views for which he fought in Congress.

One further aspect of this peculiar political machine that

Marcantonio built in the Eighteenth Congressional District bears mention here: the relationship of the organization to the Puerto Ricans who flocked to East Harlem in ever-increasing numbers after the war.

"Marcantonio's principal strength," wrote the *Daily Mirror,* "comes from hordes of Puerto Ricans enticed here from their home island, for the value of their votes, and subjected to pitiful poverty, which Marcantonio has done nothing to alleviate—except force thousands on city relief." A great many New Yorkers still remember Vito Marcantonio as "the guy who brought the Puerto Ricans to New York."[44]

Any one of several good books on these newest of the immigrants shows that the Puerto Ricans migrated to the United States after the Second World War primarily because of the depressed conditions on the island and the hope of finding economic opportunity, the same motives that have been historically important in general immigration to the United States. The bulk of the movement came after the war because of the development of swift, comparatively inexpensive air transportation between the island and New York City.[45]

Puerto Ricans settled in Marcantonio's district in such great numbers that East Harlem quickly became known to others as Spanish Harlem and to the Puerto Rican immigrants themselves as *El Barrio,* the village. New immigrants generally were forced into the city's worst slums, and East Harlem qualified as such; the Puerto Ricans were discriminated against in other sections of the city. Perhaps as important as anything else, these island people tended to settle among their own kind where their familiar Spanish was spoken and where they would not continually feel like strangers in the land.

The charge that Marcantonio forced them on relief is almost undeserving of an answer, except that knowing what the congressman *did* do is essential for an understanding of his methods. New York's Welfare Department was not established to handle American citizens whose language was

Spanish, and a slangy Spanish at that. The numerous forms that constituted an application for relief were in English. When Puerto Rican immigrants needed welfare assistance, they frequently ran into a maze of English-speaking bureaucrats and what amounted to an impenetrable language curtain. Marcantonio always managed to have on his staff Spanish-speaking secretaries and lawyers who gave these citizens the kind of advice they needed in their own language. If they then managed to get help from the proper city agencies, it was not because Marcantonio had political power but because they met the city's well-defined legal standards for receiving relief assistance.

Of course, the fact that Marcantonio also championed the Puerto Rican point of view in Congress certainly did not lose him many votes among these newer residents of East Harlem.

Service to his constituents was one component of Marcantonio's machine, and it undoubtedly convinced some people to vote for him in spite of his radical politics. But while such good works are perhaps commendable, they are hardly enough to win elections considering the opposition Marcantonio frequently faced. Charities also do good for the community, but they do not ordinarily elect their leading officers to Congress. A more formal political machine was necessary to win elections, and the peculiar affection for Marcantonio held by the rank and file of the American Labor party in New York provided him with the second component of his organization.

To a reporter's question about the existence of a machine in East Harlem, Marcantonio answered candidly, if ungrammatically: "Sure I got an organization. There ain't no substitute for door-bell ringing . . . It's stair climbing versus stair climbing. Republicans don't climb stairs. I'm talking about the Park Avenue kind Mr. Ellis is importing to fight his battles."[46]

How many individuals poured into Marcantonio's two offices and the district ALP clubs to lick envelopes, canvass lists of voters, man the sound trucks, hand out leaflets at subway entrances, and do the general "scut" work that gives breath and blood to a political campaign is unknown. In an earlier election the ALP itself estimated the number at 1,200; the campaign of 1948 was of more consequence than any previous election, and it would be safe to presume that a larger number blanketed the Eighteenth Congressional District. Left-wing unionists, members of left-wing organizations such as the Civil Rights Congress or the Young Progressives of America, and active American Laborites, all were constantly entreated to help send "Marc" back to Congress.

It was not a formal "machine" in the ordinary sense of the word, and there was nothing permanent about it. Marcantonio had to write letter after letter to local captains who had missed meetings, to trade-union leaders who had promised help and failed to live up to their pledges, and to ordinary campaign workers who had not shown up to carry out important assignments. The machine was voluntary and, like all such organizations, it was slipshod and halting rather than smoothly efficient. The picture that emerges from the documentation is one of a professional politician, fighting for his political life and sometimes growing infuriated with the political ineptness of those upon whom he had to depend.[47]

The foremost part of the machine was Vito Marcantonio. He lived in the heart of East Harlem on 116th Street in a four-room rent-controlled apartment that was decorated with a few pictures "and a couple of shelves of books. . . . Bryce, Nicolay & Hay, Claude G. Bowers, Carl Sandburg and American history generally." The moment he walked out of his house, about 9:30 A.M., after a heavy breakfast, "he is campaigning. He is known all over the district and is greeted effusively—in Italian, in Spanish, often in German, now and then in one of the Slavic tongues. Naturally he knows a lot of names and, equally naturally, he is quite adept at covering this up when he doesn't."[48]

Politics was Marcantonio's business, his total business, and it occupied all his waking hours. It was also his hobby. By 1948 he had not had a vacation in twelve years. "You don't need a vacation," he told a reporter, "if you like the work you're doing. I like the work I'm doing."[49] When he relaxed it was frequently with a history book in hand, noting the "deadly parallels of earlier periods and now. You know, Jefferson, say and Hamilton. The contest is always the same —always the people against the entrenched interests." Sometimes he played poker; sometimes, when friends came to dinner, he would labor over a spaghetti sauce.[50] But mostly it was the game of politics he played on the sprawling board spread between East Harlem and Washington.

He was proud of the fact that he had been born and raised in East Harlem, and he used it with telling effect during the campaign in 1948. "Do you want the 400," he asked an audience at 109th Street, "or do you want me, one of the 140,000,000 working Americans. I was born three blocks from here. I have shared your sorrows and our victories."[51]

Was this a pose or was it real? Did Marcantonio put on the "home folks" attitude as a typical demagogic device, or did he really feel it? Arthur Schutzer, who knew him well during this period, believed he felt it. He had, said Schutzer, a "rootedness" in the community. "He belonged in East Harlem the same way the buildings belonged. Several times, driving in from the airport with him when he'd come up from Washington, he'd change when he hit 116th Street, almost a palpable change, as if he were home and it was a good feeling. Those streets were his streets, the people were his people, their problems were his problems. The people felt it. They couldn't miss it."[52]

Marcantonio's re-election in 1948 was particularly spectacular because it was the only high spot in an otherwise dismal performance by the American left-wing movement. Henry Wallace polled only slightly more than one million votes throughout the nation. Even in New York's Twenty-fourth Congressional District, where American Laborite Leo Isaacson almost doubled the vote he had received in February's by-election, Isidore Dollinger, backed by all three New York City parties, defeated Isaacson by nearly 35,000 votes.[53]

While the political left was jubilant at Marcantonio's victory —indeed, they had to be to balance failure everywhere else— the re-elected congressman could not have been blind to the fact that in a way he had really lost. Two out of every three voters in the Eighteenth Congressional District had voted against him. It was only the huge majority he rolled up in East Harlem that had counterbalanced his failure in the southern end of the district. Marcantonio had termed Truman an "accidental" president, but he was himself a "minority" congressman.

Despite the best efforts of the American left organized into the Progressive party, the people had voted for the Marshall Plan and the Truman Doctrine. They had turned out in droves to vote for the president who had issued the loyalty order and whose attorney general had listed numerous leftist organizations as "subversive." Marcantonio's victory was tempered by the realization of the enormity of Wallace's defeat. While the Progressives complained with some justification that Truman had stolen their program on the domestic questions of the day, they also had to admit that the American people had voted for the Truman policies concerning vital foreign questions, infinitely more significant in a world torn by cold war. The Washington Vito Marcantonio returned to in January 1949 differed greatly from the national capital he had come to fifteen years before as a freshman congressman; it differed much more than the span of years alone would indicate.

The Eighty-first Congress was once again controlled by the Democratic party, but from Marcantonio's point of view it made absolutely no difference; in terms of actual accomplishments, there were no differences between Democrats and Republicans. His own position in the legislature can be summed up by the two words "in opposition." There were times, as when he voted for a administration-backed housing bill in June 1949, when he knowingly accepted the lesser of two evils; but he insisted on making his position clear. "Mr. Speaker," he said of the bill in question, "I shall vote for [it] because it is better than nothing."[54] More often he voted with the minority on important legislation, and on numerous occasions Marcantonio *was* the minority.

On two of the most vital domestic issues facing the Congress, Marcantonio was unwilling to accept any compromise: labor and civil rights. Truman had campaigned during the 1948 election on a platform promising repeal of the Taft-Hartley Act. Throughout the campaign the Progressives had insisted that the Democrats had no real interest in repealing the "Slave Labor Act." When it developed, early in the congressional session, that the administration would be willing to accept amendments to the Taft-Hartley Act rather than outright repeal, Marcantonio felt vindicated. He excoriated those labor leaders, James Carey and Philip Murray of the CIO in particular, who were willing to accept an amended act rather than continue the fight for outright repeal. During the debate over the Labor Relations Act of 1949, Marcantonio insisted that the only meaningful action by the Congress would be the "complete and absolute repeal" and the "eradication of the whole Taft-Hartley philosophy of labor relations." He accused Truman's administration of having made promises and pledges to organized labor in order to win the presidential election, promises and pledges "which today are being washed out through a series of diabolical deals."[55] The Labor Relations Act, an amended version of the Taft-Hartley Act, passed with little difficulty.

A similar political situation existed in relation to Negro rights legislation, and Marcantonio was equally vehement in his opposition. The Democratic Convention in 1948 had inserted a strong civil rights plank in the party's platform, strong enough to cause some southerners to bolt the party and support J. Strom Thurmond of South Carolina for president. In accordance with the platform promise, the new Committee on Education and Labor favorably reported a Fair Employment Practices Commission bill in mid-summer 1949.

Analyzing the political situation in January 1950, Marcantonio felt that, if brought to a vote, the bill would probably pass the House. The problem was to get it to the floor of the legislature, and this could only be done by the administration through its congressional leadership. Detailing the method by which the bill could be brought to a vote, Marcantonio as much as charged that the administration would allow the bill to die by not using its own power to bring the bill up for a vote since Truman and the Democratic party had no real interest in the legislation, needing the idea of an FEPC "as [an] issue" and "not as law."[56] The critical date set by Marcantonio was January 23, 1950. As if the Congress were following his script, Speaker Rayburn refused to recognize the congressman who was prepared to call up the FEPC bill; the measure was bypassed and allowed to die.

Marcantonio's interest in civil rights for Negroes sometimes led him into the rather peculiar position of voting favorably on amendments to bills he opposed. Thus, when Congressman Adam Clayton Powell tried to amend a bill calling for Universal Military Training so as to forbid segregation in the nation's armed forces, Marcantonio spoke in favor of the amendment although he deemed the bill "part of an insane war policy promoted at the expense of the [nation's real needs]." He explained to the members of the House that he felt it incumbent upon him "to try and perfect any legislation, even though I may be opposed [to it] especially when it seems obvious that the proposed legislation will be adopted."[57]

In September 1950, Marcantonio was one of a minority of twenty congressmen who stood in opposition to the Internal Security Act of that year, an act the majority of congressmen felt was justified in the interest of protecting the government from the influence of subversives. The nation's leading radical slashed out at the proposed legislation, insisting it was aimed not at Communists or spies but at those who disagreed with the majority opinion. Its real purpose, Marcantonio insisted, was to prevent the organization of an opposition to a militaristic, fascistic America. Legislation like the Internal Security Act, he charged, was the mother of fear and timidity, in no way protecting the nation from spies or saboteurs. What did it lead to, he asked rhetorically? "People accusing each other; whispering 'Is he loyal?' 'Is he disloyal?' We saw, even in this House of Representatives the loyalty of a man like General Marshall being impugned. This is not a healthy state of mind. It is not a healthy condition. This disease makes America really sick. You are," he charged his colleagues, "enveloping [the nation] in an atmosphere of fear."

The heyday of McCarthyism, when the junior senator from Wisconsin became the living embodiment of the disease Marcantonio diagnosed, was still dim on the horizon, but the radical congressman saw it in the atmosphere surrounding the Internal Security Act. "You are," he continued, "supplanting the Constitution with this legislation and you are killing the America of Jefferson and Paine, of Lincoln and Oliver Wendell Holmes; and the America of the abolitionists, of the men who fought and died to abolish the slave laws and repeal the alien and sedition laws. You are killing the America of the American Revolution."[58]

The Internal Security Act passed three days later.

It is almost unnecessary to detail Marcantonio's opposition to the developing foreign policy of the United States in 1949 and 1950. He had laid down his personal policy in the previous Congress when he fought against the implementation of the Truman Doctrine and the Marshall Plan. Now, in the Eighty-first Congress, he adhered to that viewpoint. Consistently, he opposed legislation appropriating funds for the Economic Cooperation Administration;[59] he opposed the Mutual Defense Assistance Act of 1949;[60] he insisted that the foreign policy the nation was following would shortly lead to the remilitarization of Germany;[61] he opposed appropriating any further funds to be used by Chiang Kai-shek in obstructing democracy in China.[62] "When will this insanity stop?" he asked plaintively. "I know—it will stop when the American people learn the truth."[63]

No single issue better illustrates Marcantonio's sharp dissent from what was becoming American dogma than his reaction to the outbreak of war in Korea in June 1950. Reacting rapidly to the invasion of South Korea by North Korean troops, President Truman, on June 27, 1950, announced that he had ordered "United States air and sea forces to give the Korean government troops cover and support." Democratic supporters and the Republican opposition rallied behind this decision in a display of overwhelming bipartisanship. In the House, Vito Marcantonio, and he alone, rose to speak for whatever opposition existed.[64]

Significantly, he had spoken of Korea just five months before when he had objected to an appropriation of $60,000,000 in aid to the Government of South Korea. Equating it with the Chiang government in China, calling it corrupt and fascistic, citing an article from *The New York Times* to prove his point, he had predicted, "This Government of Fascist Korea cannot long endure, as our $60,000,000 are not going to save it from the wrath of the Korean people."

Now, on June 27, less than an hour after Truman's announcement of military support to the Rhee government had been read to a cheering House, Marcantonio fired away at the president's policy, reminding his colleagues of his earlier speech in which he had insisted "that you cannot take a nation and draw a line through it and divide it, and split into two countries a nation which is an ethnic unity, a people united culturally and racially over centuries." The United Nations, he pointed out, had recognized that fact and had done all in its power to try to bring to fruition the "will of the people for a united and independent country." Who had prevented the successful unification of Korea? "The tyrannical rulers of South Korea [who] continued to deny this legitimate aspiration of the people to achieve this objective and thus created an irrepressible conflict."

The issue in Korea was neither aggressive communism nor Russian imperialism, both of which Marcantonio refused to admit existed. Rather the question simply concerned the right of the people of Korea to self-determination. Therefore the president's order to the armed forces was "not in the defense of the best interests of the American people." There were alternatives to war, Marcantonio said, but Truman's declaration was "an acceptance of the doctrine of the inevitability of war. I stand here and challenge that doctrine. I say that the ingenuity of Americans and people all over the world challenge this doctrine."

With this speech Marcantonio went far beyond the pale set down by the American political establishment; he knew exactly what he was doing, knew he had not the slightest chance of success, and knew the consequences.

> I would be remiss to the things in which I believe [he told his colleagues] if I did not stand up here and state my opinion on this matter. After all, Mr. Chairman, you live only once; and it is best to live one's life with one's conscience rather than to temporize or accept with silence those things which one believes to be against the interests of one's people and one's nation.[65]

Six months later, in the last speech he delivered in Congress, Vito Marcantonio chose the Korean War for his subject and called for an immediate cease-fire on both sides. "The best defense of America does not lie in this armaments race," he told the members of the House. "The best defense of America does not lie in the atom bomb. . . . The best defense of America lies in a policy of peace."[66]

Marcantonio's stand on the Korean War was not an act of political suicide. It might better be compared to the act of twisting a knife already placed deep inside his political heart. Where once he was almost good-humoredly considered an irritating gadfly, by 1950 he was more frequently viewed as a cancer that needed immediate excision in order to protect the rest of the body politic from contamination. His opposition to American participation in the Korean War was simply one more tool he handed the political surgeons.

Realistically, his political demise was writ large in the

overwhelming repudiation the American public handed the radical left in the election of 1948. His own re-election that year, as has been pointed out, was a statistical repudiation. Cracks began to show in his machine within weeks after the election.

In 1949 Marcantonio ran for mayor of New York City on the American Labor party ticket and came in a poor third.[67] The normal unanimity of the ALP began to dissolve even before Marcantonio's campaign got under way. Some factions within the party felt that since he could not possibly win, the correct position for the American Labor party was to try to use its votes to influence one of the two major parties.[68] Equally important was the fact that the ALP no longer had the resources, physical or financial, it had once been able to command. With the exception of a few left-wing unions that had been expelled from the CIO, organized labor's support of the party had dwindled to almost nothing. Marcantonio lost the mayoralty race and lost heavily. Late in 1950, when he prepared for the congressional election, he probably knew he was defeated even before the campaign got under way.

As early as February 1950 the leadership of Tammany Hall issued a statement saying, "The defeat of red Vito Marcantonio should be the first order of business of the Democratic Party in New York County in the 1950 elections."[69] The statement advocated not "the election of a Democrat," but the "defeat of red Vito Marcantonio." The following month the New York Young Republican Club called for a coalition candidate against the radical from East Harlem, and the suggestion was met with resounding cheers from various political quarters.[70] V. N. Barrington, treasurer of a Committee for Republican Action in the Eighteenth Congressional District, wrote all registered Republicans in the area that "the defeat of Marcantonio" was a primary objective of the party. "So long as a Republican candidate cannot be elected, would you not rather have an acceptable Democrat of unquestioned loyalty to our country, than more ALP misrepresentation?"[71]

The tide moved against Marcantonio. When he opposed

American participation in the Korean War, it was as if an earthquake had turned the normally powerful tide into a tidal wave. Both major parties as well as the Liberal party endorsed James Donovan, a graduate of Harvard University and of Columbia Law School, a former New York state senator, and an opponent of Marcantonio for some time.[72]

The two candidates ran in a campaign that was almost a sham. The congressman put up his usual strong fight, intensifying his efforts, calling on supporters all over the city to come to his district and aid him in his fight. If he had to go down, he was going to do it in style. The newspapers in New York heaped calumny after calumny on him with the *Daily Mirror* leading the attack. "Marcantonio's principal strength," wrote the editor, "comes from degraded and depraved slums. . . . Marcantonio has been Moscow's man" in the American Congress.[73] Even Kate Smith found time to attack Marcantonio on her nationwide radio program.[74] Donovan talked communism, the Korean War, and little else. It all made little difference, for this was not a campaign of either issues or personalities. It was simple mathematics. The three parties could probably have run anyone and beaten Marcantonio in 1950.

Considering the nature of the opposition, Marcantonio actually did quite well in the November election. His percentage of the vote increased compared with the vote in 1948, but the increase was not enough to overcome the handicap posed by an all-party candidate like Donovan. Running on the American Labor party line alone, Marcantonio amassed 36,000 votes; Donovan's total as a Democrat, Republican, and Liberal was slightly over 49,000.[75] As Marcantonio ruefully explained to a disappointed supporter, "My vote was 11,000 larger than the Democratic Party, 15,000 larger than the Republican Party and 30,000 larger than the Liberal, so that line for line I beat every Party, but I could not beat the gang-up."[76] Late on election night, when enough returns were in so that there was obviously no possibility of re-election, Marcantonio conceded. "Go home tonight," he told the crowd jammed into his headquarters, "with the full realization that the ultimate victory belongs to us."[77]

Out of office for the first time since 1938, he showed no sign of withering away. As state chairman of the American Labor party, he continued to speak and write on the significant issues of the day. He maintained the two offices in his district and continued to serve his former constituents; there were many in the neighborhood who never realized he was no longer a congressman. It was hard to think of the Eighteen Congressional District being represented by someone else.

Probably his most important activity was as a lawyer in several civil liberties cases, notably his able and victorious defense of W. E. B. DuBois, the radical Negro leader, against the government's charge of nonregistration as the agent of a foreign power, and his unsuccessful defense of the Communist party in hearings before the Subversive Activities Control Board.[78]

While he managed to keep himself in political shape, he was less successful in preventing the dissolution of the party he had helped to construct and supposedly headed. His own view led him to believe that the American Labor party had meaning only so long as it maintained its independence; under the political conditions of the 1950's, especially as the long shadow of McCarthyism spread across the land, there was no longer any point in trying to make "deals" with either of the major parties. For one thing, the ALP had no bargaining power; for another, there were no longer any practical differences between Democrats and Republicans. In the ex-congressman's mind the only point of contention between the two national parties was which was better fitted to conduct the national hunt for Communists. "Great causes," Marcantonio wrote, "were never won by sacrificing a real fight and substituting for it the seeming lesser evil."[79] There were times in the past when he would have been the first to reject such an attitude; but times had changed, and no one knew it better than Vito Marcantonio.

Others within the American Labor party held a diametrically opposite view. While the ALP lost ground after 1950,
the split did not occur until the mayoralty campaign in 1953.
The ALP ran its own candidate, Clifford McAvoy, but the
party was rather obviously not united behind him. He polled
less than 55,000 votes. The following day, Vito Marcantonio
resigned from the American Labor party.

His statement of resignation indicated that a minority
within the party had felt that the prime issue was the defeat
of the Republican candidate, while Marcantonio's own faction
had insisted, not on trying to defeat Republicans, but on
doing its best to gather the largest number of votes for Mc-
Avoy. The excessively low vote, Marcantonio declared in
his statement, "is due exclusively to the continued debate
from which ensued confusion and paralysis of the campaign. . . . The American Labor Party, because of its inherent
division, has ceased any longer to be the effective instrument
for independent political action in the State of New York. . . .
The minority still insists; the debate still continues; the house
is still divided."[80]

Significantly, while there is little doubt that the minority
Marcantonio referred to were the Communists within the
ALP, he referred to them only as "the minority." There was
no hint of what he would have termed "red-baiting" in his
public announcement. While he definitely broke with the
Communist party, he made no attempt to make political
capital of the break and he continued to represent the party
as a lawyer in appealing an adverse decision handed down
by the Subversive Activities Control Board. He generally
believed that liberty was indivisible; and, at a moment of intense personal conflict, he lived it.[81]

In January 1954, in a letter to his former constituents, he
announced the establishment of the Vito Marcantonio Political Association.[82] There were signs that the political coalition
built around Congressman Donovan was cracking, and Marcantonio prepared to fight for his old congressional seat. In
June 1954 he announced his candidacy as an independent,

intimating that he could win even if the coalition of Democrats, Republicans, and Liberals were able to agree on a single candidate as in 1950 and in 1952. Nobody scoffed at his intentions.

Monday morning, August 9, 1954, the printer delivered the first stack of independent nominating petitions to Marcantonio's law office in downtown Manhattan. They were on his desk awaiting his inspection. The fiery, fifty-one-year-old, unreconstructed radical never got there. Rushing to his office from the subway station, he slumped suddenly on the rainswept street and, almost unnoticed, died of a heart attack.[83]

Even in death he remained controversial. A lifelong Catholic, wearing a metal crucifix around his neck when he died, Marcantonio could not be buried in consecrated ground since, according to the New York Archdiocese, he "was not reconciled with the Church before his death." His widow and friends were not successful in an attempt to convince the Chancery Office to reverse its decision.[84]

While Catholic church officials refused burial to Marcantonio, the Catholics of East Harlem turned out en masse, Italians and Puerto Ricans together, to pay their last respects to the man they called "Marc," the man one writer called "a screaming, snapping, effective, tireless fighter for the man of the streets of East Harlem."[85] More than twenty thousand people passed through the funeral parlor at 115th Street and First Avenue where his body lay in state.

On August 12, 1954, some five thousand people jammed the streets and lined up on roofs and fire escapes as the funeral cortege passed along First Avenue on it way to Woodlawn Cemetery in the north Bronx, to a grave not far from where Fiorello La Guardia lay buried. Some of them cried openly, some of them watched solemnly, and some of them jeered good-naturedly at the cops directing traffic.[86]

Epilogue

Through the fourteen years he served in the House of Representatives, Vito Marcantonio was an enigma to his congressional colleagues, his political competitors, and those journalists who covered his career. It was difficult, if not impossible, for them to understand a man who played the game of politics with skill and yet chose consciously to champion unpopular causes, thus depriving himself of any opportunity to achieve real, lasting power in American politics.

It is commonplace in the popular literature about Marcantonio to find him being explained away as an agent of Moscow, a dupe of the Communist party, an ally of the Mafia, or a demagogue. Similarly, his repeated election victories are depicted as shrouded in mystery, as if some malignant force operated at a distance to guide the hand of the solitary voter in the curtained polling booth. Two days after the ex-congressman's death, an editorialist writing in New York's *Herald Tribune* insisted that precisely because Marcantonio "had color, force, mental ability," his choice of political path was "one of those riddles of human personality." The same quality of bewilderment marked many of the obituary notices.

Yet, in the final analysis, there was nothing very mysterious about Vito Marcantonio. He was an American radical, one of the last surviving members of a specie fast becoming extinct in the framework of American party politics. His career seemed enigmatic to his contemporaries only because they found it so difficult to accept the existence of an honest and constructive radical fringe in the broad range of consensus politics; thus they were led to construct complex rationaliza-

211

tions in place of the relatively simple and more obvious truths.

Just how honest and constructive the American radical has been can be judged best when one realizes that much of what passes as American liberalism in domestic affairs today was the radical position in the 1930's and 1940's. No one enunciated that radical position more forcefully or more clearly than Vito Marcantonio during his fourteen years as a congressman.

The evolution from radicalism to liberalism in domestic affairs can be followed with just one of the fields dear to Marcantonio's heart: civil rights. He had championed anti-poll-tax legislation, desegregation at least in terms of the federal government, antilynch laws, the use of federal power to assure the Negro of constitutional rights, and other similar measures. Much of this legislation has come to pass. The poll tax in national elections has been wiped out by constitutional amendment; despite the earlier warnings of the southern opposition, the Republic still stands; and despite Marcantonio's fondest hopes and predictions, democracy is not yet rampant in the South. Perhaps the cross the American radical has to bear is the watching of others pass the legislation he once advocated and the knowledge that by the time it is put into effect, it is too little and much too late.

There has been no similar evolution in terms of American foreign policy, the other major area of concern to the radicals in the United States. There seems to be two different sets of foreign policies to consider: before and after the Second World War. Yet there was a consistency of action on Marcantonio's part that is worth noting for what it indicates about American radicals in general. In both eras his position was dictated, not by events overseas, but by occurrences at home.

In the prewar period he allowed nonintervention to overcome his anti-Fascist leanings as the drive toward war served to vitiate the more progressive aspects of the New Deal program. As the reform program ground to a halt after the election of 1938, Marcantonio became an increasingly bitter opponent of the foreign policy that forced the president to abandon domestic reform.

After the war, certainly after the Republic victory at the polls in 1946, Marcantonio connected the anti-Soviet crusade with renascent conservatism at home. To him the Cold War meant, not the containment of the Soviet Union, but the Taft-Hartley Act, the burial of civil rights legislation, the repression of political minorities, and the possible destruction of American liberties.

Marcantonio's critics have implied that there was something disloyal about the foreign policies he espoused and, indeed, about the position of the radical left in general. The worst that can be said of his prewar anti-interventionist position is that he was wrong; fascism could not have been defeated without American power, and he had purposely to blind himself not to realize that fact. In the postwar period, Marcantonio stood consistently for peaceful coexistence with the Soviet Union. He may have been wrong for presuming that this was an easily attained goal, but he was neither wrong nor disloyal in standing up and fighting for peace at a time when others in America sought war.

In his last speech in Congress in 1950, he called for a cease-fire and a truce in Korea before that conflict broadened into a totally destructive third world war. A little less than three years later, a Republican administration brought about an armistice in Korea. It does not seem to have been disloyal to presume, as Marcantonio did, that the nation had nothing to gain from a nuclear war.

Like many radicals and like the abolitionists who were his own heroes in American history, Marcantonio was an intolerant human being, refusing always to compromise or to moderate his principles. More than once he explained his position for or against a particular bill by saying, "I vote my conscience." Given the general trend of American politics, it is understandable that he was relegated to the role of critic or crusader against the political establishment. In that role he served an important and useful purpose. Henry F. May, in an article on "The End of American Radicalism," stated that purpose in clear terms:

> It is the radicals who insist, from time to time, on asking the necessary but awkward questions and dragging the skeletons from the darkest closets. Especially in times of fear and confusion, when the progressive technique of compromise is less successful and progressives are likely to be dragged from one untenable position to another, radicals alone can be counted on to stand by their own clear, if partial insights, to keep unpopular causes alive.[1]

In this age of conformity it would be refreshing and useful to have at least one Marcantonio in Congress, heaping anathemas on conservative Republicans and liberal Democrats alike, attempting to prevent legislative insanity, a bigot in favor of human rights, introducing ideas which might one day become part of the American mainstream.

Bibliographic Note

The Vito Marcantonio Collection (the Marcantonio Papers), on deposit at the New York Public Library, is contained in 171 archive boxes. Almost 130 of these are filled with papers concerning cases Marcantonio and his staff handled primarily for residents of his congressional district. Except as an indication of the variety of problems brought to the congressman, this material is of little value in studying Marcantonio's political career. The remaining boxes of material have been separated into the following categories: American Tradition, Bills Introduced by Marcantonio, Civil Liberties, General Correspondence, Electoral Democracy, Honesty in Government, Housing, International Relations, Labor and Labor Unions, Peace, Personal, Appeals and Private Bills, Speeches and Press Releases, Welfare, Veterans' Affairs, Marcantonio ALP Campaigns, Legal Cases, Aides' Reports, Miscellaneous Campaigns, Office Appointments and Messages, Marcantonio Research File, and Card File.

The categorization is very general, and there is no cross-filing. Some personal material is in the eight boxes of General Correspondence, and material relating to civil liberties can be found under several other titles. The same can be said for almost every other category listed above. Yet, the breakdown is extremely helpful to the researcher; and any other system would probably lead to different, not fewer, problems.

While the Marcantonio Papers are not complete, in the sense that there are too many gaps at important points in the congressman's career, they provide a rich source of information for anyone studying the mind and workings of the American political left from approximately 1933 to the congressman's death in 1954.

I expected to find much correspondence from and to Marcantonio in the La Guardia Papers held by the Municipal Archives and Records Center in New York City. There was surprisingly little and much of it was of little significance. I suspect that the telephone deprived us of what could have been a fascinating correspondence between two very volatile and politically independent individuals.

The only other book on Marcantonio, *I Vote My Conscience: Debates, Speeches and Writings of Vito Marcantonio, 1935-1950* (New York: 1956), edited by Annette T. Rubinstein, was published by a group of the congressman's friends organized as The Vito Marcantonio Memorial. It was never very widely distributed and has long been out of print. The book has a very limited and eulogistic 34-page biographical sketch of Marcantonio and a marvelous 32-page section of pictures, many of which obviously come from private collections. The bulk of the volume's 494 pages, divided into three sections, is made up of Marcantonio's own words. The first is a strict chronological section, the second is a long section of material on Puerto Rico, and the third is composed of excerpts from the court records of four important civil liberties cases with which Marcantonio was involved in the period 1950 to 1954. While most of the material in the first two sections can be found in the *Congressional Record,* there are some speeches and radio addresses that are not in either the *Record* or in the Marcantonio Papers and can only be found in Rubinstein's book.

Notes to Chapters

I. EAST HARLEM AND A POLITICIAN'S YOUTH

1. Vito Marcantonio to Carlo Marcantonio, Sept. 5, 1947, Marcantonio Papers (New York Public Library, New York City), General Correspondence, Box 3, Marcantonio folder. Hereafter cited as MP.

2. *Manhattan Land Book: City of New York* (New York: G. W. Bromley & Co., 1934), pp. 39-41.

3. From a survey of East Harlem conducted by students at Benjamin Franklin High School and cited in Leonard Covello, *The Heart Is the Teacher* (New York: 1958), pp. 205-206; WPA Historical Records Survey, *Guide to Vital Statistics in the City of New York, Borough of Manhattan, Churches* (New York: 1942), pp. 30-38.

4. Covello, *The Heart Is the Teacher*, p. 180.

5. Edward Corsi, "My Neighborhood," *The Outlook*, Vol. 141, No. 3 (Sept. 16, 1925), pp. 90-91; Covello, *The Heart Is the Teacher*, p. 185.

6. Corsi, *The Outlook*, Vol. 141, No. 3, p. 91; Covello, *The Heart Is the Teacher*, p. 180.

7. The other was in Greenwich Village, south and west of Washington Square Park.

8. Corsi, *The Outlook*, Vol. 141, No. 3, p. 92.

9. Vito Marcantonio to Carlo Marcantonio, Sept. 5, 1947, MP, General Correspondence, Box 3, Marcantonio folder. Both families came to the United States from the province of Potenza, about a hundred miles southeast of Naples.

10. A good description of the neighborhood can be found in an article on immigrant groups in New York, "The Melting Pot," *Fortune*, Vol. XX, No. 1 (July 1939), pp. 73ff; see also Covello, *The Heart Is the Teacher*, p. 107.

11. Corsi, *The Outlook*, Vol. 141, No. 3, p. 92; see also *Fortune*, Vol. XX, No. 1, pp. 73ff.

12. Corsi, *The Outlook*, Vol. 141, No. 3, p. 90.

13. Ernest Cuneo, *Life with Fiorello* (New York: 1955), p. 158.

14. Richard Sasuly, "People's Politician," in *American Radicals: Some Problems and Personalities*, ed. Harvey Goldberg (New York: 1957), p. 147.

15. Transcript of Record, DeWitt Clinton High School, New York City.

16. Reinhard Luthin, *American Demagogues: Twentieth Century* (Gloucester, Mass., 1959), p. 307, indicates that the use of an easily memorized, affectionate nickname is one mark of the American demagogue and that Marcantonio's use of "Marc" conformed with this strategy. But Covello, *The Heart Is the Teacher*, p. 152, shows that the shortened form of the name was commonly used by Marcantonio's high school friends long before he entered the political arena. Certainly "Marc" is a more natural nickname than say "Alfalfa" Bill Murray or "The Man" Bilbo. Luthin stretched a general idea beyond recognition in this particular case. (Hereafter Luthin's work is cited as *American Demagogues*.)

17. Covello, *The Heart Is the Teacher*, p. 152.

18. *Ibid.*

19. Hillquit lost by less than 700 votes. See *The New York Times*, Nov. 3, 4, 6, 1920. Nothing indicates the changing ethnic character of the Twentieth Congressional District better than the names of the candidates in certain elections. In 1920 the two leading contenders for the House seat from the area were Morris Hillquit and Isaac Siegel. Twelve years later, Italians having replaced Jews, the campaign was waged between Fiorello La Guardia and James J. Lanzetta. By the mid-1930's some seventeen Italian language periodicals were for sale on East Harlem's newsstands, ranging from Generoso Pope's *Il Progresso* to Carlo Tresca's anarchosyndicalist *Il Martello*.

20. Covello, *The Heart Is the Teacher*, p. 156; *The New York Times* covered the rent strikes throughout the city in various issues between March 1920 and October 1921.

21. Covello, *The Heart Is the Teacher*, p. 154-156.

22. *Ibid.*, p. 152.

23. Transcript of Record, DeWitt Clinton High School, New York City.

24. Covello, *The Heart Is the Teacher*, p. 153.

25. Covello, *The Heart Is the Teacher*, p. 152-154, has a complete account of the incident. A shortened version is in Arthur Mann, *La Guardia: A Fighter Against His Time, 1882-1933* (Philadelphia & New York: 1959), p. 175; hereafter cited as *La Guardia*. Mann's book is a superb study of La Guardia in the period before he became Mayor of New York and is written with clarity, wit, and understanding.

26. Transcript of Record, New York University School of Law, New York City.

27. *Ibid.*

28. Mann, *La Guardia*, pp. 240-241.

29. Marriage License Number 12722 issued to Vito Marcantonio and Miriam Sanders, May 20, 1925, City Clerk's Office, Borough of Manhattan, Municipal Building, New York City. See also Mrs. Marcantonio's obituary, *The New York Times*, April 10, 1965.

30. Mann, *La Guardia*, p. 175.

31. Mann, *La Guardia*, pp. 132-158, 174-175, gives the story of La Guardia's political twisting and turning in copious and interesting detail. The election returns for 1922 can be followed in *The New York Times*, Nov. 8, 9, 1922.

32. Mann, *La Guardia*, pp. 171-173.

33. *Ibid.*, p. 175; see also Lowell M. Limpus and Burr W. Leyson, *This Man La Guardia* (New York: 1938), pp. 185ff.

34. Mann, *La Guardia*, p. 175; Covello, *The Heart Is the Teacher*, pp. 156-157.

35. *The New York Times*, Nov. 8, 1924; Mann, *La Guardia*, pp. 174-175.

36. Unsigned to Vito Marcantonio, Jan. 16, 1925, and Fiorello La Guardia to A. S. Cutler, Jan. 22, 1925; both in the F. H. La Guardia Papers (Municipal Archives and Record Center, New York City), Law Practice, 1924-1925. This collection is hereafter cited as the La Guardia Papers. According to Limpus and Leyson, *This Man La Guardia*, p. 129, Marcantonio worked as a clerk for La Guardia as early as 1922 but this writer finds no other confirmation of it.

37. Mann, *La Guardia*, pp. 241-242.

38. *Ibid.*

39. *Ibid.*, pp. 176, 239.

40. La Guardia to Marcantonio, Feb. 6, 1925, La Guardia Papers, Law Practice, 1924-1925.

41. Marcantonio to La Guardia, Feb. 7, 1925, *ibid.*

42. La Guardia to B. F. Foster and A. S. Cutler, Jan. 19, 1925, and La Guardia to A. S. Cutler, Jan. 22, 1925, *ibid.*

43. Mann, *La Guardia*, pp. 240-241.

44. *Ibid.*, p. 175. While it is true that Marcantonio was perhaps ill kempt at this time, it should be remembered that his salary was about ten dollars a week, hardly sufficient to keep a young man in sartorial elegance.

45. Annette T. Rubinstein (ed.), *I Vote My Conscience: Debates, Speeches and Writings of Vito Marcantonio, 1935-1950* (New York: 1956), p. 2. Cited hereafter as *I Vote My Conscience*.

46. *Ibid.*

47. Cuneo, *Life with Fiorello*, pp. 155-156.

48. Mann, *La Guardia*, pp. 319-320.

49. Cuneo, *Life with Fiorello*, p. 165.

50. *Ibid.*, p. 161.

51. Howard Zinn, *La Guardia in Congress* (Ithaca, New York: 1955), p. 155; Mann, *La Guardia*, p. 201.

52. *Ibid.*, pp. 303-304. Mann calls the feat La Guardia's "most spectacular win since he joined the House in 1917." See also Zinn, *La Guardia*, pp. 220-226.

53. See above, Chapter I, page 16.

54. Warren Moscow, *Politics in the Empire State* (New York: 1948), p. 129.

55. Luthin, *American Demagogues*, pp. 210-211. Not surprisingly Marcantonio's headquarters was in the clubhouse of the Fiorello H. La Guardia Political Association.

56. *The New York Times*, Sept. 27, 1933.

57. *Ibid.*, Sept. 29, 1933.

58. *U.S. Congressional Record*, 73d Cong., 1st Sess., 1933, p. 2585. Lanzetta took up the cudgels for the tenement landlords again the following year; see *ibid.*, 73d Cong., 2d Sess., 1934, pp. 11219-20. The only bill he introduced in 1933 dealt with minor revisions of the immigration law.

59. *Ibid.*, 73d Cong., 2d Sess., 1934, pp. 7362-63, 8449, 10269, and 12603-04.

60. *The New York Times*, Oct. 16, 1934. During the same election Marcantonio was attacked by Antonio Pacheco Padro, a leader of the Puerto Rican Nationalist party. See MP, Personal, Box 1, 1936 Campaign folder.

61. *The New York Times*, Oct. 23, 1934; for information on the Liberal party and the Knickerbocker Democrats see *ibid.*, June 27 and Nov. 11, 1933.

62. Luigi Antonini to Marcantonio, Apr. 25, 1935, MP, Labor, Box 1, ILGWU folder.

63. *The New York Times*, Nov. 6, 1934.

64. *Ibid.*, Jan. 3, 1935.

65. *Ibid.*, Oct. 30, 1934.

66. *Ibid.*, Nov. 6, 1934.

67. *Ibid.*, Nov. 7, 8, 15, 1934. There was also a Socialist party candidate in the election, E. J. Cassidy, who drew only 1,204 votes, quite a comedown from the days when the Twentieth Congressional District was "Hillquit's District."

68. James Lanzetta to Fiorello La Guardia, Oct. 8, 1934, La Guardia Papers, Correspondence with Members of the House of Representatives, 1935. La Guardia probably enjoyed Lanzetta's complaint since he had himself contested the 1932 election on the basis of Tammany intimidation of voters. See *The New York Times*, Jan. 11, 1933.

69. *Ibid.*, Jan. 3, 1935.

70. *Ibid.*, June 21, 1936.

71. *Ibid.*, Nov. 11, 1934.

II. THE OFF-COLOR REPUBLICAN

1. Arthur Schlesinger, Jr., *The Politics of Upheaval* (Boston: 1960), pp. 142-144.

2. *Congressional Record*, 74th Cong., 1st Sess., 1935, p. 10.

3. *Ibid.*, pp. 418-419; see also U.S., Congress, *Official Congressional Directory* (Washington, D.C.: 1935), p. 216.

4. Luigi Antonini to Marcantonio, April 25, 1935, MP, Labor, Box 1, ILGWU folder.

5. *Congressional Record*, 74th Cong., 1st Sess., 1935, pp. 2485-2493.

6. *The New York Times*, Feb. 23, 1935.

7. The story itself is in *The New York Times*, March 22, 1935; the scroll is in the picture section of Rubinstein, *I Vote My Conscience*.

8. *Congressional Record*, 74th Cong., 1st Sess., 1935, p. 5857.

9. *Ibid.*, 74th Cong., 2d Sess., 1936, pp. 1538ff.

10. *Ibid.*

11. Arthur Schlesinger, Jr., *The Coming of the New Deal* (Boston: 1961), p. 296.

12. Marcantonio to Robert S. Allen, Dec. 12, 1935, MP, General Correspondence, Box 1, folder A.

13. *Congressional Record*, 74th Cong., 2d Sess., 1936, pp. 6482-6486; the dialogue with Congressman McCormack is on p. 6484.

14. *The New York Times*, June 16, 1935.

15. Marcantonio and others to La Guardia, April 23, 1935, La Guardia Papers, Correspondence with Members of the House of Representatives, 1935.

16. *The New York Times*, July 6, 1935.

17. *Ibid.*

18. *Ibid.*, July 7, 1935.

19. Marcantonio to T. C. Gannon, June 26, 1935, MP, General Correspondence, Box 1, folder G.

20. Marcantonio to Robert S. Allen, July 20, 1936, MP, General Correspondence, Box 1, folder A.

21. For the Snyder-Guffey Act see *Congressional Record*, 74th Cong., 1st Sess., 1935, pp. 13432, 13435, 13448, 13466, 13481, and for his vote, p. 13667; for Marcantonio's position and his amendments to the Revenue Act see *ibid.*, pp. 12403, 12426, and for his vote see p. 14644.

22. *Ibid.*, pp. 9722-9723; *The New York Times*, June 19, 1935.

23. *Congressional Record*, 74th Cong., 1st Sess., 1935, pp. 9720-9721. It should be understood that the Wagner Act was not an administration bill and was, in fact, opposed by Roosevelt. After its passage, however, the New Deal accepted it and it is frequently considered part of the New Deal program. For a good discussion of the history of this particular piece of legislation see Basil Rauch, *The History of the New Deal, 1933-1938* (New York: 1944), pp. 185-190.

24. *Congressional Record,* 74th Cong., 1st Sess., 1935, p. 10434; he introduced the resolution on July 1. See *The New York Times,* July 2, 1935.

25. *Congressional Record,* 74th Cong., 1st Sess., 1935, p. 10435.

26. *Ibid.,* pp. 10435, 13007, 13011-13012.

27. *Ibid.,* p. 8372; *The New York Times,* May 30, 1935.

28. *Congressional Record,* 74th Cong., 2d Sess., 1936, p. 1850. This was his longest, but not his only, statement on the question of the Supreme Court's power. A week earlier, when the Congress considered legislation repealing legislation which conflicted with the Court's decision in the AAA case, Marcantonio urged a fight rather than surrender. "If there was ever a time, if we ever had an opportunity to protest against this nullification by the judiciary, to meet its challenge and assert our rights, this is the time and this is your opportunity." *Ibid.,* p. 1496. Almost a year earlier he had urged a constitutional amendment to repeal "the precedent set by the decision in the Marbury against Madison case, which is the worst piece of autocracy ever legislated by any court into the constitution of a country." *Ibid.,* 74th Cong., 1st Sess., 1935, p. 7150.

29. Rubinstein, *I Vote My Conscience,* p. 49.

30. *Congressional Record,* 74th Cong., 2d Sess., 1936, p. 3289.

31. Louis Sass to Communist Party Meeting in East Harlem, Aug. 5, 1936, MP, Personal, Box 1, 1936 Campaign folder.

32. Marcantonio to Luigi Antonini, Aug. 14, 1935, MP, Labor, Box 1, ILGWU folder.

33. Marcantonio to Girolamo Valenti, June 12, 1935, MP, General Correspondence, Box 5, folder V. Valenti had complained that since Marcantonio had spoken from the same platform as Earl Browder, there would be a tendency for the voters to connect the two men.

34. *The New York Times,* Sept. 8, 1935. The complete story can be followed in the same paper in numerous issues in July, August, and September 1935. The minor incident had far-reaching effects. The swastika became the national flag of the Third Reich as a result of the *Bremen* affair and William Dodd, American ambassador in Germany, took note of the incident by writing in his diary, "If this is not enough to make our relations with Germany critical, I do not know what could make them critical." William E. Dodd, *Ambassador Dodd's Diary, 1933-1938,* ed. W. E. Dodd, Jr., and Martha Dodd (New York: 1941), p. 264.

35. *The New York Times,* Oct. 17, 1935; undated statement on the Emergency Relief Bureau cut by Marcantonio in MP, General Correspondence, Box 4, Political Parties folder.

36. *The New York Times,* Oct. 24, 27, 1935.

37. *Ibid.,* Feb. 16, 1936.

38. *Ibid.*, Feb. 17, 1936.

39. *Ibid.*, Feb. 18, 1936. Marcantonio got in the last word by quoting Pitt's reply to a similar charge by Walpole: "I shall . . . content myself with wishing that I may be one of those whose follies may cease with their youth, and not of that number who are ignorant in spite of their experience." *Ibid.*, Feb. 19, 1936.

40. See above, page 38.

41. Vito Marcantonio, "Dusty Death," *New Republic*, Vol. LXXXVI, No. 1109 (March 4, 1936), pp. 105-106.

42. Rubinstein, *I Vote My Conscience*, p. 374.

43. *Ibid.*, pp. 377-378; *The New York Times*, May 7, 1936.

44. *Ibid.*, July 27, 1936; for an interesting account of the Nationalist viewpoint and some material on Albizu Campos, see *ibid.*, May 2, 1936.

45. *Ibid.*, Aug. 1, 2, 1936.

46. *Ibid.*, Aug. 3, 4, 1936.

47. Gruening to Marcantonio, Aug. 15, 1936, MP, Civil Liberties, Box 1, Campos folder. Gruening's motives may have been completely honest; but three months later Harold Ickes noted in his diary that Gruening, "from being a liberal, has apparently decided that the mailed fist is the proper policy in dealing with these subject people. He has gone completely in reverse." See Harold L. Ickes, *The Secret Diary of Harold L. Ickes*, Vol. II: *The Inside Struggle, 1936-1939* (New York: 1954), p. 6; hereafter cited as *The Secret Diary*, Vol. II.

48. Marcantonio's speech on the subject and the letter can be found in Rubinstein, *I Vote My Conscience*, p. 392. Thomas Mathews, *Puerto Rican Politics and the New Deal* (Gainesville, Florida: 1960), pp. 252, 266ff, and footnote 94 on p. 268, has much interesting material on the trial and the events leading up to it, but does not mention Marcantonio. The book itself, hereafter cited as *Puerto Rican Politics*, gives an excellent picture of the very complicated internal political scene on the island and of the terrible economic effects of the Depression in Puerto Rico.

III. DEFEAT AND VICTORY

1. Hamilton Fish, Jr., to Marcantonio, Oct. 30, 1936, and Marcantonio to Hamilton Fish, Jr., Nov. 5, 1936, MP, Personal, Box 1, 1936 Campaign folder.

2. Mann, *La Guardia*, p. 222.

3. Poster, MP, General Correspondence, Box 1, Antonini folder.

4. Marcantonio to Luigi Antonini, Aug. 14, 1935, MP, General Correspondence, Box 1, Antonini folder.

5. See, for example, the translation of an Italian-language pamphlet:

"My Answer to a Very Filthy False and Cowardly Attack Made on me by Luigi Antonini," *ibid.* See also Walter Davenport, "Congressional Gadfly," *Collier's*, Vol. 114, No. 16 (Oct. 14, 1944), p. 68, where Marcantonio refers to Antonini as *Emperatora Tripa Grossa* or, very loosely, "The Emperor Big Tripe."

6. Hugh Bone, "Political Parties in New York City," *The American Political Science Review*, Vol. XL, No. 2 (April 1946), p. 277.

7. Election Pamphlet, "My Position on Marcantonio," by Antonio Pacheco Padro, MP, Personal, Box 1, 1936 Campaign folder.

8. *The New York Times*, Sept. 29, 1936; see also the material in MP, Personal, Box 1, 1936 Campaign folder.

9. Heywood Broun and others to Fiorello La Guardia, Sept. 18, 1936, La Guardia Papers, Vito Marcantonio-La Guardia Correspondence, C-44, folder 120.

10. Transcript of Communist Party Meeting, May 20, 1936, MP, Personal, Box 1, 1936 Campaign folder.

11. *The New York Times*, June 22, 1936.

12. Speech delivered by Louis Sass to Communist Party Meeting, August 4, 1936, MP, Personal, Box 1, 1936 Campaign folder.

13. *The New York Times*, Oct. 26, 1936.

14. The characterization of Lanzetta came from Congresswoman Caroline O'Day who had previously thrown her support to Marcantonio. A short time later she found that her endorsement had been "hasty" and switched to Lanzetta. *The New York Times*, Sept. 26, 1936.

15. *Ibid.*, Oct. 29, 1936.

16. *Ibid.*, Oct. 10, 1936.

17. *Ibid.*, Oct. 14, 27, 28, 29, 1936.

18. *Ibid.*, Nov. 18, 1936, for the dropped charge against Silver; and Jan. 30, 1937, for the same concerning Marcantonio.

19. *Ibid.*, Nov. 4, 5, 1936.

20. *Congressional Record*, 74th Cong., 2d Sess., 1936, pp. 10723-10726.

21. Six years later Marcantonio insisted he had been beaten in 1936 because he was one of the few "Americans of Italian extraction in prominent office who refused to attend" a rally to raise funds for Mussolini held at Madison Square Garden. He said flatly, "It cost me my election in 1936." It is interesting that at the time of the election he made no such reference. *The New York Times*, Aug. 10, 1942.

22. Vito Marcantonio to International Labor Defense, Feb. 10, 1937, and Marcantonio to A. Damon, March 2, 1937, MP, Civil Liberties, Box 2, ILD, 1937-1940, folder.

23. *Ibid.*

24. Davenport, *Collier's*, Vol. 114, No. 16, p. 68.

25. *The New York Times*, Feb. 11, 1938.

26. *Ibid.*, Feb. 13, 1938; see also his speech on civil rights to the ILD, *ibid.*, Nov. 21, 1937.

27. *Newsweek*, Vol. XI, No. 19 (May 9, 1938), p. 14.

28. *Ibid.*, Vol. XI, No. 20 (May 16, 1938), p. 12.

29. *The New York Times*, May 8, 1938; *The Nation*, Vol. 146, No. 20 (May 14, 1938), p. 546.

30. Marcantonio to Leonard Covello, Nov. 3, 1938, MP, General Correspondence, Box 1, folder C; *The New York Times*, Nov. 5, 1938.

31. Moscow, *Politics in the Empire State*, Chapter VII, pp. 102ff.

32. *The New York Times*, July 16, 1938.

33. *Ibid.*, July 22, 1938.

34. *Ibid.*, Aug. 10, 1938.

35. Moscow, *Politics in the Empire State*, pp. 63-65; Moscow gives the following, rather interesting account: "The stories of how boards of election operate to preserve the status quo in a party are legion. One that comes to mind is that of the perfect set of designating petitions filed one time . . . by an independent candidate. The most careful study showed not a single thing wrong with them, not a technicality that had not been met. But something had to be done. So the Board went into a huddle and threw out the petitions on the ground that they must be fraudulent even though they did not appear so, because it was impossible to prepare legitimately so perfect a set."

36. *The New York Times*, July 27, 29, 1938.

37. *Ibid.*, Sept. 5, 1938.

38. *Ibid.*, Aug. 9, 1938. Marcantonio insisted he entered the Democratic primary only because Lanzetta had entered the ALP primary. Lanzetta promptly challenged the validity of the petitions Marcantonio used to get his name on the Democratic ballot, but the petitions were found to be perfectly legal.

39. *Ibid.*, Aug. 10, 1938.

40. *Ibid.*, Nov. 8, 1938. The witness was J. B. Matthews.

41. The statement was issued by the Executive Board of the Alliance. *Ibid.*, Aug. 21, 1938.

42. *Ibid.*, Sept. 21, 1938.

43. *Ibid.*, Sept. 22, 1938. This was the first election in East Harlem in which no candidate was entered by the Socialist party.

44. *Ibid.*, Sept. 24, 1938.

45. *Ibid.*, Sept. 27, 1938.

46. Gilbert Milstein, "Marcantonio's Fight for Re-election." This is apparently a draft of an article prepared for *The New York Times Sunday Magazine* section, MP, Personal, Box 1, 1948 Campaign folder.

47. *The New York Times*, Oct. 23 and Nov. 1, 1938.

48. Letter to the Editor from Heywood Broun, The *New Republic*, Vol. LXXXXVI, No. 1248 (Nov. 2, 1938), p. 366.

49. *The New York Times,* Nov. 4, 1938.

50. *Ibid.,* Nov. 8, 1938.

51. *Ibid.,* Nov. 9, 1938; Luthin, *American Demagogues,* p. 216. According to one reporter, T.R.B., "Washington Notes," *New Republic,* Vol. LXXXXVIII, No. 1262 (Feb. 8, 1939), p. 16. Lanzetta may not have had the full support of the Tammany organization since he was the only Tammany Democrat to support Roosevelt's Reorganization Bill. This seems unlikely however, since Lanzetta's vote in 1938 was about the normal Democratic turn-out for East Harlem in a midterm election.

52. Marcantonio to South Trimble, Nov. 19, 1938, and Trimble to Marcantonio, Nov. 21, 1938, MP, American Labor Party Campaigns, New York State Office folder; U.S., Congress, *Official Congressional Directory* (Washington, D.C.: 1939), p. 147.

IV.   GREASY STAINS ON THE LEGISLATIVE TOGA

1. Basil Rauch, *The History of the New Deal, 1933-1938* (New York: 1944), pp. 325-326.

2. T.R.B., *New Republic,* Vol. LXXXXVIII, No. 1262, p. 15.

3. Marcantonio to Rockwell Kent, July 20, 1940, MP, General Correspondence, Box 3, folder K.

4. T.R.B., "Washington Notes," *New Republic,* Vol. LXXXXVIII, No. 1271 (April 12, 1939), p. 277.

5. Roosevelt to Sam Rayburn, memorandum dated Dec. 2, 1938, Roosevelt Papers (Franklin D. Roosevelt Library, Hyde Park, New York). Cited hereafter as the Roosevelt Papers. The memo was sent in response to an earlier request to the president from La Guardia's office rather than from Marcantonio directly.

6. U.S., Congress, *Official Congressional Directory* (1939), p. 223.

7. *Congressional Record,* 76th Cong., 1st Sess., 1939, pp. 267-270.

8. *The New York Times,* Jan. 14, 1939.

9. *Ibid.,* Jan. 30, 1939.

10. *Congressional Record,* 76th Cong., 1st Sess., 1939, p. 1520.

11. *Ibid.,* p. 3299.

12. *Ibid.,* p. 338.

13. *Ibid.,* pp. 267-270, 326. Marcantonio's amendment to increase the expenditure to the figure suggested by the United States Conference of Mayors was rejected, 199 to 21.

14. *Ibid.,* p. 7367. There is no complete study of the political fight waged in and out of Congress over the Federal Theatre Project in the spring of 1939. The substance of the story can be followed in the final chapters of Hallie Flanagan's *Arena* (New York: 1940).

15. *Congressional Record,* 76th Cong., 1st Sess., 1939, pp. 2786-2787, 3139. In battling for Public Housing legislation Marcantonio excoriated those congressmen who used the issue "to array the farmers" against "the dwellers in the large cities and the wage earners of America." Instead he insisted that "the interests of the farmer and the worker . . . are essentially interdependent . . . the future of America rests on the unity of farmer and worker and on their mutual assistance."

16. Rubinstein, *I Vote My Conscience,* pp. 114-116. Marcantonio took the figure from the *Boston Evening Transcript,* Feb. 14, 1940.

17. *Congressional Record,* 76th Cong., 3d Sess., 1940, p. 1040.

18. Joseph Cadden to Marcantonio, Jan. 17, 1939, MP, Civil Liberties, Box 1, American Youth Congress folder.

19. Irving Howe and Lewis Coser, *The American Communist Party: A Critical History* (New York: 1962), pp. 359-360. Cited hereafter as *The American Communist Party.*

20. *Congressional Record,* 76th Cong., 3d Sess., 1940, p. 1527.

21. *Ibid.,* pp. 6640-6642.

22. *Ibid.*

23. *Ibid.,* 76th Cong., 1st Sess., 1939, p. 4889.

24. For Marcantonio's continuing efforts in behalf of Campos see MP, Civil Liberties, Box 1, Campos folder; the petition to the president is dated April 12, 1939, see the Roosevelt Papers.

25. *Congressional Record,* 76th Cong., 1st Sess., 1939, pp. 3123-3125.

26. *Ibid.,* pp. 5466-5477; for a brief biographical account of Iglesias see Mathews, *Puerto Rican Politics,* p. 16.

27. *Congressional Record,* 76th Cong., 1st Sess., 1939, pp. 5466-5477; virtually the same conflict was waged the following year when Marcantonio again tried to amend the Fair Labor Standards Act so that it would apply to Puerto Rico with no exceptions and again he was opposed by the resident delegate from the island; see *Congressional Record,* 76th Cong., 3d Sess., 1940, pp. 5361-5363, 5365. Mathews, *Puerto Rican Politics,* p. 324, backs up Marcantonio's contention that the New Deal was a failure as far as recovery in Puerto Rico was concerned. By November 1938, almost 1,122,000 persons were involved in the relief program on the island.

28. T.R.B., *New Republic,* Vol. LXXXXVIII, No. 1262, pp. 15-16.

29. Harold L. Ickes, *The Secret Diary,* Vol. II, p. 599; Marcantonio's full case against Governor Winship is in his long speech, "Five Years of Tyranny in Puerto Rico," *Congressional Record,* 76th Cong., 1st Sess., Appendix, 1939, pp. 4062-4069.

30. Ickes, *The Secret Diary,* Vol. II, pp. 627-628; late in April, Marcantonio had issued a statement to the press which was virtually an ultimatum. "If Governor Winship doesn't resign by the time he leaves Washington, I shall break the whole scandal about his administration.

It will not satisfy me for him to resign as of next July. I want him out immediately." At a meeting of Puerto Ricans in East Harlem the congressman insisted his charges concerning Winship would make "the historic scandalous Tea-Pot-Dome case . . . smell like lillies to my fellow legislators." Every time Marcantonio made such statements, Ickes received messages such as the one from R. Martinez Nadal, president of the Puerto Rican Senate, condemning the congressman and urging that Governor Winship be continued in his post. The story can be followed in the material on Puerto Rico for April and May 1939 in the Roosevelt Papers.

31. Marcantonio to Gilberto Concepcion, May 10, 1939, MP, General Correspondence, Box 4, La Prensa folder.

32. *The New York Times*, May 13, 1939.

33. *Congressional Record*, 76th Cong., 1st Sess., 1939, pp. 5529, 5532.

34. Luthin, *American Demagogues*, p. 221.

35. Davenport, *Collier's* Vol. 114, No. 16.

36. *Congressional Record*, 76th Cong., 3d Sess., 1940, p. 9372.

37. *Ibid.*, p. 9034; he delivered a radio address on the same subject on July 30, 1940, see Rubinstein, *I Vote My Conscience*, pp. 129-130.

38. *Congressional Record*, 76th Cong., 3d Sess., 1940, p. 9034.

39. *Ibid.*, p. 9036.

40. The bill, H.R. 9766, was introduced in June 1940 by Congressman John Lesinski (Dem., Michigan).

41. *Ibid.*, pp. 7630, 7761.

42. *Ibid.*, pp. 8181-8215; for an earlier defense of Bridges by Marcantonio, see *The New York Times*, Feb. 11, 1938.

43. *Congressional Record*, 76th Cong., 3d Sess., 1940, pp. 292-293.

44. *Ibid.*, 76th Cong., 1st Sess., 1939, pp. 1116-1119.

45. *The New York Times*, Feb. 3, 1939.

46. *Ibid.*, Oct. 18, 1939.

47. Marcantonio to James Kiernan, July 11, 1939, La Guardia Papers, Congress—Correspondence with Vito Marcantonio, C-44.

48. *Congressional Record*, 76th Cong., 3d Sess., 1940, p. 599.

V. The Divided Mind of the Left

1. Rubinstein, *I Vote My Conscience*, pp. 37-38.

2. "American Labor Party Position on Lend-Lease Bill," Feb. 24, 1941, MP, American Labor Party Campaigns, New York County Office folder.

3. *Congressional Record*, 74th Cong., 2d Sess., 1936, p. 6486.

4. *Ibid.*, 76th Cong., 3d Sess., 1940, p. 6642.

5. A typical popularization of the idea can be found in "Arms and the Men," *Fortune*, Vol. IX, No. 3 (March 1934), pp. 53-57ff.

6. *Congressional Record,* 74th Cong., 1st Sess., 1935, pp. 5038-5040.

7. *The New York Times,* May 2, 1936; Marcantonio was joint author of a bill proposing a constitutional amendment outlawing American participation in war except in the event of an attack upon the United States. *The New York Times,* May 3, 1936.

8. Marcantonio to La Guardia, May 3, 1935, La Guardia Papers, Correspondence with Members of the House of Representatives, 1935.

9. *The New York Times,* Sept. 21, 1935.

10. *Ibid.,* April 23, 1937.

11. Marcantonio to W. Feinberg, May 12, 1937, MP, Personal, Box 3, People's Voice folder.

12. *The New York Times,* Nov. 21, 1938.

13. Marcantonio to various groups and individuals, Dec. 14, 1938, MP, General Correspondence, Box 4, *Il Popolo* folder.

14. Marcantonio to L. S. Beller, Feb. 8, 1939, MP, General Correspondence, Box 1, folder A.

15. Rauch, *The History of the New Deal, 1933-1938,* p. 329.

16. Marcantonio to Father Sebastian Schaff, Jan. 16, 1939, and Marcantonio to *Comite Antifascista Espanol,* Jan. 12, 1939, MP, General Correspondence, Box 1, folder C; Luthin, *American Demagogues,* pp. 225-226, insists Marcantonio's Catholicism was only a political expedient, but there is no evidence to support this contention.

17. Howe and Coser, *The American Communist Party,* pp. 315-316.

18. Marcantonio to Eugene Connolly, Oct. 7, 1939, MP, American Labor Party Campaigns, New York County Office folder.

19. Selig Adler, *The Isolationist Impulse: Its Twentieth Century Reaction* (New York: 1961), pp. 257-258.

20. *Daily Worker,* Nov. 3, 4, 1939.

21. *Congressional Record,* 76th Cong., 2d Sess., 1939, p. 1389.

22. Rubinstein, *I Vote My Conscience,* pp. 125-129.

23. Marcantonio to Anna Damon, June 5, 1940, MP, Civil Liberties, Box 2, International Labor Defense folder.

24. Marcantonio to Rockwell Kent, July 20, 1940, MP, General Correspondence, Box 3, folder K.

25. Marcantonio to L. B. Harrison, Feb. 16, 1940, MP, Civil Liberties, Box 1, American Youth Congress folder.

26. *The New York Times,* May 29, 1940.

27. Marcantonio to J. Cadden, March 14, 1940, and Cadden to Marcantonio, undated but from the same period, MP, General Correspondence, Box 1, American Youth Congress folder; Marcantonio to N. Brooks, Aug. 16, 1940, MP, General Correspondence, Box 1, American Student Union folder; *The New York Times,* Aug. 1, 15, Sept. 5, 20, 1940.

28. Bone, *The American Political Science Review,* Vol. XL, No. 2, p. 278.

29. Marcantonio to Alex Rose, Jan. 30, 1939, and L. Rosner to Marcantonio, Jan. 31, 1939, MP, American Labor Party Campaigns, New York State Office folder.

30. *The New York Times*, May 29, 30, 1940; the paper took note of Marcantonio's position in an editorial, *ibid.*, May 31, 1940.

31. "American Labor Party Position on Lend-Lease Bill," Feb. 24, 1941, MP, American Labor Party Campaigns, New York County Office folder.

32. *The New York Times*, Aug. 9, 10, 12, Sept. 18, 19, 1940.

33. Morris Watson to the author in a letter, March 12, 1964.

34. *Ibid.*

35. *The New York Times*, Sept. 25, 1940.

36. Election broadside, 1940 campaign, MP, Personal, Box 1, 1940 Campaign folder.

37. La Guardia to J. Boccia, Nov. 2, 1940, MP, Personal, Box 1, 1940 Campaign folder; *The New York Times*, Nov. 5, 1940.

38. La Guardia to Mrs. L. White, March 8, 1941, La Guardia Papers, Correspondence with Members of the House of Representatives, C-43, folder 144.

39. Interview with Arthur Schutzer, Jan. 12, 1962.

40. *The New York Times*, Nov. 6, 1940.

41. W. M. Whittington to J. J. Lanzetta, Dec. 2, 1940, MP, Personal, Box 1, 1940 Campaign folder.

42. U.S., Congress, *Official Congressional Directory* (Washington, D.C.: 1941) p. 151; for the second time he was relegated to the committees on invalid pensions, mines and mining, and public lands. *Ibid.*, p. 222.

43. "American Labor Party Position on Lend-Lease Bill," Feb. 24, 1941, MP, American Labor Party Campaigns, New York County Office folder.

44. Gen. R. E. Wood to Marcantonio, Feb. 18, 1941, and American Student Union to Marcantonio, May 2, 1941, MP, General Correspondence, Box 1, folder A; Luthin, *American Demagogues*, p. 217; *The New York Times*, Feb. 1, 9, March 7, 20, 23, 1941.

45. Marcantonio to L. Criscuolo, June 5, 1941, MP, General Correspondence, Box 2, Criscuolo folder.

46. *The New York Times*, March 20, 1941.

47. *Ibid.*, March 23, 1941.

48. Eugene Lyons to Marcantonio, July 10, 1941, MP, General Correspondence, Box 1, folder A.

49. *The New York Times*, Aug. 23, 1941.

50. *Ibid.*, Oct. 16, 1941.

51. *Ibid.*, Oct. 17, 1941. "I am not only for this bill," he said, "I go far beyond it. I am for repeal of the entire neutrality act, and I go

further than that. I think the United States should do everything that is possible to open up a western front."

52. *Congressional Record,* 77th Cong., 1st Sess., 1941, pp. 7987-7989.

53. Eugene Connolly to Marcantonio, Dec. 8, 1941, MP, American Labor Party Campaigns, New York County Office folder.

VI. The All-Party Congressman

1. "Editorial," *New Republic,* Vol. 106, No. 22 (June 1, 1942), p. 748.

2. "Editorial," *Ibid.,* Vol. 107, No. 9 (Aug. 31, 1942), p. 246.

3. Roland Young, *Congressional Politics in the Second World War* (New York: 1956), pp. 243-244, 254-256. Cited hereafter as *Congressional Politics.*

4. *Congressional Record,* 77th Cong., 2d Sess., 1942, pp. 1718, 1743; Rubinstein, *I Vote My Conscience,* p. 159.

5. Young, *Congressional Politics,* pp. 59-60.

6. Rubinstein, *I Vote My Conscience,* p. 159; *Congressional Record,* 77th Cong., 2d Sess., 1942, p. 1743.

7. *Ibid.,* p. 1759; for subsequent efforts to enact similar legislation see Young, *Congressional Politics,* pp. 60-61.

8. *Congressional Record,* 77th Cong., 2d Sess., 1942, p. 1796.

9. Marcantonio to Roosevelt, Sept. 4, 1942, Roosevelt Papers.

10. *Congressional Record,* 77th Cong., 2d Sess., 1942, pp. 5150-5151; Young, *Congressional Politics,* p. 24.

11. Young, *Congressional Politics,* pp. 128-130; Rubinstein, *I Vote My Conscience,* p. 165.

12. MP, Legislative Record, General Correspondence, Box 1; *Congressional Record,* 77th Cong., 2d Sess., 1942, p. 6423.

13. *The New York Times,* June 29, 1942.

14. "Editorial," *New Republic,* Vol. 107, No. 5 (Aug. 3, 1942), p. 133.

15. *Congressional Record,* 77th Cong., 2d Sess., 1942, p. 8069; yet, in talking to a reporter about Marcantonio, Cox said, "He is a likeable person and his word is good." Sydney Shalett, "They Couldn't Purge Vito," *The Saturday Evening Post,* Vol. 219, No. 28 (Jan 11, 1947), p. 110.

16. *Congressional Record,* 77th Cong., 2d Sess., 1942, p. 8072.

17. *Ibid.,* p. 8168.

18. *The New York Times,* Nov. 27, 1942.

19. *Congressional Record,* 77th Cong., 2d Sess., 1942, p. 2299.

20. Marcantonio to Roosevelt, Feb. 19, 1942, and Roosevelt to Marcantonio, Feb. 24, 1942, Roosevelt Papers.

21. The verbal battle over Dies' committee went on through February and March 1942. Marcantonio's longest and most important speech on

the subject is in the *Congressional Record,* 77th Cong., 2d Sess., 1942, pp. 2055-2066.

22. *The New York Times,* Sept. 25, 1942; Marcantonio wrote the president asking clemency for Earl Browder, head of the Communist party, who was serving a sentence in federal prison at the time. Marcantonio to Roosevelt, Mar. 26, 1942, Roosevelt Papers.

23. Joseph North, editor of the magazine, to Marcantonio, Nov. 18, 1942, and Jan. 20, 1943, MP, General Correspondence, Box 4, *New Masses* folder.

24. *The New York Times,* July 10, 1942.

25. New York *Herald Tribune,* July 30, 1942.

26. *The New York Times,* July 30, 1942.

27. *Ibid.,* Aug. 6, 1942; New York *Herald Tribune,* July 30, 1942.

28. *The New York Times,* Aug. 6, 1942.

29. *Ibid.*

30. *Ibid.,* Aug. 12, 1942.

31. "Editorial," *Ibid.,* Aug. 14, 1942.

32. *Ibid.,* Aug. 6, 13, 1942.

33. Moscow, *Politics in the Empire State,* pp. 98-100.

34. Marcantonio to La Guardia, Oct. 16, 1939, La Guardia Papers, Congress, Correspondence with Vito Marcantonio, C-44.

35. Stanley Howe to Marcantonio, Feb. 27, 1940, and Marcantonio to Howe, Feb. 29, 1940, La Guardia Papers, Political Correspondence of Stanley Howe, H-16, folder 213.

36. Marcantonio to La Guardia, May 2, 1940, La Guardia Papers, Congress, Correspondence with Vito Marcantonio, C-44.

37. J. Raymond Jones to Marcantonio, Aug. 31, 1944, MP, General Correspondence, Box 2, folder D.

38. J. G. Ford to Eugene Connolly, June 9, 1944, MP, American Labor Party Campaigns, New York County Office folder; Moscow, *Politics in the Empire State,* pp. 114ff.

39. *The New York Times,* July 19, Aug. 2, 1942.

40. Shalett, *The Saturday Evening Post,* Vol. 219, No. 28, p. 109.

41. Moscow, *Politics in the Empire State,* p. 98.

VII.   The Leftish Phenomenon

1. U.S. Congress, *Official Congressional Directory* (Washington, D.C.: 1943), p. 147.

2. *The New York Times,* Jan. 4, 1943.

3. *Ibid.,* Jan. 16, 1943.

4. *Ibid.,* Jan. 17, 1943.

5. A sample of the letters that poured into his office are in MP, General Correspondence, Box 3, Judiciary Committee folder.

6. MP, Electoral Democracy, Election Irregularities folder.

7. *The New York Times,* Jan. 20, 1943.

8. For Marcantonio's statement on being refused the position on the Judiciary Committee see MP, General Correspondence, Box 3, Judiciary Committee folder.

9. I. F. Stone, "Capitol Notes," *The Nation,* Vol. 156, No. 4 (Jan. 23, 1943), p. 115.

10. *Congressional Record,* 78th Cong., 1st Sess., 1943, p. 663; *The New York Times,* Feb. 6, 1943.

11. Rubinstein, *I Vote My Conscience,* p. 175.

12. *Congressional Record,* 78th Cong., 1st Sess., 1943, pp. 4092-4093.

13. *The New York Times,* May 11, 1943; in an editorial backing efforts to wipe out the poll tax, the *Times* strangely failed even to mention Marcantonio's name as one of the leading figures in the fight. See, for example, the issue for May 16, 1943.

14. *Ibid.,* May 26, 1943.

15. "Editorial," *The Nation,* Vol. 156, No. 23 (June 5, 1943), p. 794.

16. *The New York Times,* April 8, 1944; an editorialist for *The Nation,* Vol. 156, No. 22 (May 29, 1943), p. 758, wrote: "A country that tolerates no work stoppages in industry should make matters uncomfortable for political strikers who would paralyze the Senate of the United States in war time."

17. MP, General Correspondence, Box 2, Committee for the Protection of the Consumer folder.

18. *The New York Times,* June 25, 1943.

19. Young, *Congressional Politics,* p. 65.

20. *Ibid.,* MP, Legislative Record, General Correspondence, Box 1.

21. Young, *Congressional Politics,* p. 83; *The New York Times,* June 12, 1943.

22. Rubinstein, *I Vote My Conscience,* pp. 176-179.

23. Young, *Congressional Politics,* p. 87.

24. *The New York Times,* April 16 and May 16, 1944; Marcantonio had no illusions about the ability of the Congress to take any effective action on civil rights. In the summer of 1943 he wrote the president a long letter detailing discriminatory acts against Negroes, including those in the armed forces. He urged Roosevelt to "speak out" in an historic fireside chat "against the forces attempting to tear the fabric of national unity" and "to place your high office back of guarantees that Negro people and other minority groups will be freed from every hindrance which prevents their full participation in our war effort." Marcantonio to Roosevelt, June 16, 1943, Roosevelt Papers.

25. *Congressional Record,* 78th Cong., 2d Sess., 1944, p. 5058.

26. "Editorial," *The Nation*, Vol. 158, No. 24 (June 10, 1944), p. 667.

27. *Ibid.*, Vol. 159, No. 1 (July 1, 1944), p. 2; "Editorial," *New Republic*, Vol. 110, No. 24 (June 12, 1944), p. 777; for a good explanation of the necessity for a permanent FEPC see a letter to the editor from Anna A. Hedgeman, National Executive Secretary, National Council for a Permanent FEPC in *The Nation*, Vol. 159, No. 3 (July 15, 1944), p. 83.

28. *Congressional Record*, 77th Cong., 2d Sess., 1942, pp. 8810-8812 and Appendix, pp. 2809-2810. In this last speech Marcantonio urged the Congress at least to allow Puerto Rico the right to elect its own governor. This, he insisted, was not a substitute for independence but would be "an improvement within the colonial structure."

29. Davenport, *Collier's*, Vol. 114, No. 16, p. 68.

30. Rubinstein, *I Vote My Conscience*, p. 165.

31. *The New York Times*, July 26, 1943.

32. *Congressional Record*, 78th Cong., 2d Sess., 1944, pp. 8134-8136; Marcantonio to Roosevelt, Jan. 31, 1944, Roosevelt Papers.

33. The Greek and Yugoslav communities in the United States hurled imprecations at the congressman for the mere suggestion that Italy be made an ally. See, for example, Greek-American Progressive Association to Roosevelt, Aug. 14, 1944, and other telegrams and letters between Aug. 1 and Aug. 14, 1944, Roosevelt Papers.

34. Marcantonio to Roosevelt, June 6, 1944, Roosevelt Papers.

35. Milstein, "Marcantonio's Fight for Re-election."

36. U.S., Congress, *Biographical Directory of the American Congress, 1774-1961*. House Document No. 442 (Washington, D.C.: 1961).

37. Luthin, *American Demagogues*, p. 220; *The New York Times*, March 21, 1944.

38. *Ibid.*, March 29, April 5, 1944.

39. *Ibid.*, April 2, 5, 1944. A week earlier, on March 30, 1944, in an editorial the *Times* had called for the exodus of "genuine liberals and progressives" from the ALP.

40. Richard H. Rovere, "Marcantonio: Machine Politican, New Style," *Harper's Magazine*, Vol. 88, No. 1127 (April 1944), p. 397.

41. *The New York Times*, June 3, 1944.

42. *Ibid.*, July 31, 1944.

43. *Ibid.*, July 31, 1944.

44. *Ibid.*, July 29, 1944.

45. The New York *Daily Mirror*, July 31, 1944.

46. *The New York Times*, Aug. 2, 1944; Rubinstein, *I Vote My Conscience*, p. 6.

47. Marcantonio to M. Schein, Sept. 11, 1944, MP, Personal, Box 1, 1944 Campaign folder.

48. *The New York Times,* Aug. 1, 1944.

49. *Ibid.,* Aug. 2, 1944.

50. *Life,* Aug. 14, 1944, p. 32; "Editorial," *The Nation,* Vol. 159, No. 7 (Aug. 2, 1944), pp. 170-171.

51. *The New York Times,* Aug. 3, 1944.

52. *The New York Times,* Aug. 15, Oct. 25, 1944.

53. *Ibid.,* Aug. 11, 31, 1944; almost 3,500 signatures had been submitted.

VIII. CONSISTENCY IN A CHANGING WORLD

1. Eric F. Goldman, *The Crucial Decade: America, 1945-1955* (New York: 1956); hereafter cited as *Crucial Decade.*

2. Robert S. Allen and William V. Shannon, *The Truman Merry-Go-Round* (New York: 1950), pp. 211-212.

3. *Congressional Record,* 79th Cong., 1st Sess., 1945, p. 18.

4. *Ibid.,* pp. 5290-5291.

5. *Ibid.,* pp. 5892ff.

6. *Ibid.,* p. 5812; Rubinstein, *I Vote My Conscience,* p. 198.

7. *The New York Times,* July 4, Oct. 9, 1945.

8. *Ibid.,* April 25, 1965; *Congressional Record,* 79th Cong., 1st Sess., 1945, p. 3904.

9. *Ibid.,* 79th Cong., 2d Sess., 1946, pp. 3227, 3231.

10. *Ibid.*

11. *Ibid.,* 79th Cong., 1st Sess., pp. 645, 649; for a general discussion of this type of legislation see Young, *Congressional Politics,* pp. 76-82.

12. *Congressional Record,* 79th Cong., 2d Sess., 1946, pp. 4847-4848.

13. Rubinstein, *I Vote My Conscience,* p. 215.

14. *Ibid.,* pp. 217-218; *Congressional Record,* 79th Cong., 2d Sess., 1946, pp. 5864, 5924-5945.

15. *Ibid.,* p. 5924; *The New York Times,* May 30, 1946.

16. *Congressional Record,* 79th Cong., 2d Sess., 1946, pp. 7510-7511.

17. Goldman, *Crucial Decade,* p. 25; *The New York Times,* Aug. 9, 1946.

18. Unsigned to Marcantonio, undated, MP, General Correspondence, Box 5, folder U; *The New York Times,* Sept. 30, 1946.

19. *Congressional Record,* 79th Cong., 2d Sess., 1946, p. 4470.

20. For the sequence of letters see Abner Green to Marcantonio, March 9, 1945, MP, American Tradition, American Committee for the Protection of the Foreign Born folder. Marcantonio scribbled his comment on this letter and forwarded it to Congressman Dickstein. Dickstein to Marcantonio, March 15, 1945, and Abner Green to Marcantonio, May 12, 1945, both filed with the original letter.

21. *Congressional Record,* 79th Cong., 2d Sess., 1946, pp. 2745-2752.

22. *Ibid.,* pp. 5213-5216; see also *The New York Times,* May 18, 1946, for Marcantonio's protest on the congressional appropriation for the House Committee on Un-American Activities.

23. *Congressional Record,* 79th Cong., 2d Sess., 1946, p. 7598; *The New York Times,* May 18, 1946.

24. *Congressional Record,* 79th Cong., 1st Sess., 1945, Appendix, p. 501.

25. Goldman, *Crucial Decade,* pp. 37-38.

26. *Ibid.,* p. 60.

27. *Congressional Record,* 79th Cong., 2d Sess., 1946, p. 8949.

28. *The New York Times,* Sept. 27, 1946; for earlier defenses of Wallace by Marcantonio see *ibid.,* March 1, 24, 1945.

29. The story can be followed in *The New York Times* news columns, May 21, 30, June 5, and in an editorial, June 7, 1946.

30. Arthur W. Bingham, "The Congressional Elections of Vito Marcantonio" (unpublished undergraduate thesis on deposit at Widener Library, Harvard University), pp. 98-99.

31. *The New York Times,* May 9, 1946.

32. *Ibid.,* May 15, 1946; Bingham, "The Congressional Elections of Vito Marcantonio," p. 99.

33. *The New York Times,* July 12, 1946.

34. For examples of Marcantonio's speeches see *ibid.,* Aug. 4, 15, 1946.

35. *Ibid.,* Aug. 4, 1946.

36. Bingham, "The Congressional Elections of Vito Marcantonio," p. 101.

37. *The New York Times,* Aug. 19, 1946.

38. *Ibid.,* Aug. 15, 1946.

39. The New York *Daily Mirror,* Aug. 1-15, 1946.

40. *The New York Times,* Aug. 22, 1946.

41. *Ibid.,* Oct. 19, 1946; Bingham, "The Congressional Elections of Vito Marcantonio," pp. 98–99.

42. *The New York Times,* Oct. 4, 1946.

43. *Ibid.,* Oct. 16, Nov. 4, 1946.

44. *Ibid.,* Nov. 1, 1946.

45. *Newsweek,* Vol. XXVIII, No. 22 (Nov. 25, 1946), pp. 31-32; the description of Marcantonio comes from Milstein, "Marcantonio's Fight for Re-election."

46. *The New York Times,* Nov. 5, 1946.

47. *Ibid.,* Nov. 6, 1946.

48. Shalett, *The Saturday Evening Post,* Vol. 219, No. 28, p. 17.

49. *The New York Times,* Nov. 6, 1946.

50. *Ibid.*

IX. THE TIDE TURNS

1. *The New York Times,* Nov. 12, 1946.
2. *Ibid.; Newsweek,* Vol. XXVIII, No. 22 (Nov. 25, 1946), p. 31.
3. *Ibid.*
4. New York *Daily Mirror,* Dec. 21, 1946.
5. Transcript of Statement by Congressman Vito Marcantonio, made before Mr. Robert B. Barker, Assistant General Counsel and Chief Investigator of the special committee of the House to investigate campaign expenditures pursuant to House Resolution No. 645, December 21, 1946, p. 7, MP, Electoral Democracy, Election Irregularities folder.
6. *The New York Times,* Nov. 15, 1946. Marcantonio was a diabetic, a factor that complicated complete recovery in this instance.
7. Transcript of Statement. . . , *passim,* MP, Electoral Democracy, Election Irregularities folder. The kind of intimidation by implication Marcantonio referred to can be seen in a single sentence in a book by Jack Lait and Lee Mortimer, *New York Confidential!* (Chicago: 1948), pp. 101-102: "But in Congressman Marcantonio's East Harlem the poorest and most crime-ridden Little Italy in all the world begrimes New York." While the statement is perhaps debatable, the implication is quite clear.
8. Shalett, *The Saturday Evening Post,* Vol. 219, No. 28, p. 112.
9. Interview with Arthur Schutzer, Jan. 12, 1962.
10. Quoted in Goldman, *Crucial Decade,* p. 57.
11. K. M. Le Compte to Marcantonio, March 30, 1948, MP, Personal, Box 1, Committee folder.
12. *The New York Times,* Jan. 4, 1947.
13. Ralph de Toledano, *Lament for a Generation* (New York: 1960), pp. 227-228.
14. *Congressional Record,* 80th Cong., 1st Sess., 1947, pp. 3418-3419.
15. New York *Herald Tribune,* June 4, 1947; *The New York Times,* June 4, 1947.
16. New York *Herald Tribune,* June 5, 1947.
17. Marcantonio to the Editor, New York *Herald Tribune,* June 5, 1947, MP, Personal, Box 3, Letters to Newspaper Editors folder.
18. *Congressional Record,* 80th Cong., 1st Sess., 1947, p. 3534.
19. *Ibid.,* pp. 2011-2013.
20. *Ibid.,* 80th Cong., 2d Sess., 1948, pp. 2356, 2357.
21. *Ibid.,* 80th Cong., 1st Sess., 1947, pp. 2752, 2774-2775.
22. *Ibid.,* Appendix, p. 357.
23. *Ibid.,* pp. 1911, 1913.
24. *Ibid.,* 80th Cong., 2d Sess., 1948, p. 10220.
25. *Ibid.,* p. 318; *ibid.,* 80th Cong., 1st Sess., 1947, p. 9578.
26. *Ibid.,* pp. 10886ff; *The New York Times,* April 23, 1947.

27. Karl M. Schmidt, *Henry A. Wallace: Quixotic Crusade 1948* (Syracuse: 1960), one of the best sources to date on the Wallace campaign. Cited hereafter as *Quixotic Crusade*.

28. Rubinstein, *I Vote My Conscience;* pp. 241-243.

29. *Congressional Record,* 80th Cong., 1st Sess., 1947, pp. 9123ff.

30. *Ibid.,* 80th Cong., 2d Sess., 1948, p. 5999; see also pp. 6283, 6264, 6287.

31. *Ibid.,* pp. 5988-5989.

32. Marcantonio to Baron House Plan, College of the City of New York, March 29, 1947, MP, General Correspondence, Box 1, folder B.

33. Quoted in Rubinstein, *I Vote My Conscience,* p. 318.

34. *Congressional Record,* 80th Cong., 2d Sess., 1948, pp. 3622-3625.

35. *Ibid.,* p. 3533; for other comments see pp. 3545, 3537.

36. Rubinstein, *I Vote My Conscience,* pp. 259-260.

X. In Victory Lies Defeat

1. *The New York Times,* March 9, Aug. 12, 29, 1947.

2. E. S. Griffith to Marcantonio, July 28, 1947, MP, General Correspondence, Box 4, Progressive Party folder.

3. Schmidt, *Quixotic Crusade,* pp. 36-40.

4. Marcantonio to Mrs. Elliott Dexter, Jan. 8, 1948, MP, General Correspondence, Box 2, folder D. A decade earlier Marcantonio himself had backed an Italian-language newspaper as a way of reaching the public of East Harlem. While the project failed because it cost too much, he was apparently quite conscious of the problems involved in trying to run a political campaign without press support. See Marziale Sisca to Marcantonio, Nov. 22, 1938, and other letters, MP, General Correspondence, Box 3, "La Follia" folder.

5. "The New Party's Smoke Filled Room," *New Republic,* Vol. 119, No. 4 (July 26, 1948), p. 18.

6. *The New York Times,* Feb. 18, 23, 1948; Schmidt, *Quixotic Crusade,* pp. 69-70.

7. *The New York Times,* Feb. 23, 1948.

8. *New Republic,* Vol. 119, No. 4, p. 18.

9. In January 1948 Marcantonio was elected state chairman of the American Labor party, a job he did not particularly want and tried to get rid of in order to devote more time to the problem of re-election in his own district. *The New York Times,* Jan. 8, Feb. 23, 1948.

10. Moscow, *Politics in the Empire State,* pp. 100-101, has a good discussion of the meaning of the Wilson-Pakula Act and states flatly: "It was aimed primarily at Marcantonio." For the Court of Appeals

decision upholding the constitutionality of the measure see *The New York Times,* July 3, 1947; the rumor about Marcantonio running as a Democrat is in *ibid.,* Aug. 5, 1947; similar legislation had been discussed in New York political circles as early as 1945, for which see *ibid.,* Jan. 17, 25, Feb. 28, 1945.

11. *Ibid.,* Nov. 6, 1946.

12. *Ibid.,* May 19, June 28, 1948.

13. *Ibid.,* July 22, 1948.

14. Eugene Connolly to Marcantonio, undated but from this period, MP, American Labor Party Campaigns, New York County Committee folder; Marcantonio to E. J., Sept. 27, 1947, MP, Personal, Box 2, Miscellaneous Correspondence folder; the conflict among O'Dwyer, the leadership of Tammany Hall, and Marcantonio is ably discussed in Gus Tyler, "The Roosevelt or the Tiger," *The New Republic,* Vol. 120, No. 20 (May 16, 1949), pp. 9-11.

15. "National Affairs," *Time,* Vol. LII, No. 17 (Oct. 25, 1948), p. 24.

16. Milstein, "Marcantonio's Fight for Re-election," p. 13; *The New York Times,* Nov. 11, 1948; Bingham, "The Congressional Elections of Vito Marcantonio," p. 116.

17. Milstein, "Marcantonio's Fight for Re-election," p. 13; Bingham, "The Congressional Elections of Vito Marcantonio," p. 117.

18. *The New York Times,* July 13, 1948.

19. *Ibid.,* Oct. 12, 14, 15, 1948.

20. *Ibid.,* Oct. 29, 1948.

21. *Ibid.,* Sept. 30, 1948.

22. Milstein, "Marcantonio's Fight for Re-election," p. 2.

23. *Ibid.,* p. 12.

24. Marcantonio to the Editor, *The New York Times,* Oct. 28, 1948, MP, Personal, Box 1, 1948 Campaign folder. The letter was printed in *The New York Times,* Oct. 30, 1948.

25. *The New York Times,* Nov. 3, 1948.

26. Milstein, "Marcantonio's Fight for Re-election," pp. 1-2.

27. Davenport, *Collier's,* Vol. 114, No. 16, p. 68.

28. Shalett, *The Saturday Evening Post,* Vol. 219, No. 28, p. 112.

29. Marcantonio to G. Tarantino, June 5, 1944, MP, Veterans Affairs, American Legion folder.

30. Milstein, "Marcantonio's Fight for Re-election," p. 1; a good picture of the kinds of cases the congressman handled can be seen best by sampling any of the 129 archive storage boxes under the category "18th Congressional Cases" in the Marcantonio Papers.

31. Milstein, "Marcantonio's Fight for Re-election, p. 9.

32. The correspondence covering these cases, all between 1942 and 1945, are in the La Guardia Papers, Marcantonio-La Guardia Correspondence, folder 120, C-44.

33. Shalett, *The Saturday Evening Post*, Vol. 219, No. 28, p. 112.

34. Marcantonio to La Guardia, July 15, 1944, La Guardia Papers, Congress, Correspondence with Vito Marcantonio, C-44.

35. Marcantonio to La Guardia, June 25, 1945, *ibid*. The letter illustrates Marcantonio's interest in seeing that the workingman received a fair deal: "I hate to pressure you," he wrote. "These people are neither constituents nor are they clients. I have no interest in them [but] it seems to me to be grossly unfair to have men work for the city and then not have them paid."

36. Marcantonio to La Guardia, Jan. 8, 1945, *ibid*.

37. La Guardia to Marcantonio, Oct. 4, 1945, *ibid*.

38. Marcantonio to A. A. Bass, April 3, 1947, MP, General Correspondence, Box 1, folder B.

39. Anonymous to Marcantonio, Oct. 5, 1948, MP, Personal, Box 3, Marcantonio Personal Miscellaneous folder.

40. Davenport, *Collier's*, Vol. 114, No. 16, p. 70.

41. W. Thiess to V. N. Barrington, treasurer, Committee for Republican Action, May 10, 1950, MP, Personal, Box 1, 1950 Campaign folder.

42. Covello, *The Heart Is the Teacher*, pp. 156-157.

43. Luthin, *American Demagogues*, p. 235.

44. New York *Daily Mirror*, Oct. 23, 1950.

45. See for example Oscar Handlin, *The Newcomers: Negroes and Puerto Ricans in a Changing Metropolis* (Cambridge: 1959) and Christopher Rand, *The Puerto Ricans* (New York: 1958).

46. Milstein, "Marcantonio's Fight for Re-election," p. 7.

47. The 1948 campaign folder in MP, Personal, Box 1, is filled with letters that indicate Marcantonio's frustration with his subordinates and especially with the leaders of those organizations who had promised physical help and had failed to deliver. At one point Marcantonio showed up for a meeting at a school building only to find out the meeting had been canceled without anyone informing him in advance.

48. Milstein, "Marcantonio's Fight for Re-election," p. 9.

49. *Ibid.*, p. 10.

50. Interview with Arthur Schutzer, Jan. 12, 1962; when questioned about his hobbies, Marcantonio said, "I . . . like a poker game. The gang meets Saturday nights at a friend of mine's house. He's a well-to-do contractor, conservative, reactionary. We were raised together. His career was to make money." Milstein, "Marcantonio's Fight for Re-election," p. 10.

51. *Ibid.*, p. 13.

52. Interview with Arthur Schutzer, Jan. 12, 1962.

53. *The New York Times*, Nov. 3, 1948.

54. Rubinstein, *I Vote My Conscience*, p. 302.

55. Marcantonio to J. Selly, June 25, 1949, MP, General Correspondence, Box 4, folder S; *Congressional Record*, 81st Cong., 1st Sess., 1949, pp. 5192-5193.

56. Marcantonio to C. Howard, Jan. 23, 1950, MP, General Correspondence, Box 3, folder H; New York *Daily Compass*, Jan. 15, 1950.

57. *Congressional Record*, 81st Cong., 2d Sess., 1950, p. 7679.

58. *Ibid.*, p. 15288.

59. *Ibid.*, 81st Cong., 1st Sess., 1949, p. 4194.

60. *Ibid.*, pp. 11663-11664.

61. Rubinstein, *I Vote My Conscience*, p. 321.

62. *Congressional Record*, 81st Cong., 2d Sess., 1950, pp. 1605-1607.

63. *Ibid.*, 81st Cong., 1st Sess., 1949, p. 11664.

64. Goldman, *Crucial Decade*, pp. 145-159; *Congressional Record*, 81st Cong., 2d Sess., 1950, p. 9265.

65. *Ibid.*, pp. 9268-9269.

66. *Ibid.*, pp. 16662-16663.

67. The campaign can be followed best in *The New York Times* for 1949; no individual citations are necessary here.

68. New York *Herald Tribune*, April 4, 1949; New York *Daily Compass*, Nov. 12, 1950.

69. *The New York Times*, Feb. 1, 1950.

70. New York *Herald Tribune*, March 12, 1950.

71. V. N. Barrington, treasurer, Committee for Republican Action, form letter, May 10, 1950, MP, Personal, Box 1, 1950 Campaign folder.

72. U.S. Congress, *Official Congressional Directory* (Washington, D.C.: 1951), p. 88; Luthin, *American Demagogues*, p. 232.

73. New York *Daily Mirror*, Oct. 23, 1950.

74. Marcantonio to Arthur Schutzer, May 5, 1951, MP, ALP Campaigns, Miscellaneous folder.

75. *The New York Times*, Nov. 8, 1950.

76. Marcantonio to Jack Hall, Dec. 26, 1950, MP, Personal, Box 1, 1950 Campaign folder. The folder is filled with messages of regret from people living in the district, college professors, labor leaders, left-wing luminaries, and one from the National Gypsy Association.

77. *National Guardian*, Nov. 10, 1950.

78. Rubinstein, *I Vote My Conscience*, p. 65.

79. *Ibid.*, p. 10.

80. Statement issued by Honorable Vito Marcantonio on Nov. 4, 1953, on occasion of his resignation as chairman and member of the American Labor party, MP, Personal, Box 1, ALP folder.

81. Sasuly, "People's Politician," p. 152.

82. Letter to constituents, Jan. 11, 1954, MP, Personal, Box 1, ALP folder.

83. *The New York Times*, Aug. 10, 1954.

84. *Ibid.*, Aug. 11, 12, 13, 1954.

85. Shalett, *The Saturday Evening Post,* Vol. 219, No. 28, p. 17.

86. *The New York Times* and the *Herald Tribune* carried the story of the funeral on Aug. 13, 1954. Jeering the cops was, of course, in the best tradition of both East Harlem and of the left wing. The *Herald Tribune* had an editorial on Marcantonio's death on Aug. 11, 1954. Gus Tyler, in a letter to the editor, *The New Republic,* Vol. 131, No. 8 (Aug. 23, 1954), p. 6, threw a few darts at the dead ex-congressman, darts which Luke W. Wilson attempted to remove in a reply in *ibid.*, Vol. 131, No. 10 (Sept. 6, 1954), p. 22. In separate letters to the editor, *The Nation,* Vol. 179, No. 11 (Sept. 11, 1954), p. 200, David L. Weissman and James Imbrie paid tribute to Marcantonio.

EPILOGUE

1. Henry F. May, "The End of American Radicalism," *American Quarterly,* Vol. II, No. 4 (Winter 1950), pp. 291-292.

Index